Thomas F. Torrance and the Orthodox-Reformed Theological Dialogue

Thomas F. Torrance and the Orthodox-Reformed Theological Dialogue

JASON ROBERT RADCLIFF

☙PICKWICK *Publications* · Eugene, Oregon

THOMAS F. TORRANCE AND THE ORTHODOX-REFORMED THEOLOGICAL DIALOGUE

Copyright © 2018 Jason Robert Radcliff. All rights reserved. Except for brief quotations in critical publications or reviews, no part of this book may be reproduced in any manner without prior written permission from the publisher. Write: Permissions, Wipf and Stock Publishers, 199 W. 8th Ave., Suite 3, Eugene, OR 97401.

Pickwick Publications
An Imprint of Wipf and Stock Publishers
199 W. 8th Ave., Suite 3
Eugene, OR 97401

www.wipfandstock.com

PAPERBACK ISBN: 978-1-4982-2630-1
HARDCOVER ISBN: 978-1-4982-2632-5
EBOOK ISBN: 978-1-4982-2631-8

Cataloguing-in-Publication data:

Names: Radcliff, Jason.

Title: Thomas F. Torrance and the Orthodox-Reformed theological dialogue / Jason Robert Radcliff.

Description: Eugene, OR: Pickwick Publications, 2018 | Includes bibliographical references and index.

Identifiers: ISBN 978-1-4982-2630-1 (paperback) | ISBN 978-1-4982-2632-5 (hardcover) | ISBN 978-1-4982-2631-8 (ebook)

Subjects: LCSH: Torrance, Thomas F. (Thomas Forsyth), 1913–2007 | Theology, Doctrinal—History—20th century | Orthodox Eastern Church—Doctrines | Reformed Church—Doctrines | Orthodox Eastern Church—Relations—Reformed Church.

Classification: BX4827.T67 R35 2018 (paperback) | BX4827.T67 (ebook)

Manufactured in the U.S.A.   10/05/18

This book is dedicated to George Dragas who embodies the ethos of the Orthodox-Reformed Dialogue in all that he does.

Contents

Preface | ix

Introduction: Thomas F. Torrance and the Orthodox-Reformed Theological Dialogue | 1

Part 1: A Critical Appreciation of the Orthodox-Reformed Theological Dialogue

CHAPTER 1
The Catholic and Patristic Roots of the Orthodox-Reformed Dialogue: A Trinitarian, Christocentric, and *Homoousion*-Centered Approach | 13

CHAPTER 2
The Friendship of Thomas Torrance and Methodios Fouyas: Underlying Similarities and Differences between Reformed and Orthodox at the Dialogue | 37

CHAPTER 3
The Five Consultations: Toward an Agreed Statement on the Holy Trinity | 56

CHAPTER 4
The Agreed Statement on the Holy Trinity: A Trinitarian Theology Ahead of Its Time | 80

CONCLUSION
A Proposed Way Forward from "The Agreed Statement" | 99

Part 2: Primary Sources from the Orthodox-Reformed Theological Dialogue

CHAPTER 1
Address by President Dr. James I. McCord, W.A.R.C. President to his All-Holiness the Ecumenical Patriarch, Dimitrios I, Istanbul, July 26, 1979 | 125

CHAPTER 2
Address by his All-Holiness the Ecumenical Patriarch Dimitrios I to the Delegation of the World Alliance of Reformed Churches, Istanbul, July 26, 1979 | 127

CHAPTER 3
Memoranda on Orthodox/Reformed Relations | 129

CHAPTER 4
Agreed Statement on the Holy Trinity | 144

CHAPTER 5
Significance Features: A Common Reflection on the Agreed Statement | 151

CHAPTER 6
Photos | 155

Bibliography | 161
Index | 171

Preface

UPON REACHING THE REFORMATION one is reminded of both the great importance and the great tragedy of the Protestant Reformation. Concerning the great importance, as Robert Farrar Capon puts it, "The Reformation was a time when men went blind, staggering drunk because they had discovered, in the dusty basement of late medievalism, a whole cellar full of fifteen-hundred-year-old, two-hundred proof Grace—bottle after bottle of pure distillate of Scripture, one sip of which would convince anyone that God saves us single-handedly" (*Between Noon and Three*, 109–10). Yet, as Joseph McLelland says in the discussion following the Third Preliminary consultation of the Orthodox-Reformed Dialogue (in 1983) "we Reformed tend to overemphasize the uniqueness of the 16th century Reformation." The Reformation was a movement of rediscovery of the radically unconditional grace of God as witnessed by the Scriptures and church fathers; but, it was one movement of many throughout history and, it was never meant to be decisively schismatic in the way that it eventually became.

As Thomas F. Torrance says at the beginning of "Memorandum A" on Orthodox/Reformed relations, "'The Reformed Church' does not set out to be a new or another Church but to be a movement of reform within the One, Holy Catholic and Apostolic Church of Jesus Christ . . . " (p. 10). Elsewhere Torrance states, "the Reformed Church is the Church reformed according to the Word of God so as to restore to it the face of the ancient Catholic and Apostolic Church." (*Conflict and Agreement in the Church: Volume 1*, 76). In other words, we should never be happy with being "Protestant." We must always, as Protestants, work toward rapprochement with Rome and Constantinople.

As we pass by the 500th anniversary of the Protestant Reformation these words of Torrance are as relevant today as they ever were. As we commemorate the Reformation and celebrate the wonderful rediscovery of the

Preface

radical grace of God in Jesus Christ, the inherently ecumenical and catholic approach of Torrance and the Orthodox Reformed Dialogue remind us that being Protestant was not the point of the Reformers. Torrance and the Dialogue remind us that we are not faithful to the spirit of the Reformation if we cease working for reform and renewal within the the one universal church. As Protestants, Torrance reminds us that we should bewail the necessity of the Reformation and, indeed, the continued existence of Protestantism. Torrance reminds us that Protestants faithful to the Reformation should regularly work towards rapprochement with the other two wings of the One, Holy, Catholic, and Apostolic Church: Roman Catholicism and Eastern Orthodoxy. He reminds us that Protestantism is not the Church. We are a prophetic movement of reform within it; if we cease working for reform and rapprochement, we cease to follow the Reformers.

The type of ecumenical rapprochement offered by the Orthodox-Reformed Dialogue also provides an example of real ecumenical dialogue. The agreement reached by Orthodox and Reformed was authentic and substantial. It was not the "agree to disagree" compromise so often settled for in ecumenical conversations today. The Orthodox and Reformed confessed together a doctrine of the Trinity that bridged East and West on the basis of the Trinitarian and Christocentric theology of Athanasius and Cyril.

I hope this book, above all else, points away from itself to Torrance and the Orthodox-Reformed Dialogue as an example. I hope it points to them as an example of Trinitarian theology. I hope it points to them as an example of the best of Third-Wave Trinitarianism (before there was even such a thing). I hope it points to them as an example of creative usage of the church fathers. Above all, I hope it points to them as an example of how to do ecumenical theology.

The present book has come into existence through the help and support of many parties. I am grateful to The Stony Brook School and Dr. Sean Riley for generous support in the form of grants for the archival research for this book as well as for subsequent conference presentation of the material. Kenneth W. Henke, Curator of Special Collections and Archivist at Princeton Theological Seminary, assisted me greatly in my research of the Torrance Manuscript Collection for this project. I am most grateful to The Very Rev. Dr. Iain Torrance for his immense kindness and generosity in permitting me to scan material in the archives, helping me to identify various memorabilia (pectoral crosses in particular) and photos in The Torrance Manuscript Collection, and for so generously granting me permission to include photos from the Dialogue as well as the "Memoranda on Orthodox/Reformation Relations" and "The Common Reflection," previously published by now defunct journals and publishers, both written by his late father, in this book. Thank you as well to Princeton Theological Seminary, who hold the copyright to the photos, "Memoranda on Orthodox/Reformed Relations," and "The Common Reflection," for allowing the publication of the abovementioned photos and materials, with the permission of Very Rev. Dr. Torrance, in this book. I am grateful to the World Communion of Reformed Churches, who hold the copyright to The Official Minutes from the Dialogue, for allowing me to publish selections from them in the book as well. Thanks also to Fr. George Dragas for helping to identify figures in the photos. I also thank His Eminence Job of Telmessos, the Permanent Representative of the Ecumenical Patriarchate to the World Council of Churches, for helping me to discover the public nature of "The Agreed Statement on the Holy Trinity," which is also published in this book. I am grateful to Tom Noble, Gary Deddo, and The Executive Committee of *The Thomas F. Torrance Theological Fellowship* for inviting me to give the fellowship's Annual Meeting lecture in November 2017, particularly inasmuch as this invitation has helped to sharpen many aspects of the book and its arguments. I am also grateful to my editors at Wipf & Stock, Robin Parry and Dave Belcher, who, as always, offered great guidance, assistance, and support as I completed the project. I am, finally, most grateful of all to my wife Alexandra, who has served this project very generously as my unofficial proofreader, editor, and copyeditor, as well as my children, Nicholas and Matilda, for their gift of time and support to complete this project.

Jason Radcliff
Stony Brook, NY
All Saints Day 2017

Introduction

Thomas F. Torrance and the Orthodox-Reformed Theological Dialogue

It is my plea to the Orthodox that they should resist the temptation to take their main stand today, somewhat one-sidedly, on the Cappadocian development from Athanasius, but reconsider the centrality of the Athanasius-Cyril axis on which there can be deep agreement . . . it is my plea to Roman Catholics that a rapprochement be made with Greek patristic understanding of the Trinity and the vicarious humanity of Christ . . . My plea to Protestants is that they learn to look behind the pluralist society and the fragmented patterns of the Reformation Churches to the "wholeness" that belongs to the apostolic foundation of the Church in Christ.

Thomas F. Torrance[1]

INTRODUCTION

HAILED BY MANY AS one of the greatest and most significant theologians of the twentieth century,[2] Thomas F. Torrance was at his core an ecumenical[3] theologian. He understood true, dogmatic theology to necessarily be

---

1. *Theology in Reconciliation*, 9–10.
2. See, e.g., Molnar, *Thomas F. Torrance*, 1; and McGrath, *Thomas F. Torrance*, xi, 107.
3. From the Greek οἰκουμένη meaning "universal" and, in this context, "the whole church." Lampe defines it as "inhabited land," "world," "earth," "whole world," "inhabited

ecumenical and to involve the whole church.[4] In the introduction to one of his earliest texts, *The School of Faith,* Torrance states:

> Theology must engage in ecumenical studies just because it is the dialogue of the one Covenant people with God, and therefore the exposition of theology as hearing of the Word and understanding of the Truth cannot be private to one particular Church any more than it can be private to one generation.[5]

Thus for Torrance, who had a massive output of publications in the fields of Christian dogmatics, the interrelation between theology and science, and historical theology, engaged in scholarship from a perennially ecumenical perspective.[6] The theological conversation partners in Torrance's many writings are from all traditions, ranging from Russian Orthodox and Vatican II Catholicism to Federal Calvinist and from the second century to the twentieth.

Torrance's ecumenical theology was certainly not "inter-faith" in the sense that the term "ecumenicity" is often used today. Rather, ecumenical theology for Torrance was Christocentric, traditionally orthodox,[7] and ecumenical in both the "vertical"[8] and "horizontal"[9] senses. For Torrance, this basic theological commitment to a thoroughly christocentric ecumenicity

---

world," and "another world." See Lampe, *A Patristic Greek Lexicon,* 944. The meaning in this context is "whole church."

4. Radcliff, *Thomas F. Torrance and the Church Fathers,* 60.

5. See further Torrance, "Introduction to *The School of Faith,*" lxvii–lxvii.

6. See McGrath, *Thomas F. Torrance,* 249–96, for a very full bibliography. Regarding the distinction between the three areas in which Torrance wrote, George Hunsinger aptly states: "I like to think there were at least three T. F. Torrances all rolled up into one: the distinguished Reformed dogmatic theologian, the apologetic proponent of dialogue between theology and science, and (least well known) the historian of doctrine who wrote on almost every major figure from the fourth through the twentieth century. He was also a pastor and teacher, an ecumenical dialogue partner, one of Karl Barth's very best students (whom Barth at one point hoped would become his successor), the editor of the English translation of Barth's *Church Dogmatics,* not to mention of Calvin's New Testament commentaries, and the editor and founder of a major theological journal, *The Scottish Journal of Theology,* which still exists." See Hunsinger, "Foreword," iii.

7. That is, committed to the Ecumenical Councils, particularly the Council of Nicaea.

8. That is, engaged with theologians from throughout church history. Torrance's favorites were of course Athanasius and Cyril of Alexandria. See Radcliff, *Thomas F. Torrance and the Church Fathers,* for an examination and assessment of Torrance's reading and use of the church fathers.

9. That is, engaged with theologians from other denominations during his own time. Torrance's favorites, as shall be seen, were the Eastern Orthodox.

was of course more than just theory; Torrance practiced ecumenical theology from his very genesis as an academic and pastoral theologian.[10] As a professor at the University of Edinburgh, students from all over the world from many different denominational backgrounds came to study both theology and also patristics with Torrance during 1952–1979.[11] During Torrance's tenure at New College, Edinburgh he made the School of Divinity something of a center of theological studies for students of many different denominations from around the world.

Torrance's entire career as a theologian was without doubt marked by ecumenical *foci*, however it was not until he became Moderator of the General Assembly that his ecumenical activity began in full force.[12] Traditionally, newly elected Moderators of the Church of Scotland began their tenure with visitations to key Reformed churches throughout the world. Upon his election as Moderator of the General Assembly of the Church of Scotland for 1976–1977, Torrance, however, embarked from his position of leadership in the Reformed world on two very unique and important endeavors, both of which flowed from his commitment to ecumenical theology: (1)

---

10. See, e.g., two of Torrance's early edited texts: Torrance, *Conflict and Agreement in the Church*, vols. 1–2. See Molnar, *Thomas F. Torrance*, 1; McGrath, *Thomas F. Torrance*, 107. The two *Conflict and Agreements* volumes are his first two directly ecumenical relations and they are immensely practical and pastoral.

11. For example, George Dragas and Constantine Dratsellas of Greek Orthodox background and Thomas Noble of a Wesleyan background. See Baker "Introduction," vi.

12. Torrance seems to have understood his role as Moderator of the Church of Scotland as something like a bishop and so it makes sense that he, as the "Bishop of Scotland," a center of the Reformed churches, would approach the Ecumenical Patriarch (the clear head Bishop of the Orthodox churches). See Baker and Dragas, "Interview," 10, for Dragas's account of an interaction where Methodios Fouyas, no doubt with a wink, calls Torrance the "Patriarch of Scotland." See Torrance, *Royal Priesthood*, 88–108, for Torrance's theological interpretation of the Moderator as, basically, Presiding Bishop. For an early proposal in dialogue between the Church of Scotland and the Anglican Church, which is essentially a combined Presbyterian-Episcopal structure ("corporate episcopate"), see The Thomas F. Torrance Manuscript Collection. Special Collections, Princeton Theological Seminary Library. Box 89. See also T. Torrance, *Conflict and Agreement*, 1:83–98, for further elaboration upon this point. In the Orthodox-Reformed Dialogue Torrance states, "It became distinctive of the Reformed Church that the *episcope* was held to be lodged not individually in the persons but corporately in the body of Presbyters i.e. in the Presbytery as a whole . . . the "Bishop" was understood as the presiding Presbyter . . . the Reformed Church sought to take its pattern of reform from the pattern of the Early Church before the bishop became separated from the presbytery over which he presided . . . " (See Torrance, "Memoranda on Orthodox/Reformed Relations," 9).

he visited the then Archbishop of Aksum,[13] Methodios Fouyas, a visit both out of friendship[14] and ecumenical rapprochement, and (2) he visited the Archbishop of Constantinople with the suggestion of opening up an Official Dialogue between the Orthodox and Reformed churches. These two important events highlight splendidly Torrance's unique understanding of the Reformed tradition not as a church itself but as a prophetic movement within the western church.[15] By visiting the ancient Episcopal Sees of Alexandria and Constantinople in his capacity as Moderator, and staying with Archbishop Methodios in his Episcopal Palace in Adis Adaba, Torrance was making a statement about how he understood his Reformed tradition and his role as moderator, namely, a part of the one, holy, and catholic church.

SCOPE OF THE BOOK

This book examines the history and theology of the Orthodox-Reformed Dialogue of the late nineteenth and early twentieth century. In particular, the book explores the theological rapprochement that occurred between the Orthodox and Reformed traditions, presenting a critical examination of the Orthodox-Reformed Ecumenical Dialogue especially its patristic roots and constructively extending the Dialogue from the early 1990s into contemporary theological conversation, suggesting that it has much to offer the current theological conversation,[16] despite being largely unutilized in current Trinitarian theology.

The present volume therefore explores the history and theology of the Orthodox-Reformed Dialogue, spearheaded by T. F. Torrance (on the Reformed side) and Methodios Fouyas (on the Orthodox side). The Reformed and Orthodox, although vastly different in expression, overlap substantially in theological content with their focus on the Trinitarian and Christocentric theology of the Greek fathers. Utilizing both the small handful of

---

13. An Archbishopric in Ethiopia "founded by the great Athanasius." See Torrance's speech in honor of Methodios's at the Rotary Club of Athens in The Thomas F. Torrance Manuscript Collection. Special Collections, Princeton Theological Seminary Library. Box 172.

14. See chapter 2 of this book for elaboration upon the relationship, both personal and theological, between Torrance and Archbishop Methodios.

15. Torrance, *Conflict and Agreement in the Church: Volume*, 1:76–77; Torrance, "Memoranda on Orthodox/Reformed Relations," 3.

16. So-called "Third-Wave Trinitarianism," to utilize Sarah Coakley's categories. See "Afterword: 'Relational Ontology,' Trinity, and Science," 184–99.

published texts from the Dialogue and "reading in between the lines" via unpublished Minutes and Correspondence, the book introduces the reader to the Orthodox-Reformed Dialogue as well as, more generally, differences in approach yet important similarities in core theology between the Reformed and Orthodox traditions. The argument emerges throughout the book that, whilst meritorious in countless ways, the Orthodox-Reformed Dialogue of Torrance is also dated in certain areas. The book suggests specific elements that should be left with Torrance and the Dialogue in the 1980s and 1990s and constructively explores which elements may provide fruitful soil for further ecumenical and Trinitarian conversation, ultimately aiming to point to the Dialogue and the texts produced by it as relevant for the current ecumenical and theological conversations, not least on the doctrine of the Trinity.

In the current resurgence of interest in Eastern Orthodoxy, the patristic doctrine of the Trinity, and T. F. Torrance, the book examines all three through the important point of convergence in the Orthodox-Reformed Dialogue. On account of these three elements, the book is relevant in four specific ways. First, the book is relevant most generally as an historical study of how two traditions explored their common roots in the Greek fathers and, relevantly, how they might do so today. Second, the book is more specifically relevant during this present time when so many Protestants (particularly evangelicals) are interested in the fathers and in Orthodoxy; Torrance and the Dialogue show a way for Protestants to engage the fathers and the Orthodox whilst remaining faithfully Protestant, but understanding themselves, not as a separate church, but as part of the One, Holy, Catholic, and Apostolic Church. Third, the book (and the Dialogue, especially "The Agreed Statement on the Trinity," the theological "fruit" of the Dialogue) is most specifically relevant in contemporary Trinitarian theology, which states that East and West are at least complementary if not identical (as opposed to the traditional distinction between East vs. West on the doctrine) in which conversation Torrance and the Orthodox-Reformed Dialogue are both seriously underutilized. Fourth, it is the hope that this book will fill a lacuna in the growing field of secondary literature on Torrance. Torrance wrote profusely in his time and it is only in recent years that books on Torrance have been published. As of yet, however, nothing has been published in the form of a monograph on Torrance and the Orthodox-Reformed Dialogue; the story needs to be told.

Building upon *Thomas F. Torrance and the Church Fathers* (Pickwick, 2014) and also *T. F. Torrance and Eastern Orthodoxy* (Wipf and Stock, 2015) this book presents a critical examination of the Orthodox-Reformed ecumenical dialogue. Focusing upon the Patristic foundations of the Dialogue as seen in Torrance as well as the theological outcome of the Dialogue, "The Agreed Statement on the Holy Trinity," this book also highlights some of the notable conversations about patristic theology, inter alia, that went on "behind the scenes" of the Dialogue as seen in the unpublished Official Minutes as well as correspondence between Torrance and other major figures in the Dialogue, namely, George Dragas, Methodios Fouyas, and the Archbishop of Constantinople himself about such topics such as the Athanasian doctrine of the Trinity, Barthian christocentrism, and John Zizioulas.

Ultimately this book hopes to point to Torrance and the Dialogue as an example *par excellence* of Trinitarian and ecumenical theology. As Donald Fairbairn aptly puts it in his review of *Thomas F. Torrance and the Church Fathers*,

> Torrance's approach to patristic theology is deeply provocative and—if it is even partially correct in its main assertions—profoundly significant . . . we disregard Torrance's interpretations at our own peril. At a time when not only scholars but even lay people are increasingly interested in the early Church, Torrance's *consensus patrum* deserves a broader hearing than it has received thus far.[17]

Fairbairn notes that the book, ultimately, points to Torrance as a good example and herein lies its value.[18] Similarly, this present book aims to point to Torrance and the Orthodox-Reformed Dialogue as a good but overlooked example of Third-Wave Trinitarianism, notwithstanding certain critiques, which deserves a place in the current Trinitarian conversation. Indeed, like St. John in Karl Barth's beloved Grünewald crucifixion scene from the Isenheim Altarpiece, and Barth who understood the piece to capture splendidly his task and calling as a theologian as ultimately witnessing to the crucified Christ, this book hopes to point away from itself and to Torrance and the Orthodox-Reformed Dialogue as a good example of ecumenical Trinitarian theology and, through them, to God's self-revelation in Christ. Or, as Peter Kreeft puts it in his inimitable fashion, like a little boy,

---

17. Fairbairn, "Review of *Thomas F. Torrance and the Church Fathers*," 118.
18. Ibid.

this book hopes to point away from itself and say "look!"[19] Accordingly, the book not only introduces the Patristic foundations of the Dialogue in the Torrancian-Athanasian *homoousion* but also critically examines and suggests areas where Torrance and the Dialogue may say more about the Trinitarian issues of the 1980s than the 380s. The book ultimately argues that the incredible ecumenical agreement and conclusions at the Dialogue between Orthodox and Reformed Churches on the basis of the *homoousion*-centered Trinitarian and Christocentric theology of the Greek fathers and also "The Agreed Statement on the Holy Trinity" produced by the Dialogue presents a Trinitarian Theology that is, if anything, Third-Wave Trinitarianism (but a better, more nuanced version) and it deserves a much stronger consideration in the conversations theologians and historians are having about the doctrine of the Trinity today. Ultimately, this book seeks to point to the Orthodox-Reformed Dialogue and the texts surrounding it as a movement in Trinitarian Theology that should be a part of the current conversation.

In the book, the doctrine of the Trinity discussed and agreed upon in the Dialogue will be examined and constructively engaged in light of contemporary discussions in systematic theology on the doctrine of the Trinity, in which conversation Torrance is seriously underutilized and usually entirely unutilized.[20] Ultimately, the book will argue that Torrance, Dragas, Methodios, and the wider Orthodox-Reformed Dialogue arrived at a much better nuanced version of Third-Wave Trinitarianism decades before Third-Wave Trinitarianism existed inasmuch as they "got behind" the problem of the *filioque*[21] and articulated a Trinitarian theology that says there are real differences in Trinitarian language between East and West but the theological substance is the same from the patristic era to the present day.

---

19. Kreeft, *Protestants and Catholics in Dialogue*, 9.

20. See also Radcliff, "T. F. Torrance and the Patristic Consensus on the Doctrine of the Trinity," 21–38.

21. Latin for "and the Son," i.e., stating that the Holy Spirit proceeds from the Father *and the Son*. This was officially added to the Creed by the Council of Lyons in 1274 and then again at the Council of Florence in 1439. See Fouyas, *Orthodoxy, Roman Catholicism, and Anglicanism*, 206.

OUTLINE OF THE BOOK

The present book seeks to do three things (1) tell the story of Torrance and the Orthodox-Reformed Dialogue, (2) argue for the theological relevance of Torrance and the Orthodox-Reformed Dialogue, particularly the relevance of "The Agreed Statement on the Holy Trinity" for contemporary conversations in Trinitarian Theology, and (3) make available for use by those who wish to build off of the good work of the Dialogue useful but difficult-to-access and out-of-print texts as well as previously unpublished documents from the Official Minutes.

Part One of the book is a critical appreciation of the Orthodox-Reformed Dialogue. In Chapter One, the historical and theological details of the Orthodox-Reformed Dialogue are introduced and examined, particularly the ecumenical, catholic, and Trinitarian Greek patristic basis which undergirds Torrance's approach and the Dialogue at large in both content and method. Chapter Two examines the friendship between Torrance and Methodios Fouyas, the two spearheads of the Dialogue, whose theological and personal relationship based on agreed commitments to the Greek Patristic doctrines of the Trinity, Christology, and Soteriology provided the impetus and fulcrum of the Dialogue. Chapter Three explores the events and people of the Dialogue, providing an account of the meetings, papers, and subsequent conversation, utilizing especially correspondence and Official Minutes to help read in between the lines of the publications and get behind the scenes, as it were. This chapter aims to trace the development of the Orthodox-Reformed Dialogue, particularly the theological route to "The Agreed Statement on the Holy Trinity." Chapter Four examines "The Agreed Statement on the Holy Trinity," which was the outcome of the Dialogue. Here, the doctrine of the Trinity that emerges for the Greek fathers, as articulated through the Dialogue via "The Agreed Statement," is examined and it shall be argued that "The Agreed Statement" does what current Trinitarian Theology is doing, but did it a quarter of a century prior and in a more nuanced fashion. This chapter argues that the Orthodox-Reformed Dialogue was a Third-Wave Trinitarianism before its time. The Conclusion explores the key points of agreement and disagreement between Reformed and Orthodox and weeks to extend and apply the many contributions in the Dialogue in both content and method. As shall be seen, there were many points of disagreement as well, but the foci of the Dialogue became on the many points of agreement that arose out of their shared commitment to the Greek fathers' Trinitarian and Christocentric theology. The Conclusion also highlights some of the shortcomings of the Dialogue. It suggests that some points of disagreement can be forgotten today and critically explores ways in which the Dialogue can proceed.

The second part of the book contains Primary Sources produced by the Orthodox-Reformed Dialogue, some of which are published here for the first time. Included are Torrance's "Memoranda on Orthodox/Reformed Relations" (Memorandum A was written by Torrance and Memorandum B was written by George Dragas, but both were presented to Patriarch Dimitrios I during the 1979 initial visit to Phanar and the official opening of the Orthodox-Reformed Dialogue),[22] "The Agreed Statement on the Holy Trinity," "A Common Reflection, Significant Features on the Agreed Statement," and the speeches by Dr. James McCord (from the Reformed) and Patriarch Dimitrios I (from the Orthodox), contained in the 1979 Official Minutes.

The Patriarch's speech to the Reformed delegates and Dr. McCord's speech to the Orthodox Delegates, both from the 1979 meeting, each offer a glimpse into the warm cordiality and mutual appreciation that undergirded the entire Dialogue. The "Memoranda," especially "Memorandum A," offer Torrance's understanding of the Reformed church and tradition and its place in the One, Holy, Catholic Church and, as such, exhibit Torrance's unique understanding of Reformed and Protestant Catholicity and, thus, the very possibility of and impetus for ecumenical Dialogue. "The Agreed Statement," written by Torrance and Dragas, offers the unprecedented agreement between East and West, Reformed and Orthodox on the doctrine of the Trinity and the "Common Reflection" offers Torrance's own interpretation of the content, method, and significance of the document.

CONCLUSION

This introductory chapter has introduced many of the themes that the remainder of this book will unpack more fully. In particular, it has considered the inherent ecumenicity of Torrance's theology, his friendship with Archbishop Methodios Fouyas, the unprecedented agreement in "The Agreed Statement on the Holy Trinity" and its relevance for Third-Wave Trinitarianism, and the good example of the Trinitarian, Christocentric, and patristic approach of the Dialogue. There is indeed much more to be explored regarding the history and theology of the Orthodox-Reformed Dialogue,

22. See Baker and Dragas, "Interview," 12.

the relationship between T. F. Torrance and Methodios Fouyas, and the Trinitarian theology of the Greek fathers that emerges from the Dialogue. Prior to exploring the important details of the Dialogue, a basic historical and theological overview is necessary. Therefore, this book now turns to an overview prior to critically examining the historical and theological detail.

PART 1

A Critical Appreciation of the Orthodox-Reformed Theological Dialogue

CHAPTER 1

The Catholic and Patristic Roots of the Orthodox-Reformed Dialogue

A Trinitarian, Christocentric, and *Homoousion*-Centered Approach

> *Both the Orthodox and the Reformed readily acknowledged that they have different emphases in their approaches to the doctrine of the Holy Trinity, but they insisted that they agree on the content of the doctrine.*
>
> Thomas F. Torrance[1]

INTRODUCTION

COLIN GUNTON STATES THAT Thomas F. Torrance offers "a reopening of a major historical conversation and George Dragas elaborates that "few contemporary theologians in [Torrance's] tradition have so thoroughly and consistently appropriated the spiritual wealth of Greek Patristic Theology . . ."[2] It was the Reformed, led by Torrance, who approached the Orthodox and initiated the Dialogue. Indeed, Torrance is an important figure in two

---

1. "Memoranda on Orthodox/Reformed Relations," xxi.

2. Dragas, "The Significance for the Church of Professor Torrance's Election As Moderator of the General Assembly of the Church of Scotland," 216.

movements in the latter half of the twentieth century: the *ressourcement* of the church fathers and the very much connected revival of Trinitarian theology from an ecumenical perspective. A cursory glance at a bibliography of Torrance indicates that he clearly was heavily influenced by the Greek fathers and sees himself as returning to the patristic consensus on, *inter alia,* the doctrine of the Trinity.[3]

Torrance's vast work on the doctrine of the Trinity, as seen not least in his books *The Christian Doctrine of God* and *The Trinitarian Faith* are, to use the words of George Hunsinger, "studded with Greek patristic citations."[4] Torrance's approach to all aspects of his theological scholarship and teaching was undergirded by the church fathers. This approach is perhaps best illustrated by a humorous story oft-told by Fr. George Dragas to his patristics students at Holy Cross. As Fr. George recounts, in his first interaction with his beloved Edinburgh teacher, a bright-eyed Fr. George arrived to Edinburgh to study theology with the famed Professor Tom, who, according to Fr. George, told the University of Basel when they asked him to succeed Karl Barth, that theologians used to come to Basel, now they could come to Edinburgh. Fr. George sat down in his new professor's New College office and he immediately noticed two pieces of art: an icon of Athanasius and a painting of John Calvin.[5] Fr. George recounts that, upon inquiry, Torrance exhorted the young theologian, "*always* follow the example of St. Athanasius." When Fr. George asked about the other figure, Torrance apparently responded, "well, you should read him." This anecdote, with which Fr. George's students are familiar, illustrates Torrance's approach to a theology guided by the Nicene fathers wonderfully. One could look at nearly any one of Torrance's books to see that the fathers are in the background, if not the foreground of what he is doing. From the connection between Nicene theology and Einstein's relativity theory in *Space, Time, and Incarnation* and the realist Nicene theology of the *homoousion* and the realist philosophy of John Philoponus in *Theological Science* to the explicitly Nicene *Christian Doctrine of God* and *Trinitarian Faith*, the Trinitarian and Christocentric theology of the Greek fathers undergirds all that Torrance does. In his teaching, the connection of Greek patristic and Scottish Reformed theology shines clear not only in his New College lectures recently edited and published by Robert Walker but also in his New College

---

3. See, e.g., Torrance, *The Trinitarian Faith*; Torrance, *The Christian Doctrine of God*.
4. Hunsinger, "Foreword," iii.
5. Baker and Dragas, "Interview," 3.

seminars, where, according to the course syllabus, Athanasius' *Letters to Serapion* was one of three key texts studied (the other two were Anselm's *Cur Deus Homo* and Kierkegaard's *Philosophical Fragments*).[6]

Torrance's patristic study was not, however, done for purely academic or pedagogical reasons. Torrance's unique "turn to the east" was a part of his greater ecumenical vision which entailed a reunion of churches on the basis of the Trinitarian and Christocentric theology of the Greek Nicene fathers. Torrance practiced this ecumenical theology with Presbyterians, Anglicans, and Roman Catholics from the very beginning of his career as a theologian, professor, and churchman as seen through his published *Conflict and Agreement Volumes 1 and 2*.[7] Torrance's early vision of ecumenical rapprochement seemed to be largely reunion on the basis of Greek patristic forms of ministry, sacrament, and episcopacy, but by the 1980s, however, Torrance's great work with the Eastern Orthodox began as a rather different type of vision of ecumenical rapprochement, namely one of theological agreement. This theological ecumenical work, based on the Greek fathers, is unique and, as George Hunsinger puts it, "[Torrance's] profound interest in Eastern Orthodoxy—not only in the legacy of the Greek church fathers, but also in face-to-face encounter with Eastern Orthodox theologians . . . may prove crucial to interpreting his entire legacy for present day theology."[8] It was, indeed, in the Orthodox-Reformed Dialogue that Torrance's great interest in Greek patristic theology provided the substantial theological and ecumenical ground for a dialogue with the Eastern Orthodox and produced fruit not only for ecumenical theology but also for Trinitarian theology today.

Scope of the Chapter

The Reformed and Orthodox churches interacted in significant ecumenical conversation during the last two decades of the twentieth century; a dialogue spearheaded by Torrance. The Orthodox-Reformed Dialogue

---

6. Torrance, "Course Syllabus," in The Thomas F. Torrance Manuscript Collection. Special Collections, Princeton Theological Seminary Library. Box 51. See also Baker and Dragas, "Interview," 3–4. According to Dragas, Torrance said that "these books . . . bring us face to face with the basis of Christian dogmatics, the event of the Incarnation, the fact that God has become man." See ibid., 4.

7. Torrance, *Conflict and Agreement in the Church*, vols. 1 and 2.

8. Hunsinger, "Foreword," iii.

took place during the 1980s and 1990s, although more informal dialogue had been going on prior to this between the two traditions. At the Orthodox-Reformed Dialogue, participants gathered, presented papers, and discussed. Torrance published the papers as *Theological Dialogue Between Orthodox and Reformed Churches Volume 1*[9] and *Theological Dialogue Between Orthodox and Reformed Churches Volume 2*[10] and he wonderfully saved and preserved copies of correspondence surrounding the Dialogue and copies of the Official Minutes, both of which contain comments and notes on many of the discussion points raised after the papers and in between official meetings; these are preserved in the *Thomas F. Torrance Manuscript Collection* in the Princeton Theological Seminary Library Archives in Princeton, New Jersey. George Dragas, who as shall be seen in subsequent chapters of this book, was a major player in the Dialogue, also provides a fair amount of insight and commentary in his "Interview" with Matthew Baker published in Baker and Speidell's *T. F. Torrance and Eastern Orthodoxy*.[11] The correspondence and minutes in particular help one to "read in between the lines" and gain a fuller picture of what happened at the Orthodox-Reformed Dialogue, and learn more of the story.

The present chapter offers an introduction to the Orthodox-Reformed Dialogue spearheaded by Torrance. It begins to explore in particular how Torrance and the Dialogue's ecumenical use and creative interpretation of the Trinitarian and Christocentric theology of the church fathers has much to offer contemporary Trinitarian theology, raising questions and ideas that will be explored in the subsequent chapters of the book. The aim of the present chapter is to outline the historical and theological contours and context of the Orthodox-Reformed Dialogue, Torrance's approach and understanding in initiating it in particular, prior to examining the history and theology of the Dialogue in further detail in subsequent chapters of this book. This chapter will thus focus in particular on the ecumenical and patristic understanding of Torrance which enabled him to uniquely turn East in the Orthodox-Reformed Dialogue. Ultimately, this chapter will argue that the ecumenical, Trinitarian, and *homoousion*-centered theology of Athanasius as seen by Torrance provided the grounds and impetus for the Orthodox-Reformed Dialogue which was itself a truly ecumenical and

---

9. Torrance, *Theological Dialogue between Orthodox & Reformed Churches*, vol. 1.
10. Torrance, *Theological Dialogue between Orthodox & Reformed Churches*, vol. 2.
11. See Baker and Speidell's *T. F. Torrance and Eastern Orthodoxy*, 1–18.

Third-Wave Trinitarian theology that deserves far more utilization in today's scholarly conversations in Trinitarian Theology.

THE HISTORICAL CONTEXT OF THE ORTHODOX-REFORMED DIALOGUE

Informal ecumenical dialogue between the Reformed and Orthodox traditions occurred in the years preceding the official Orthodox-Reformed Dialogue. From the very outset of the Reformation, the Protestant Reformers began to turn East in some form or another.[12] Calvin returned to the Eastern church fathers, as did Zwingli and Bucer, most notably in their articulation of the doctrine of the Trinity.[13] Despite certain overgeneralizations and misunderstandings, such as Calvin's view of the Seventh Ecumenical Council and the use of icons as idolatrous,[14] as Joseph Small puts it,

> Calvin's high regard for the Fathers and the (first four) ecumenical councils carried into seventeenth-century Reformed scholasticism and beyond. Patristic scholarship deepened and Reformed theology continued to draw on the Fathers, particularly with regard to the doctrine of the Trinity . . . it was not coincidental that it was a Reformed theologian and patristics scholar who initiated twentieth-century Reformed engagement with the Orthodox churches.[15]

Informal ecumenical dialogue between the Reformed and Orthodox traditions occurred in the years preceding the official Orthodox-Reformed Dialogue spearheaded by Torrance[16] but the formal Dialogue in which Torrance was involved happened between the Reformed (headed by the World Alliance of Reformed Churches) and the Orthodox (headed by the Greek Orthodox Patriarchate) in 1981, 1983, 1988, and 1990. Prior to the

12. See, e.g., Mastrantonis, *Augsburg and Constantinople,* for correspondence between Lutheran and Orthodox theologians in the sixteenth century, esp. pp. 3–20 for the history of their dialogue and correspondence.

13. See Small, "Orthodox and Reformed in Dialogue," 103–9, for an excellent outline. As Small notes, however, the Reformers' use of the fathers was largely polemical in an attempt to prove that the Reformation was rooted in the ancient church.

14. See ibid., 104.

15. Ibid., 108–9.

16. See the Memoranda and Introductions in both volumes of *Theological Dialogue between Orthodox and Reformed Churches* for outlines of the history surrounding the Dialogue and also for the historical precedent. Protestants and Orthodox had really been in dialogue in some form since shortly after the Reformation.

Part 1: A Critical Appreciation of the Orthodox-Reformed Theological Dialogue

official Dialogue, the Reformed churches and Eastern Orthodox churches had been engaged in dialogue for some time. A letter written by the Orthodox to the World Alliance of Reformed Churches highlights previous dialogue which had been transpiring since the mid-twentieth century, for example, in North America, the World Alliance of Reformed Churches and the Standing Conference of Canonical Orthodox Bishops in the Americas had been in theological dialogue since 1968; in Eastern Europe and Russia, the World Alliance of Reformed Churches had been in dialogue with churches connected to the Moscow Patriarchate since 1972; in Romania, the Reformed Church in Romania had been in dialogue with the Orthodox Church since 1964.[17] Notably, there was also Orthodox involvement in the Edinburgh Missionary Conference (1910) and the Faith and Order Conferences in Lausanne (1927) and Edinburgh (1937).[18]

Whilst the Reformed proposed the Dialogue, the Orthodox responded with great enthusiasm, stating in a letter to Torrance: "We greet you in love and we received you with great honour. You represent in the most official way the large and well-respected world of the Reformed Churches. You came here with the sacred and concrete purpose to make the official proposal for the opening of the Theological Dialogue with Orthodoxy."[19]

The Orthodox-Reformed Dialogue attempted to investigate the common roots between the Reformed and Orthodox traditions on the basis of the Greek patristic theology in which both traditions are rooted and, as such, the patristic doctrines of Trinity and Christology steered the Dialogue. According to the Minutes from the meeting where the Reformed officially proposed the Dialogue, in his introductory greeting to the Orthodox Patriarchate during their official proposal for dialogue, James McCord "stressed how the Reformed feel themselves historically very close to the Orthodox in a common concern for the truth of the Apostolic Faith and for the unity of the Church in that same faith."[20] The Minutes also record that Torrance notes he established his opinion while Moderator of the General Assembly of the Church of Scotland that any Orthodox and Reformed theological

---

17. See the letter in The Thomas F. Torrance Manuscript Collection. Special Collections, Princeton Seminary. Box 170. See also Radcliff, "T. F. Torrance and the Reformed-Orthodox Dialogue," 32–53.

18. Small, "Orthodox and Reformed in Dialogue," 109.

19. See this letter in The Thomas F. Torrance Manuscript Collection. Special Collections, Princeton Theological Seminary Library. Box 170.

20. See the 1979 Minutes in The Thomas F. Torrance Manuscript Collection. Special Collections, Princeton Theological Seminary Library. Box 170.

dialogue should begin on the doctrine of the Trinity and move forward from there.[21] So, the Reformed and Orthodox, spearheaded by Reformed Torrance and Orthodox Methodios, began the Orthodox-Reformed Dialogue on the basis on their common fount: the Apostolic Faith as preserved by the Greek fathers and encapsulated in their Trinitarian and Christocentric theology.

A letter from Prof Jan Lochman, Chairman of the Department of Theology for the World Alliance of Reformed Churches, elucidates with clarity the approach from the Reformed side of the Dialogue.[22] In the letter, dated February 18, 1977, Lochman writes a letter to support Torrance as a representative of the World Alliance of Reformed Churches (W.A.R.C.) and the Reformed tradition more generally in his visit to the Ecumenical Patriarch in Constantinople. In the letter, Lochman unpacks what he sees as the patristic rootedness of the Reformed tradition and suggests this as a way forward for continuing ecumenical dialogue between Reformed and Orthodox churches.

Lochman highlights three bases in particular from which he believes the Reformed and Orthodox churches can proceed in ecumenical dialogue, at least from the Reformed perspective: (1) Reformed Catholicity, (2) the Reformed tradition's patristic rootedness, and (3) the precedent of recent ecumenical dialogue between the two traditions, especially in North America. First, by way of greeting, Lochman states: "That the bearer [of this letter], the present Moderator of the General Assembly of the Church of Scotland, the Right Rev. Prof. T. F. Torrance, is able to visit your Holiness in his capacity as representative of the Church of Scotland is a great source of satisfaction to many of us in the Reformed family of churches." Herein, Prof Lochman supports Torrance as representing the W.A.R.C. and the Reformed church more generally. Second, Lochman identifies the Reformed churches as "143 autonomous denominations throughout the world with approximately 60 million communicant members." Lochman traces the Reformed churches to Jan Hus, Ulrich Zwingli, and John Calvin, suggesting that Calvin is the primary root of the Reformed tradition and Calvin himself was rooted in the patristic tradition. Lochman says "the theology of Calvin was deeply rooted in patristic thought and doctrine, embracing

---

21. Ibid.

22. For this and subsequent references to this letter, see The Thomas F. Torrance Manuscript Collection. Special Collections, Princeton Theological Seminary Library. Box 170.

the early fathers of the east and the west," and that the ecumenical councils and creeds are equally received in the Reformed tradition as they are in the Orthodox.[23] Third, Lochman identifies the precedent, particularly in North America, for such a dialogue. He lists three particular instances that he thinks augur well for ecumenical dialogue between the Reformed and Orthodox churches: (1) the dialogue in North America as seen in John Meyendorff and Joseph McLelland's edited volume, *The New Man*,[24] (2) the dialogue in Eastern Europe from 1972–1976 in Romania, Hungary, Debrecen, and Leningrad, and (3) the dialogue between Reformed churches and the Roman Catholic Church officially sponsored by the W.A.R.C. and the Secretariat for Promoting Christian Unity of the Roman Catholic Church. Lochman concludes by stating his hope that Torrance and the Ecumenical Patriarch will proceed with discussing the beginnings of this dialogue.

The Ecumenical Patriarch provides a response[25] to Lochman intimating a positive reception of the W.A.R.C. proposal via Torrance to begin ecumenical dialogue. In a handwritten piece of correspondence from 1983, the Ecumenical Patriarchate in Phanar, Constantinople says "In March 1977 an approach was made by the W.A.R.C. to the Ecumenical Patriarchate, and the other Patriarchs and Archbishops in Greece, Cyprus, Egypt, and Jerusalem with a view of opening up dialogue between Orthodox and Reformed churches bearing on the very centre of the catholic faith beginning with the doctrine of the Holy Trinity." In this important piece, the Ecumenical Patriarchate agrees to proceed in dialogue on the basis of the patristic doctrines of the Trinity, Christology, and soteriology. As shall be seen, this indeed becomes the very basis of the Dialogue.

Ultimately, then, the Reformed proposed the Dialogue and the Orthodox responded with great enthusiasm, stating in a letter to Torrance: "We greet you in love and we received you with great honour. You represent in the most official way the large and well-respected world of the Reformed Churches. You came here with the sacred and concrete purpose to make the official proposal for the opening of the Theological Dialogue with Orthodoxy."[26] The Orthodox-Reformed Dialogue attempted to investigate

---

23. As shall be seen, this will be central to Torrance's approach throughout the Dialogue and his theological writings more generally.

24. *The New Man: An Orthodox and Reformed Dialogue*.

25. For this and subsequent references to this letter, see The Thomas F. Torrance Manuscript Collection. Special Collections, Princeton Theological Seminary Library. Box 170

26. See this letter in The Thomas F. Torrance Manuscript Collection. Special

the common roots between the Reformed and Orthodox traditions on the basis of Greek patristic Trinitarian theology. Common points of agreement and overlap between the two traditions were stressed from the beginning of the Dialogue.

The Minutes note that Torrance established the view while Moderator of the General Assembly of the Church of Scotland that any theological dialogue between the two traditions should begin on the doctrine of the Trinity and proceed from that grounding.[27] So, the Reformed and Orthodox, spearheaded by Reformed Torrance and Orthodox Methodios, began the Orthodox-Reformed Dialogue on the basis on their common fount: the Apostolic Faith as preserved by the Greek fathers and encapsulated in their Trinitarian and Christocentric theology. They emphasized points of agreement and aimed to avoid focus on points of different historical and pietistic development. In many ways, however, it was Torrance's understanding of the Reformed tradition as inherently ecumenical that enabled him to approach the Orthodox and begin the incredibly unique and unprecedented Orthodox-Reformed Dialogue.

THE THEOLOGICAL CONTEXT OF THE ORTHODOX-REFORMED DIALOGUE

Torrance, Fouyas, and the Orthodox-Reformed Dialogue, led largely by Torrance and George Dragas, eventually constructed an ecumenically and theologically significant document: "The Agreed Statement on the Holy Trinity" which cuts behind the issue of the *filioque*, bridging a chasm that had grown between East and West for centuries on the doctrine of the Trinity. The document which states a doctrine of the Trinity, rooted in Scripture and the church fathers, exhibits not only great ecumenical rapprochement, therefore, but also a significant theological development: Third-Wave

---

Collections, Princeton Theological Seminary Library. Box 170.

27. See the 1979 Minutes in The Thomas F. Torrance Manuscript Collection. Special Collections, Princeton Theological Seminary Library. Box 170.

Trinitarianism,[28] to use Coakley's term,[29] before there was such a thing. The Orthodox-Reformed Dialogue arrived at the theological place that Third-Wave Trinitarianism claims to be arriving just now, yet they arrived at, arguably a better and more nuanced version 30 years earlier. Yet, Third-Wave Trinitarians—and Trinitarian theologians more generally—hardly refer to the Orthodox-Reformed Dialogue, if they do at all.[30]

At its core, therefore, this book wonders why the Orthodox-Reformed Dialogue is under (indeed entirely un) utilized and seeks, ultimately, to point to the Dialogue and the texts associated with it and produced by it as not only relevant for the current theological conversation but as a better and more nuanced example in both content and method of ecumenical theological dialogue that successfully accomplished what Third-Wave Trinitarianism and all forms of ecumenical theology seek—or at least should seek—to accomplish: real theological rapprochement and agreement on the basis of the Trinitarian, Christocentric, and Patristic theology of the church fathers. Torrance's approach to the Orthodox-Reformed Dialogue was ultimately driven by three convictions: his (1) the catholicity of the Reformed tradition, (2) the Greek patristic nature of the Reformed tradition, and (3) the importance of a Christocentric (*homoousion*-centered) reading of the church fathers.

---

28. In short, this is the view that says the so-called de Régnon thesis, which said East and West were completely divergent on the doctrine of the Trinity, is false and East and West, rather than the former emphasizing the three Persons and the latter emphasizing the one Being, in fact speak with one voice on the doctrine and thus the *filioque* clause is neither necessary nor cause for concern. Third-Wave Trinitarianism claims this on an historical level (e.g., Ayres, *Nicaea and Its Legacy*) and on a theological level (e.g., Holmes, *The Holy Trinity*). Despite their variagated conclusions, Third-Wave Trinitarian claims are, however, consistent and unanimous in their departure from the de Régnon thesis and Second-Wave/Social Trinitarianism views that emphasize God's plurality over his unity.

29. See "Afterword: 'Relational Ontology,' Trinity, and Science," 184–99.

30. Holmes says that Torrance does not fit the story he is telling (of how theology arrived at Third-Wave Trinitarianism)! See Holmes, "Response: In Praise of Being Criticized," 151. Of course, there are exceptions, see Molnar, *T. F. Torrance, Theologian of the Trinity*; and Molnar, "Theological Issues Involved in the *Filioque*"; Habets, *Ecumenical Perspectives on the Filioque for the 21st Century*; and Baker, "The Eternal 'Spirit of the Son': Barth, Florovsky and Torrance on the Filioque," 382–403.

TORRANCE AND THE CATHOLICITY OF THE REFORMED TRADITION

First, Torrance held that the Reformed tradition in which he was a part was inherently ecumenical and, as such, very much rooted in the Greek fathers, thus the Dialogue was a true ecumenical work of attempted reunion. Herein Torrance understands himself to be approaching estranged brethren rather than members of a different church. As such, Torrance goes to great lengths to prove the similarity not only in theology but also in order between Reformed and Orthodox. For example, Torrance articulates a similarity between Orthodox autocephalous churches[31] and the autonomous nature of the Reformed churches.[32] As such, part of the basis for the Dialogue came from Torrance's understanding of the Reformed tradition as inherently "catholic." In Torrance's "Memorandum" published in *Theological Dialogue Between Orthodox and Reformed Churches Volume 1*, he stresses how the Reformed tradition has never sought to be a "new" church but rather sees itself as a prophetic movement of reform within the western church.[33] As Torrance says elsewhere:

> The Reformation was not a movement to refound the Church, or to found a new Church; for the whole reforming movement would undoubtedly have continued within the Roman Church had it not been for the bigoted and arrogant recalcitrance of its hierarchy, which insisted in binding the movement of the Word and Spirit by the traditions of men and making it of none effect, and when that failed, in throwing it out altogether, just as the early Christians were thrown out of the synagogues and followed with maledictions and anathemas."[34]

Thus, Torrance argues, "the Reformed Church is the Church reformed according to the Word of God so as to restore to it the face of the ancient

---

31. From αὐτοκεφαλία, self (αὐτο)-heading (κεπαλία). Orthodox autocephalous churches are not under an archbishop.

32. Torrance, "Memoranda on Orthodox/Reformed Relations," 10. Notably, the Orthodox found this interesting. See the minutes from the 1981 meeting in The Thomas F. Torrance Manuscript Collection. Special Collections, Princeton Theological Seminary Library. Box 170.

33. See also the 1979 minutes in Thomas F. Torrance Manuscript Collection. Special Collections, Princeton Theological Seminary Library. Box 170.

34. See Torrance, *Conflict and Agreement in the Church*, 1:77

Catholic and Apostolic Church."[35] The Reformed tradition, says Torrance, "does not set out to be a new or another Church but to be a movement of reform within the One Holy Catholic and Apostolic Church of Jesus Christ . . . ."[36] As a part of the Western tradition inheriting the tradition of the Greek fathers and their theology as much if not more so than the Orthodox,[37] Torrance explains that the Reformed Churches have always been guided by "classical Greek theology," the "great Alexandrian and Cappadocian theologians," the Augustinian doctrine of grace, and the Trinitarian theology of the Greek fathers.[38]

Ultimately, Torrance sees the Reformed tradition rooted in the foundation of the Apostolic and catholic Faith. According to Torrance, both the Orthodox and Reformed should embrace their own pietistic and historical distinctiveness as developed within their respective "cultural and historical milieu,"[39] but seek to return to their shared theological core in the Trinitarian theology of the Greek fathers. For Torrance, the Reformed tradition, while being unique from Orthodoxy in many ways, is rooted in the very same catholicity.[40] Torrance felt that it was on this common basis that the two traditions could hope for rapprochement and real theological agreement. Furthermore, Torrance sees a shared commitment to the substance

---

35. Torrance, *Conflict and Agreement in the Church*, 1:76.

36. Torrance, "Memoranda on Orthodox/Reformed Relations," 3. As Lukas Vischer states during the Third Consultation, "the Reformed Churches see themselves as within the Christian tradition which seeks ancient catholicity, rather than as a separate tradition." Joe McLelland adds to this that this too is "a spirit of movement," i.e., one of many movements of reform within the western church, not simply *the* Reformation. He states "we Reformed tend to overemphasize the uniqueness of the 16th century Reformation." See The Thomas F. Torrance Manuscript Collection. Special Collections, Princeton Seminary. Box 170. The point seems to be that Luther was like Francis of Assisi and, indeed, the other medieval movements of reform, often monastic, inasmuch as what he was doing was not unheard of, nor meant to explode in the way that it did.

37. See Radcliff, *Thomas F. Torrance and the Church Fathers*, for an elaboration on this argument.

38. Torrance, "Memoranda on Orthodox/Reformed Relations," 4. He understands John Calvin as particularly indebted to Gregory Nazianzen. See, e.g., Torrance, *Trinitarian Perspectives*, 21–40.

39. Torrance, "Memoranda on Orthodox/Reformed Relations," 5, 10.

40. Although, the 1981 Minutes record the Orthodox wondering how the Reformed could hold to any doctrine (the question of authority) and the Reformed pointing to the Reformed emphasis on synodical and conciliar consensus. See the 1981 Minutes in The Thomas F. Torrance Manuscript Collection. Special Collections, Princeton Theological Seminary Library. Box 170.

of the theology of the Greek fathers, making the Reformed and Orthodox traditions both ecumenical and catholic. He argues that the Reformed tradition adheres to the Apostolic Faith[41] and practice[42] and contends for a way forward in ecumenicity with a focus on the truly catholic and Apostolic Deposit of Faith and *kerygma* as captured best in the Trinitarian theology of the Greek fathers.[43]

TORRANCE AND THE GREEK PATRISTIC NATURE OF THE REFORMED CHURCHES

Second, for Torrance, the Reformed church not only shares catholicity and apostolicity with the Orthodox but also, as distinct from the Roman Church, a commitment to the Greek patristic tradition. Important for Torrance in the Dialogue in this regard was Torrance's conviction that the Reformed church is rooted in the fulcrum of the "Athanasius-Cyril axis of classical theology"[44] and, especially, in Athanasius of Alexandria himself "the foundation of classical theology."[45] In Torrance's "Memoranda on Orthodox and Reformed Relations," he highlights the "patristic character" of Reformed theology.[46] In his dialogue with the Orthodox, Torrance understood his position as a Reformed Christian in the Church of Scotland as more specifically a part of the evangelical Scottish tradition of theology, a classical stream which can be traced back specifically to the ancient patristic church, as juxtaposed with the "hyper-Calvinist" stream more prevalent in

---

41. Torrance, "Memoranda on Orthodox/Reformed Relations," 6. Torrance says: "While the Reformed Churches in the sixteenth and seventeenth centuries produced catechetical and confessional formulations for the guidance of their life, teaching and proclamation of the Gospel, these were and are held only as 'secondary standards' subordinate to the Apostolic Faith as mediated through the New Testament, and to the Catholic doctrine as defined by the Apostles' and Nicene-Constantinopolitan Creeds."

42. Ibid., 8–10.

43. Torrance, "The Trinitarian Foundation and Character of Faith and of Authority in the Church," 91. Torrance states: "The *kerygma* refers not merely to proclamation about Christ but to the Reality proclaimed, Jesus Christ who is personally, actively and savingly at work through the *kerygma*." See pp. 91–107.

44. Torrance, *Theology in Reconciliation*, 9.

45. See Torrance's essay "Athanasius: A Study in the Foundations of Classical Theology," 215–56.

46. See the 1979 Minutes in The Thomas F. Torrance Manuscript Collection. Special Collections, Princeton Theological Seminary Library. Box 170.

Scotland.[47] Torrance views figures such as Robert Boyd[48] and John Forbes of Corse[49] in this line and he considers John McLeod Campbell's emphasis upon the personal nature of the atonement to be inherently patristic and evangelical, fitting therein as well.[50]

TORRANCE'S TRINITARIAN PATRISTIC ORTHODOXY[51]

Third, Torrance's unique reading of the church fathers undergirded his approach to the Orthodox-Reformed Dialogue and, in many ways the overall trajectory of it. Torrance understood himself to be able to turn to the Greek fathers because of the Reformed tradition's catholic and Greek patristic rootedness. Torrance's turn to and utilization of the church fathers was a major aspect of his ecumenical work, driving not least his work in the Orthodox-Reformed Dialogue, and it needs to be viewed in its particular context inasmuch as his approach certainly fell within the historical and theological movements of the late twentieth century. However, that notwithstanding, it is equally important to note at the same time that Torrance's use of the fathers was very much a part of how he approached his vocation as an ecumenical churchman and theologian and was thus its own entity and can be difficult to categorize with a pre-existing paradigm. Indeed, Torrance's use of the church fathers was totally unique and can be described much like Barth describes the Person of Christ in his account of the "miracle of Christmas" and the virgin birth: "marked off in the first instance, not by our own understanding or our interpretation, but by itself."[52] As has been argued in *Thomas F. Torrance and the Church Fathers*, Torrance's reading of the fathers was absolutely unique and creative, consisting of key catholic themes and figures, centered around the fulcrum of the Nicene *homoousion*, that central assertion that the son is of the same essence as the Father,

---

47. See Torrance, *Scottish Theology*, 66–74.

48. See ibid. See also some correspondence between Torrance and George Dragas on this subject in The Thomas F. Torrance Manuscript Collection. Special Collections, Princeton Theological Seminary Library. Box 104.

49. Torrance, *Scottish Theology*, 80.

50. Ibid., 287–315.

51. See Radcliff, *Thomas F. Torrance and the Church Fathers* for an overview and examination of Torrance and the church fathers. It is argued that Torrance's unique approach to the fathers was more than a simple reading for he reconstructed the fathers in light of the evangelical and Christocentric theology of the Reformation.

52. Barth, *Church Dogmatics*, 1/2:182.

albeit interpreted by Torrance using the very method it centers. In other words, Torrance's approach to the fathers was Christocentric in a creatively synthesized Reformed-Patristic theology.[53]

Torrance's approach to the fathers was unique in that it was neither that of a church historian nor a patrologist as traditionally understood, nor, it must be said, as a purely Reformed dogmatic theologian. As Robert Walker draws out splendidly in his review of *Thomas F. Torrance and the Church Fathers,* "he is a dogmatician, concerned to listen to the fathers and think out with them the evangelical faith. He looks through their eyes to know the same realities of God and faith as he sees through Reformed eyes."[54] Torrance's Reformed-Patristic synthesis is at the same time creative, imaginative, historical, theological, Reformed, evangelical, ecumenical, and patristic. Pui Him Ip summarizes it nicely in "'Back to the Fathers': The Nature of Historical Understanding in 20th century Patristic *Ressourcement*" as "constructive-systematic.[55] In a letter to Torrance in 1988, Torrance's partner in the Orthodox-Reformed Dialogue and the then Greek Orthodox Archbishop Methodios of Aksum, writes "I admire your patristic

---

53. However, more deeply this approach was central to Torrance's understanding of himself as a theologian and churchman. As Torrance says in his introduction to *The School of Faith,* theology is inherently catholic. By this Torrance means that theology is "dialogical" both vertically between God and his people and horizontally between God's people, which is why, as he says, "the exposition of theology as hearing of the Word and understanding of the Truth cannot be private to one particular church." See Torrance, "Introduction" in *The School of Faith,* lxv. Torrance was ecumenical from his childhood. He reflects in his unpublished intellectual autobiography, *Itinerarium Mentis In Deum,* that he recalls an ecumenical atmosphere in his home life, which began as a missionary child in China, instilled into his family by a Presbyterian father and Anglican mother. Torrance, *Itinerarium Mentis In Deum: T. F. Torrance—My Theological Development.* The Thomas F. Torrance Manuscript Collection. Special Collections. Princeton Theological Seminary Library, Series II, Box 10. Ecclesiologically, Torrance understood himself to be part of the Scottish evangelical tradition, standing in a line of theological succession from the patristic era through John Calvin and brought into Scotland by figures such as Robert Bruce, Robert Boyd, and Robert Forbes of Corse, and states as such not only in his published works but also in correspondence with George Dragas about the connection between the Scottish church and the ancient Greek church. See also Torrance, *Preaching Christ Today,* 18–19; Torrance, *Theology in Reconciliation,* 83–84; Torrance, *The Mystery of the Lord's Supper,* 32. So, Torrance's approach to the fathers was in so many ways a part of an ecumenical approach instilled in him from his birth.

54. Walker, Review of "Thomas F. Torrance and the Church fathers: a reformed, evangelical, and ecumenical reconstruction of the patristic tradition," 67–69.

55. Him Ip, "'Back to the Fathers,'" 4–13.

expressions and your use of catholic terms . . . ."[56] The Archbishop's language captures the essence of Torrance's approach to the fathers inasmuch as Torrance does not simply return to them attempting to offer a narrow representation of their concepts but instead constructs, or to use his own language, "reconstructs,"[57] the fathers around catholic themes and figures.[58] As Dragas puts it, Torrance: "seeks to build up his theology on the one, historical common ground of all three traditions and . . . he is prepared at the same time to confess in full modesty and sincerity their historical particularities and fortify himself only with their positive forces."[59]

In short, Torrance essentially extrapolates what he sees as best of the patristic era, the best of the Reformation, and the best of the modern eras of the theological tradition and synthetically combines them, re-centering them upon Jesus Christ and his Gospel of grace. As Robert Walker states, Torrance's "theology is highly original, which does not mean first and foremost that he developed new concepts, although he did, but that he made new connections between known theological ideas and concepts. For him, originality was not necessarily thinking new thoughts but making new connections."[60] The combination makes Torrance a theological figure of great ecumenical import inasmuch as his reconstruction bridges theological chasms between Christian traditions that need not exist except for historical, not theological, differences. Torrance's reading of the church fathers is ultimately a creative attempt to produce a Reformed and evangelical version of the patristic consensus creating significant changes to both the standard interpretations of the fathers and Torrance's own Reformed tradition. Dragas calls Torrance's approach an "ecumenical historical reconstruction," a "synthetic approach," and a "theological reconstruction."[61] The truly Torrancian reconstruction has many insights which have been overlooked by his commentators and his contemporaries on account of his

---

56. See the correspondence in The Thomas F. Torrance Manuscript Collection. Special Collections, Princeton Theological Seminary Library. Box 172.

57. Torrance, *Theology in Reconstruction*.

58. See Torrance, *The Trinitarian Faith,* for arguably the *magnum opus* of Torrance's reconstruction.

59. Dragas, "The Significance for the Church of Professor Torrance's Election As Moderator of the General Assembly of the Church of Scotland," 226.

60. Walker, "Recollections and Reflections," 43.

61. Dragas, "The Significance for the Church of Professor Torrance's Election As Moderator of the General Assembly of the Church of Scotland," 214–18.

being evaluated simply through a patrological, Reformed, or, as shall be argued, Second-Wave Trinitarian lens.

The central theme in Torrance's imaginative reconstruction is the *homoousion*, namely a Christocentric assertion that salvation and revelation are absolutely centered in Christ and a Reformed-Patristic statement of the divine-initiative in salvation and revelation. The central theme of the *homoousion* drives Torrance's approach to the church fathers and, as shall be seen, it became the patristic basis of the Orthodox-Reformed Dialogue. The Nicene doctrine of *homoousion*[62] serves as the cornerstone of Torrance's creative reconstruction of the church fathers.[63] It is taken from Nicene theology and it is, in many ways, a synthetic combination of the Reformation principle of *Solus Christus* (Christ alone) with the patristic principle of the incarnation of the Son of God, exemplifying Torrance's creative approach to the church fathers more generally.

Torrance understands the term to mean "God Himself is the actual content of his revelation and God Himself is really in Jesus Christ reconciling the world to Himself."[64] For Torrance all theology must be centered around the term and in this way it affects all other doctrines, functioning as a lynchpin for all dogmatics.[65] Torrance defines it as

> what God is 'toward us' and 'in the midst of us' in and through the Word made flesh, he really is in himself; that he is in the internal relations of his transcendent being the very same Father, Son and

---

62. Greek: ὁμοούσιον. The word comes from the combination of the Greek words ὁμο (same) and οὐσια (stuff/essence) and means "of the same substance or stuff" deriving from the Nicene-Constantinopolitan Creed: "We believe . . . in the Son . . . who is light of light, very God of very God, *of one essence with the Father*."

63. Scholars such as John Behr commend Torrance for this Christological emphasis. See Behr, Review of *Divine Meaning: Studies in Patristic Hermeneutics*, 105.

64. Torrance, *The Christian Doctrine of God*, 7.

65. Torrance says that it is "the organic pattern integrating all the doctrines of the Christian faith." See Torrance, *Theology in Reconciliation*, 264. Scholars today share this approach. For example, John Behr has initiated a project in which he contends that the way in which the fathers did theology was through Christology. See Behr, *Formation of Christian Theology*; Behr, *The Nicene Faith: Part I and II*; Behr, *The Mystery of Christ*; Behr, "Introduction" to *Saint Athanasius the Great: On the Incarnation*. For Torrance, then, the Nicene *homoousion* ultimately preserves the key evangelical assertion that "God is really like Jesus." See Torrance, *Preaching Christ Today*, 55–56; Torrance, *Trinitarian Perspectives*, 86. In turn, this means that due to the *homoousion* God can be known internally *in himself*. See Torrance, *Theology in Reconciliation*, 241; Torrance, *Atonement*, 236; Torrance, *Trinitarian Faith*, 66–68, 72.

Holy Spirit that he is in his revealing and saving activity in time and space toward mankind.[66]

The *homoousion* is the center of the Torrancian vision of the patristic tradition and Torrance's entire imaginative reading of the church fathers is done on the basis of it and through it and he reconstructs everything around it. Torrance's reconstruction of the patristic dogmatic tradition begins with Christology, for which the *homoousion* is central, and remains anchored there throughout. For him, everything in theology—not least historical theology and interpretation of the church fathers—rests upon this Father-Son relationship and, accordingly, every single one of the themes which arise in Torrance's interpretation of the fathers rests upon and arises from the *homoousion*. The other themes[67] Torrance draws out of the church fathers, a doctrine of the Trinity and Pneumatology centered in the *ousia* of the Father, a natural and a revealed theology both rooted in God's self-revelation, and a Christological and Pneumatological rooting of ecclesiology and the sacraments, are all undergirded by Athanasius and the Nicene doctrine of the *homoousion.*

Torrance then reconstructs the patristic tradition around the *homoousion* into "streams" or "threads" in theological history. These theological streams will, as shall be seen in the next two chapters of this book, drive Torrance and the Orthodox-Reformed Dialogue's approach to discussion and ultimately agreement on the doctrine of the Trinity and many of these texts lie in the background—and the foreground—of "The Agreed Statement on the Holy Trinity." In terms of his reconstruction of the patristic tradition around the Nicene doctrine of the *homoousion* into streams/threads, Torrance believes that certain eras of theological history captured the inner structure of the Gospel best[68] and sees these eras connected to one another as something of a golden thread running throughout theological history as part of the overarching stream into which all orthodox streams/thread trace their roots. Within this evangelical stream of theological history, the three instances that best captured this aforementioned inner structure are: Nicaea (particularly Athanasius), the Reformation (particularly Calvin), and contemporary evangelical theology (particularly Karl Barth).[69]

---

66. Torrance, *Trinitarian Faith*, 130. Bold in original.

67. See Radcliff, *Thomas F. Torrance and the Church Fathers*, 54–111.

68. See also Colyer, *How to Read T. F. Torrance*, 360.

69. Torrance, *Reality and Evangelical Theology*, 14–15; Torrance, *Preaching Christ Today*, 20; *Theology in Reconciliation*, 235–37, 285; Torrance, *Theology in Reconstruction*, 267.

The Catholic and Patristic Roots of the Orthodox-Reformed Dialogue

Very much connected to this, Torrance views the Reformation emphasis on grace as complementary to the Nicene emphasis on oneness in essence between the Father and the Son.[70] Indeed, the Reformation, according to Torrance, is thus "not contrary to but complementary to that of Nicaea, Ephesus, Chalcedon, etc."[71]

When Torrance approaches and uses the church fathers, he understands them in a creative and constructive fashion allowing his Reformed theology to inform his understanding of patristic theology and allowing the fathers to inform his understanding of Reformed theology, all the while reconstructing both around the Nicene doctrine of the *homoousion* understood through the great strides made by Karl Barth on the connection of God's revelation and God himself in the *Church Dogmatics*. As Paul Molnar puts it, "It is no secret that one of his favourite modern theologians was his own mentor, Karl Barth, whom he counted among the great theologians of the church, on the same level as Athanasius, Augustine, Thomas Aquinas and John Calvin."[72] In many ways Karl Barth functions as the funnel through which Torrance pours—or perhaps the mold into which Torrance shapes—his creative mixture of patristic theology and Reformed theology. Ultimately, then, Torrance sees Karl Barth as inheriting the patristic and Reformed and funneling them out into contemporary evangelical theology.[73] In many ways Torrance sees Barth as a modern Athanasius, or to put it another way, Athanasius as an ancient Barth. At the very least, Torrance sees Barth as the theologian who brought the Trinity back to the forefront

---

70. Torrance, *Theology in Reconstruction*, 225. Furthermore, Torrance states: "[It is] when Greek Patristic Theology is studied and interpreted in the strong Biblical perspective restored through the Reformation of the Church in the West that its permanent place in the foundations of Evangelical Theology may be appreciated in a new way . . .[and] when Reformed Theology is reassessed and interpreted in light of its ancient roots in the evangelical theology of the early centuries that its essential catholicity and its unifying force are to be understood." See Torrance, *Trinitarian Perspectives*, 21–22. The Reformers, argues Torrance, attempted "to carry through a Christological correction of the whole life and thought of the Church. It was an attempt to put Christ and his Gospel once again into the very centre and to carry through extensive reform by bringing everything into conformity to him and his Gospel." See Torrance, *Theology in Reconstruction*, 265.

71. Ibid. Torrance, "Karl Barth and the Latin Heresy," 462–63.

72. Molnar, "Introduction," xi.

73. Cf. Roldanus, *Le Christ Et l'homme dans la Théologie d'Athanase d'Alexandrie*, who argues for a connection between Barth and Athanasius. See especially pp. 2, 4, 218–19, 359, and 373.

of theology and in doing so returning modern theology to the classical Trinitarian theological foundation of the church fathers.[74]

It is in this imaginative synthesis of the church fathers with the issues of his own day that Torrance offers perhaps his greatest, or at least most creative, contribution to patristic study. Like Newman before him,[75] Torrance reads the church fathers into contemporary debates and reads contemporary debates back into the church fathers.[76] In his article "Karl Barth and the Latin Heresy," Arius's division of the divine Logos from the human Jesus sheds light on nineteenth-century liberalism's division of the Christ of faith from the Christ of history. In Torrance's "Memoranda on Orthodox/Reformed Relations," Nestorian dualism between the human and divine Jesus sheds light on Federal Calvinism's doctrine of Limited Atonement. In his chapter on the Holy Spirit in *The Trinitarian Faith*, the problem with the Cappadocian fathers' emphasis on the Person of the Father as *arche* of the Trinity sounds just like John Zizioulas's work in Social Trinitarianism. Throughout *Preaching Christ Today*, Augustine's implicit pagan dualism sounds almost exactly like the critiques Karl Rahner had of post-Scholastic Roman Catholicism; critiques which Torrance greatly appreciates and says as such in his chapter on Rahner in *Trinitarian Perspectives*. In his essay "The Legacy of Karl Barth" Torrance even states that both Barth and Athanasius were fighting "Contra Mundum" for the evangelical and catholic faith of the *homoousion* against forms of liberal dualism in their day.[77] Torrance's amalgamation of contemporary theological debate with patristic debate is, perhaps, his greatest strength inasmuch as he applies the fathers to his own context. Torrance has a very dynamic way of using historical texts and he jumps from the fourth century to the sixteenth century to the twentieth century, often in one sentence. He uses fifth-century heresies to critique much later theological problems. This can be an extremely helpful application of the Fathers to contemporary problems and a successful attempt at what Georges Florovsky has called a neopatristic synthesis; yet it can also be highly confusing. Here, Torrance's greatest strength may have also been his greatest weakness. He made the fathers highly relevant to his

---

74. Torrance, *The Christian Doctrine of God*, 7–10; Torrance, "Karl Barth and the Latin Heresy," 462.

75. See Daley, "The Church Fathers," 3

76. See in particular Torrance, *Space, Time, and Incarnation*; and Torrance, "Karl Barth and the Latin Heresy."

77. See Torrance, "The Legacy of Karl Barth," 160–61.

contemporary time by, for example, viewing the ways that Athanasius' attack on Arianism overlapped with his own contemporary battle with liberal theology. However, this was somewhat oversimplified simply because Arianism, though similar, was not the same as nineteenth-century liberal theology. Despite the strong similarities between Barth/Athanasius and Arianism / nineteenth-century liberal theology, the two surely had their differences. For example, in "Karl Barth and the Latin Heresy," Torrance paints a picture of Athanasius and Barth as both fighting the same perennial battle against dualism. In many ways, this is typical of Torrance and his favorites throughout church history tend to sound very similar to one another in their commitments and in the theological battles they fought. As will be argued in the conclusion, it is these areas which could perhaps be reconsidered as theologians revisit the Orthodox-Reformed Dialogue today.

TORRANCE'S USE OF THE FATHERS AND THE TRINITARIAN THEOLOGY OF THE ORTHODOX-REFORMED DIALOGUE: SECOND-WAVE TRINITARIANISM?

Myk Habets, in his critical introduction to the new edition of *Trinitarian Faith*, suggests, albeit hesitantly, that Torrance's work on the church fathers on the doctrine of the Trinity, and thus the very much connected Orthodox-Reformed Dialogue, might reasonably be placed within the context of Second-Wave Trinitarianism. As Habets says, "this certainly seems to be the unstated implication of third-wavers."[78] Sarah Coakley, from whom the concept of "three waves" originates, outlines the "three waves" of Trinitarian thought from the twentieth century until today. The First-Wave, consisting of figures like Karl Barth, Karl Rahner, and Vladimir Lossky, were united in their "concern to loose Trinitarian thinking from any vulnerability to critique from secular philosophy or science, and thereby to evade the metaphysical roadblock that had seemingly been constructed impassibly by Kant against all doctrinal speculation about God-in-Godself."[79] The Second-Wave, building off the First Wave's recovery of the doctrine of the Trinity, no longer had the enemy of the enlightenment's avoidance of metaphysics, rather, according to Coakley, the "bogeyman in the second wave

---

78. Habets, "The Essence of Evangelical Theology," xxi.
79. Coakley, "Afterword: Relational Ontology, Trinity, and Science," 187.

was now modernity's 'turn to the subject' and in particular its anthropological emphasis on individualism and atomism."[80] Exemplified in figures like John Zizioulas and Colin Gunton, the Second-Wave championed the social doctrine of the Trinity which focuses on God's threeness and all it has to offer in its understanding of a personhood that exhibits the interconnectedness of humankind. According to Coakley, the Third-Wave rejected the Second-Wave and the assumed distinction between east and west embedded within the de Régnon thesis.[81]

Torrance was certainly writing on the doctrine of the Trinity and engaging in the Orthodox-Reformed Dialogue during the height of Second-Wave Trinitarianism (the 1980s and 1990s). Yet, as Habets makes clear, Torrance does not use the church fathers in the stereotypically Second-Wave fashion, for, "in Torrance's hands, the fathers are not "a static monolithic 'thing' to be reckoned with. Rather, Tradition is one aspect of the church universal, as, together, under the Spirit and in the Word, the people of God discern the mind of Christ."[82] Indeed, as has been argued in *Thomas F. Torrance and the Church Fathers,* Torrance's approach to the Fathers is a creative reconstruction of the patristic Greek East into Reformed and ecumenical theological themes. There are a variety of catholic themes and figures that dictate and undergird Torrance's approach to the Fathers, making his work at the Orthodox-Reformed Dialogue absolutely unique and difficult to categorize outside of the categories it provides for itself. Indeed, Habets acknowledges the difficulty in taxonomizing Torrance within any of Coakley's categories. Notably, one Third-Wave Trinitarian, telling the story of Second-Wave Trinitarianism as largely a failure, writes "Torrance does . . . not fit the story . . . ."[83] Ultimately, as Habets concludes, "Torrance's work on patristic theology has been largely ignored by Third-Wave Trinitarians like Coakley, Ayres, and Holmes" and thus "one can only conclude that Torrance's work does not fit the narrative of Coakley's three waves."[84]

---

80. Ibid., 188–89.

81. The de Régnon thesis says there is a sharp distinction between Greek (Cappadocian) Triadology, which focuses on the threeness of the Persons in God, and Latin (Augustinian) Triadology, which focuses on the oneness of the Being of God, see Théodore de Régnon, *Études de théologie positive sur la Sainte Trinité.*

82. Ibid.

83. "Response: In Praise of Being Criticized," 151. See further Radcliff, "T. F. Torrance in light of Stephen Holmes's critique of contemporary Trinitarian thought"; and Radcliff, "T. F. Torrance and and the Patristic Consensus on the Doctrine of the Trinity."

84. Habets, "The Essence of Evangelical Theology," xxi.

Torrance's work on the Trinity does not fit the East-West divide so often caricatured by Third-Wavers as being completely divided by those in the Second-Wave. Rather, Torrance's understanding of the church fathers on the Trinity is very ecumenical and seeks to understand the fathers as a part of a living tradition of East and West. Thus, despite Torrance seemingly being lumped into the Second-Wave slot by many Third-Wavers, implicitly if not explicitly, he does not really fit into this category neatly, if at all. Thus, it is important to consider what wave, if any, Torrance fits in his work on the Trinity and in the Orthodox-Reformed Dialogue. Ultimately, Torrance's understanding of the church fathers was something entirely different than the categories presented by the "three waves." The real evidence of this is his work on the Orthodox-Reformed Dialogue and "The Agreed Statement" which offers a better, more nuanced version of Third-Wave Trinitarianism; yet it continues to be unutilized in the current Third-Wave conversations.

The real evidence of Torrance's project as "Third-Wave Trinitarianism before its time" is his work in the Orthodox-Reformed Dialogue. Here, Torrance's Third-Wave Trinitarianism before there was such a thing becomes clear, particularly in his work on "getting behind" the *filioque* through his work constructing, with George Dragas, "The Agreed Statement on the Holy Trinity." Through Torrance's work in the Orthodox-Reformed Dialogue he exhibits a clear cut Third-Wave Trinitarianism that deserves consideration in the Third-Wave Trinitarian conversations today.

CONCLUSION

Torrance and the Orthodox-Reformed Dialogue bequeath to contemporary ecumenical dialogue and theological thought seeking to be truly catholic an approach that is centralized upon the Trinitarian and Christocentric theology of the Greek fathers. This positively and objectively tethered approach offers a basis that has already proven fruitful and will no doubt continue to serve future generations of ecumenical theology, should they turn to Torrance and the Orthodox-Reformed Dialogue. However, there was much more to the Dialogue than pure theological agreement: the (indeed, theological) friendship between T. F. Torrance and Methodios Fouyas served very much as part of the basis of the Orthodox-Reformed Dialogue. These two theologians, preeminent in the Dialogue, offer not only insight into the basis of the Dialogue (agreement on the Christocentric and Trinitarian theology of the Greek fathers), but also a window into the differences of approach exhibited in the Dialogue. Therefore, the present book now turns to an exploring of this personal basis of the Dialogue: the theological and personal friendship of T. F. Torrance and Methodios Fouyas, the two founders of the Orthodox-Reformed Dialogue.

CHAPTER 2

The Friendship of Thomas Torrance and Methodios Fouyas
Underlying Similarities and Differences between Reformed and Orthodox at the Dialogue

> Tom Torrance . . . would really like to be Patriarch of Alexandria, and that we cannot give him; but we would recognize him as Patriarch of Scotland!"
>
> Archbishop Methodios Fouyas[1]

> [Methodios Fouyas is]the outstanding Church Father of Orthodoxy in the world today.
>
> Thomas F. Torrance[2]

> The Greek Orthodox Church make [sic.] me a Protopresbyter within the Alexandrian Patriarchate, which astonished me! This is an act of ecumenical union, on the ground of patristic theology, which I appreciate greatly.
>
> Thomas F. Torrance[3]

1. Baker and Dragas, "Interview," 8.

2. Torrance, "His Eminence Archbishop Methodios of Thyateira and Great Britain." The Thomas F. Torrance Manuscript Collection. Special Collections, Princeton Theological Seminary Library. Box 172.

3. Baker, "Correspondence Between Torrance and Florovsky," 319.

Part 1: A Critical Appreciation of the Orthodox-Reformed Theological Dialogue

INTRODUCTION

TORRANCE STATES: "THE IMPETUS for [the Orthodox-Reformed Dialogue] came from a deep theological rapport that had developed between Archbishop Methodios of Aksum (as he then was) and myself over the understanding of classical Alexandrian theology, as represented above all by St. Athanasius and St. Cyril, and our appreciation of its scientific basis."[4] Furthermore, Torrance says in his introduction to *Theological Dialogue Between Orthodox and Reformed Churches*: "At that first meeting in Istanbul considerable attention was given to problems of method and the underlying assumptions that gave rise to divergence in doctrinal formulation and in the structure of the ministry."[5] This chapter seeks, accordingly, to explore the "theological rapport" between Torrance and Fouyas and to draw out the similarities and divergences between the Orthodox and Reformed at the Dialogue.

Having explored the nature and scope, both theological and historical, of the Orthodox-Reformed Dialogue in Chapter One, particularly its catholic nature and Greek patristic rootedness, the second chapter of this book now explores the similarities and differences of approach between the Reformed and the Orthodox in general and the manifestation of this in particular in the friendship between T. F. Torrance and Methodios Fouyas. Furthermore, this chapter will explore how this manifests itself in the Dialogue. The underlying difference can be seen in the Word-centered theology (on the Reformed side) and the synthetic church theology involving a broader tradition (on the Orthodox side). Utilizing not only the published (*Theological Dialogue Volumes 1 and 2*) but also unpublished (from the *Torrance Manuscript Collection*) materials, this chapter explores the manifestation of the different approaches in the Dialogue itself as well as other key Orthodox and Reformed texts undergirding the approach of the theologians in the Dialogue through a focus on the key figures prevalent in the Dialogue, particularly T. F. Torrance and Methodios Fouyas and their deep theological and personal friendship. This chapter will also explore some of the similarities and differences in the theological approaches of the two figures and the two traditions they represented in light of the conversations at the Orthodox-Reformed Dialogue and in light of their friendship.

---

4. Torrance, "Memoranda on Orthodox/Reformed Relations," x.

5. Torrance, "Introduction" to *Theological Dialogue between Orthodox and Reformed Churches*, 1:xxi.

Scope of the Chapter

The present chapter first explores the deep theological friendship between Torrance and Fouyas. Expanding from the friendship, the chapter, furthermore, examines the similarities between Reformed and Orthodox that surfaced at the Dialogue. Ultimately, this chapter will argue that the Trinitarian theology of the Greek fathers, as understood initially by Torrance and Fouyas, provided fertile ground for the Orthodox-Reformed Dialogue and its ultimate fruit, "The Agreed Statement on the Holy Trinity."

A THEOLOGICAL INTRODUCTION TO THE FRIENDSHIP BETWEEN TORRANCE AND FOUYAS: THE BASIS OF THE DIALOGUE

Torrance states at the very beginning of his introduction in *Theological Dialogue Between Orthodox and Reformed Churches*, published in 1985 after the first three consultations in Istanbul and Geneva, that the Orthodox-Reformed Dialogue was a new ecumenical movement borne out of contacts made at the Missionary Conference in 1910 in Edinburgh, the Faith and Order Conferences held at Lausanne in 1927 and Edinburgh in 1937 which subsequently fed into more formal dialogue at the First Assembly of the World Council of Churches in Amsterdam in 1948 and the Third Council of Faith and Order held at Lund in 1952.[6] According to Fouyas, however, the relationship is even deeper. He states that nearly immediately after the Protestant Reformation, "the Protestants attempted to establish relations with the Patriarch of Constantinople."[7] Beginning in the late sixteenth century, Protestants, particularly in the British Isles, began to turn to the Orthodox and the Patriarch of Constantinople and substantial ecumenical conversations began.[8] Notably, the Nonjurors and then the Oxford Movement reached out most substantively for reunion with Constantinople as well.[9] Torrance then notes that the dialogue continued to develop after the

---

6. Torrance, "Memoranda on Orthodox/Reformed Relations," ix.

7. Fouyas, *Orthodoxy, Roman Catholicism, and Anglicanism*, 34–35.

8. Ibid., 34–37. Fouyas had a very catholic understanding of non-Orthodox and non-Roman churches, as seen, e.g., in his statement that "Anglicanism is not a Protestant Church, but a reformed Catholic Church, which maintains its unity with the ancient undivided Church." See ibid., 88.

9. Ibid., 37–38.

Fourth World Conference of Faith and Order in Montreal in 1962 between the World Alliance of Reformed Churches and various Orthodox Churches (he lists Romanian, Hungarian, and the Moscow Patriarchate).[10]

All of the movements above, however, were concerned primarily with order and form rather than theology.[11] Torrance notes that a different route was taken with the Orthodox-Reformed Dialogue, beginning with "theological consultations" that had "a rather different objective."[12] As Torrance states: "the impetus for this new move came from a deep theological rapport that had developed between Archbishop Methodios of Aksum (as he then was)[13] and myself over the understanding of classical Alexandrian theology, as represented above all by St. Athanasius and St. Cyril, and our appreciation of its scientific basis."[14] In particular, says Torrance, the goal was "clarifying together the classical bases of Orthodox and of Reformed theology and in the hope of reaching the same kind of profound accord with respect to the 'theological axis' of Athanasian/Cyrilline theology, to which the Reformed Church has looked as having regulative force in its

---

10. Ibid., ix–x.

11. Although, Fouyas notes that the Orthodox sent the Nonjurors a list of Orthodox dogma to see if they agreed. See ibid., 37. The form-focused approach of the Faith and Order conferences and the connected two-volume published *Conflict and Agreement in the Church* is perhaps best exemplified by Torrance's work on an ecumenical understanding of episcopacy in dialogue between the Church of Scotland and the Anglican Church: a combined Presbyterian-Episcopal structure ("corporate episcopate"). See a document outline of this proposal (which did not develop) in The Thomas F. Torrance Manuscript Collection. Special Collections, Princeton Theological Seminary Library. Box 89.

12. Torrance, "Introduction" to *Theological Dialogue between Orthodox and Reformed Churches*, 1:x. Torrance does not explicitly unpack the objective of the earlier dialogues, but the implication is that they focused more on issues of order and structure as opposed to the content of the faith. It should also be noted that in the late 1980s and early 1990s Torrance's brother, James Torrance, was engaged in Trinitarian ecumenical dialogue with John Zizioulas, Alisdair Heron, Colin Gunton, Tom Smail, and Sarah Coakley, *inter alia*, in the "British Council of Churches Study Commission on Trinitarian Doctrine Today." See the published volumes related to this: *The Forgotten Trinity* (3 volumes). The published volumes suggest both a moving away from the *filioque* clause (much like the Orthodox-Reformed Dialogue) but with a strong "social Trinitarian" emphasis à la Gunton and Zizioulas. Torrance mentions this study appreciatively in *Trinitarian Perspectives* (see preface, p. 5), but he does not engage it any more than that, which would suggest he did not find it all that relevant for the Orthodox-Reformed Dialogue.

13. Methodios Fouyas was at the time Archbishop of Thyateira and Great Britain. This is an Orthodox diocese covering Orthodox Christians living in the United Kingdom, Ireland, the Isle of Man, and the Channel Islands.

14. Torrance, "Memoranda on Orthodox/Reformed Relations," x.

understanding of Christian doctrine hardly less than the Greek Orthodox Church."[15] Thus it was through the ecumenical and theological friendship between Torrance and Fouyas, in particular their agreement that the Trinitarian and Christocentric theology of Athanasius and Cyril is central to any theological dialogue, that the Orthodox-Reformed Dialogue was borne. Before exploring the Dialogue they founded and some of the underlying similarities and differences of approach, it is essential to first understand each figure and their ecumenical approach.

T. F. TORRANCE: A RADICAL ECUMENICAL SCOTTISH MODERATOR

It was the Reformed who approached the Orthodox with a proposal for Dialogue. It was also Torrance who initiated the initial proposal for Dialogue through his visits to Alexandria as Moderator and, earlier, through his collaboration with Methodios Fouyas which ultimately led to his ordination as "Honorary Protopresbyter" by Fouyas in the Greek Orthodox Patriarchate of Alexandria. Where did these radically ecumenical inclinations come from? What drove Torrance's unique approach?

As explored in the previous chapter, Torrance's approach to theology and churchmanship was inherently ecumenical which certainly undergirded his approach in the Orthodox-Reformed Dialogue. In Torrance's introduction to *The School of Faith*,[16] he writes, "it belongs to the nature of theology to be *catholic*," which he sees as involving both historicity and ecumenicity.[17] Torrance believes that theology is inherently "dialogical" and conversational, between God and his people.[18] Thus, for Torrance, theology is necessarily historical and ecumenical. It is historical "because it is historical dialogue with God" and it is ecumenical because "the exposition of theology as hearing of the Word and understanding of the Truth

---

15. Torrance, "Introduction" to *Theological Dialogue between Orthodox and Reformed Churches*, 1:x.

16. Torrance, "Introduction" to *The School of Faith*, xi–cxxvi. Torrance's important introduction outlines in short form many of his theological convictions and commitments. According to Robert Walker and Tom Noble, two former students of Torrance's, Torrance used to recommend this introduction to his students as preparatory reading for his dogmatics lectures. See Torrance, *Atonement*, lxxxiv.

17. Torrance, "Introduction" to *The School of Faith*, lxv.

18. Ibid., lxv–lxvii.

cannot be private to one particular Church."[19] Torrance understands theology to be inherently catholic, historical, and ecumenical; to be otherwise would point to "theology" not having its grounding in God himself. For Torrance this means looking at theology's object, God revealed in Christ, alongside other denominations. Furthermore, Torrance sees himself within the Scottish evangelical tradition of theology, which he sees in line with classical patristic Christianity through John Calvin.[20] Torrance did not understand himself to be outside the catholic church seeking *reunion*; rather, he understood himself as standing within the one catholic church seeking *rapprochement*.

Torrance was active ecumenically throughout his professional life. Early in his career (in the 1950s and 1960s), Torrance published the two-volume work, *Conflict and Agreement in the Church*, concerning ecumenical dialogue with Anglicans, Presbyterians, and Roman Catholics.[21] Whilst Moderator of the General Assembly of the Church of Scotland Torrance was ordained "Honorary Protopresbyter" of the Orthodox Archdiocese of Alexandria. As this book is exploring, during the 1980s and 1990s Torrance led the Reformed side of the Orthodox-Reformed Dialogue, and subsequently edited and published the two-volume output of this discussion.[22] Torrance's role, therefore, in the ecumenical movement in the twenty-first century was vast, widespread, and very much a consistent part of his theological career from beginning to end.

As something of the apex of his ecumenical work, Torrance turns to the Orthodox, and not the Roman Catholics, for a plethora of reasons.

19. Ibid., lxvii–lxviii.

20. Torrance, *Preaching Christ Today*, 18–19; Torrance, *Theology in Reconciliation*, 83–84; Torrance, "Introduction" to *The Mystery of the Lord's Supper; Sermons on the Sacrament Preached in the Kirk of Edinburgh by Robert Bruce in AD 1589*, 32. Torrance sees Robert Bruce, a minister at St Giles in Edinburgh in the sixteenth century, as steeped in classical Christian theology. See also Torrance, *Scottish Theology*. Torrance sees Robert Boyd as following in the Greek patristic tradition. See further his correspondence with George Dragas on this subject. The Thomas F. Torrance Manuscript Collection. Special Collections, Princeton Theological Seminary Library. Box 104. Torrance also sees John Forbes of Corse as indebted to the Greek patristic tradition. See Box 178. It is perhaps apt to mention McGrath's observation that British evangelicals tend to see themselves in continuation with historical Christianity (ancient and medieval) more so than their North American counterparts who see themselves more as a distinct, even separate, movement from the wider church. See McGrath, "Trinitarian Theology," 52.

21. Torrance, *Conflict and Agreement in the Church*, vols. 1–2.

22. Torrance, *Theological Dialogue between Orthodox & Reformed Churches*, vols. 1–2.

Why? Perhaps it was because Torrance saw himself within the Western Church already.[23] Ecumenical dialogue for Torrance seems not so much entail dialogue with Roman Catholics[24] because he sees his own Reformed tradition as a part of the same Western tradition of the Roman Catholics.[25] Torrance understands his tradition to have arisen out of and to still be a part of the same Western Christian tradition of which Roman Catholics are also a part[26] and thus a dialogue with Roman Catholics would have not been significantly different in form[27] from a dialogue between the Reformed and Anglicans.[28] Perhaps Torrance saw the need for rapprochement with Catholics as smaller than the need for rapprochement with the Orthodox. Or perhaps Torrance saw himself, as Reformed, as a representative of the Western Church at large. Indeed, Torrance regularly speaks of the Western Church as having problems such as the "Latin Heresy," a dualism that Torrance throughout his life argued against in both the Roman Catholic form and the Westminster Calvinist form.[29] So, perhaps Torrance did not see a need for rapprochement with the Romans inasmuch as the Reformed are a protest movement within the Western Church; it seemed to be the East that needs to be engaged in the first instance for the kind of rapprochement Torrance had mind.

Regardless, Torrance approaches the Orthodox ultimately on account of a shared love of the church fathers in general and the Greek fathers in particular. Whereas disagreements do arise between the Reformed and Orthodox on the place of the later Byzantine tradition, Torrance sees that the Reformed and the Orthodox share in their love of the classical Greek tradition of Athanasius and Cyril of Alexandria and their emphasis on

---

23. Conversely, perhaps as Nesteruk says, "Thomas Torrance knew Greek Patristics well and in his personal contacts with the present author he clearly indicated that in his perception of Christianity he was an orthodox with a capital "O." See "Universe, Incarnation, and Humanity," 214.

24. Though, he does include an article on Rahner and Vatican II in a collection of essays in ecumenical perspective (*Trinitarian Perspectives*, 77–102) and he writes about Catholics in his *Forward* to *Theology in Reconciliation*.

25. See, e.g., Torrance, "Memoranda on Orthodox/Reformed Relations," 3.

26. The similarity between Torrance and Schaff on this point is notable. See Schaff, *History of the Church: Reformation A.D. 1517–1530*, 4.

27. But there would perhaps be differences in substance.

28. See Torrance, *Conflict and Agreement in the Church*, vols. 1–2.

29. Torrance, "Karl Barth and the Latin Heresy," 461–82.

Christology and the Trinity.[30] In this, Torrance departs from the typical approach of Protestants, especially those in the Reformed tradition, of emphasizing Augustine and the crucifixion, also done by the Roman Catholics.[31] Torrance wants to avoid this typically Western emphasis of which his own Reformed tradition is no less guilty and sees this as a possibility in dialogue with the Orthodox.

According to Gunton, Torrance's reading of the church fathers has provided a "reopening of a major historical conversation."[32] Though there had certainly been informal dialogue between the Reformed and Orthodox churches since the mid-twentieth century, as discussed earlier in this book, the Orthodox-Reformed Dialogue formally occurred in 1981, 1983, 1988, and 1990. Torrance notes that Georges Florovsky, in particular, impacted the beginnings of the Dialogue, stating Florovsky is "at once catholic and evangelical."[33] Torrance and Florovsky interacted with one another at an ecumenical level during The Faith and Order meetings during the 1950s.[34]

The stated goal of the Orthodox-Reformed was to explore the common roots between the two churches on the basis of Apostolic, Trinitarian,

---

30. See also Torrance, "The Orthodox Church in Great Britain," 325–31; and "The Relevance of Orthodoxy," 332–40. The latter text in particular suggests that Torrance appreciated far more than just the shared commitment to the Greek fathers. After a detailed account of a recent discovery that the Byzantine liturgy is a Christian adaptation of the Temple liturgy before its destruction by Jewish priests who converted to Christianity, Torrance says "I have just been describing the worship of the Early Christians, but that is just what the worship of the Orthodox Church is." See Torrance, "The Relevance of Orthodoxy," 339.

31. See further chaps. 1 and 2 of *Thomas F. Torrance and the Church Fathers*.

32. Colin, *Father, Son, and Holy Spirit*, 51.

33 Torrance, "Introduction" to *Theological Dialogue Between Orthodox and Reformed Churches*, 1:ix. Torrance says of the early ecumenical dialogue (pre Orthodox-Reformed) in which he was a part: "Again and again however, when passages of the Bible were being interpreted by others—Professor Florovsky, for example—I had to take a new, hard look at the Greek text of the New Testament to see whether it really did mean what he said, and again and again found that I had been misreading the New Testament because I had been looking at it through Presbyterian spectacles." See Torrance, "The Relevance of Orthodoxy," 333. As Baker puts it, "Father George Dragas has recalled how Torrance once remarked to him that Florovsky was one of the few who could force him to reconsider his position on a given theological point." See Baker, "Correspondence between Torrance and Florovsky," 292. According to Baker, Dragas also says that Florovsky said a similar thing about Torrance. See ibid., 292n15. For more on on the overlap between Torrance and Florovsky, see Irving, "Fr. Georges Florovsky and T. F. Torrance on the Doctrine of Creation," 301–22.

34. Baker, "Correspondence between Torrance and Florovsky," 289–92.

and Christocentric faith and order as explicated in classical Christianity. According to the Minutes, in his introductory greeting to the Orthodox patriarchate during their official proposal for dialogue, James McCord, then-president of the World Alliance of Reformed Churches, "stressed how the Reformed feel themselves historically very close to the Orthodox in a common concern for the truth of the Apostolic Faith and for the unity of the Church in that same faith"[35] and Torrance notes how he developed the view, while Moderator, that Orthodox-Reformed Dialogue should usefully begin on the doctrine of the Trinity.[36] The impetus for the Dialogue ultimately came, however, from "deep theological rapport" between Torrance and Methodios Fouyas over the understanding of classical Alexandrian theology as represented especially by Athanasius and Cyril.[37]

METHODIOS FOUYAS: A RADICALLY ECUMENICAL ORTHODOX BISHOP

The friendship and shared theological commitment of Torrance and Fouyas undergirded the Orthodox-Reformed Dialogue. Born in Corinth in 1925,[38] Fouyas[39] joined the monastery at Penteli when he was twenty. He then studied theology at The University of Athens from 1946–1951, was ordained a priest in 1950, and became an Archimandrite in 1951. He served as Priest in Charge of the Greek Orthodox Church in Munich, the Secretary General of the Patriarchate of Alexandria, Priest in Charge of the Greek Orthodox Church in Manchester, Secretary to the Holy Synod of the Church in Greece, and Bishop of Aksum in Ethiopia.

George Dragas, a former student of Torrance's who played a central role in the Orthodox-Reformed Dialogue[40] was ordained by Fouyas in

35. See the Minutes from the 1979 meeting in Istanbul contained in The Thomas F. Torrance Manuscript Collection. Special Collections, Princeton Theological Seminary Library. Box 170.

36. See ibid.

37. Torrance, "Introduction" to *Theological Dialogue between Orthodox and Reformed Churches*, 1:x.

38. He died in 2006.

39. See Torrance's speech at the Rotary Club for this and subsequent biographical details. In it, Torrance calls Fouyas "the outstanding Church Father of Orthodoxy in the world today." See The Thomas F. Torrance Manuscript Collection. Special Collections, Princeton Theological Seminary Library. Box 172.

40. He contributed to the Dialogue not least by co-writing "The Agreed Statement on

1980[41] and recounts the relationship between Fouyas and Torrance in his interview with Matthew Baker in *T. F. Torrance and Eastern Orthodoxy*: "Fouyas did his doctorate in the 1960s in Manchester, before becoming a bishop in the Patriarchate of Alexandria. Fouyas' *Doktorvater*, Arnold Ehrhardt, was a friend of Torrance. When I first met Fouyas in Edinburgh on the occasion of his receiving the doctorate in 1970, he told me that he had exchanged extensive correspondence with Torrance . . . "[42] Dragas goes on to state: "Tom and Methodios collaborated through the 1970s and 1980s and in various academic and publishing venues."[43] These venues included *Ekklestikos Pharos, Abba Salama, Texts and Studies,* and *Ekklesisia kai Theologia.* The relationship between Fouyas and Torrance was therefore based upon a deep professional appreciation for one another; and, as shall be seen, this provided a solid undergirding for co-leading the Orthodox-Reformed Dialogue.[44]

In 1977 Fouyas became Archbishop of Thyateira and Great Britain, a role he would hold until 1988.[45] Under Archbishop Methodios, the Ortho-

---

the Holy Trinity" with Torrance. Dragas wrote his PhD thesis under Torrance, starting at Edinburgh and finishing at Durham. See "St. Athanasius contra Apollinarem." Dragas has contributed greatly to research on Athanasius, particularly his understanding of the vicarious humanity of Christ, via his argument for the Athanasian authorship of *Contra Apollinarem.* See, e.g., *Saint Athanasius of Alexandria: Original Research and New Perspectives.*

41. Baker and Dragas, "Interview," 7. Dragas states: "It was Torrance who also introduced me to Archbishop Methodios."

42. Ibid., 9. Fouyas became bishop of Aksum in Ethiopia.

43. Ibid. Torrance states: "[I]n 1969 Archbishop Methodios Fouyas had refounded the ancient Journal of Historical Greek Theology, *Ekklesiastikos Pharos*, and in 1970 had founded a new Journal, *Abba Salama*, with a view to clarifying the foundations of Greek Conciliar Theology upon which all Christendom had come to rest, and with a view also towards reconciling Chalcedonian and non-Chalcedonian theology, in all of which I had come to be deeply associated." See Torrance, "Introduction" to *Theological Dialogue between Orthodox and Reformed Churches,* 1:x.).

44. See, e.g., Torrance's nomination of Fouyas for the Templeton Prize in 1984 and his speech on the occasion of Fouyas receiving the Gold Medal and Diploma of Honour from the Rotary Club of Athens joined by the Rotary Club of London. Torrance was invited to give the lecture on Fouyas' induction. In it, he calls Fouyas "one of the most eminent and colourful personages of our time." See The Thomas F. Torrance Manuscript Collection. Special Collections, Princeton Theological Seminary Library. Box 172. In his speech at the Rotary Club, Torrance calls Fouyas "the outstanding Church Father of Orthodoxy in the world today." See The Thomas F. Torrance Manuscript Collection. Special Collections, Princeton Theological Seminary Library. Box 172.

45. Fouyas was "dismissed" as Archbishop of Thyateira and Great Britain in 1988.

He was apparently accused of "coveting other thrones," i.e., was trying to take over the churches in Great Britain, presumably the national churches (Church of England and Church of Scotland) for the Orthodox. Fouyas argued that the real reason for his dismissal was his success at expanding the Orthodox community in Britain, which had "provoked the leaders of other churches facing decline" and his dismissal was thus influenced by the then Archbishop of Canterbury, Robert Runcie. Runcie, however, denied these charges and said that Fouyas's dismissal was "entirely a matter for the Ecumenical Patriarchate." See Gledhill and Longley, "Methodios tells of 'envious rivals.'" Torrance states of the great growth of Orthodoxy in Great Britain under Fouyas, "He is not at all interested in winning for the Orthodox Church members from other communions—in fact he postively discourages that sort of thing—but insists that the task of the Orthodox Church is to help renew the foundations of historic Christendom, embracing all Churches and Communions." See Torrance's letter of nomination on behalf of Methodios for the Temple Prize in Religion in The Thomas F. Torrance Manuscript Collection. Special Collections, Princeton Theological Seminary Library. Box 172. It seems Fouyas thought that the Church of England played a big role in dismissing him from his position, perhaps due to certain critiques he had of the Anglican Church, stating "[relations with the Anglican Church] played a very important role [in my dismissal]" and "in the society of the Church of England, the principles of Christian doctrine, of canon law, of morality, etc. have no meaning at all." See Brown, "Sacked Greek Orthodox leader attacks church." The dismissal of Fouyas as Archbishop had larger implications for the Orthodox-Reformed Dialogue and also the ecumenical dialogue between the Orthodox and the Church of England. Whereas Gregorious Theocharous replaced Methodios Fouyas as Archbishop (a Cypriot now leading a largely Cypriot Orthodox community in Great Britain), John Zizioulas replaced Fouyas in his key role as leader of the Orthodox in ecumenical dialogues with the Anglicans. Torrance was incredibly concerned with the second development in particular, stating in a letter to Fouyas dated May 19th, 1988: "I was most shocked and astounded to learn that you had been relieved of your sacred office . . . and that you had been replaced in such a high-handed and, as far as I can see, quite uncanonical way." See The Thomas F. Torrance Manuscript Collection. Special Collections, Princeton Theological Seminary Library, Box 172. He wrote a letters to the Archbishop of Canterbury (Anglican) and the Archbishop of Constantinople (Orthodox) expressing his concern about this move. See, e.g., a letter written to Dimitrius I on March 22nd 1988 in Box 170 which references an earlier letter in which Torrance wrote to the Ecumenical Patriarchate urging them to reconsider replacing Fouyas with Zizioulas for theological and ethical reasons. The Ecumenical Patriarchate states in response to Torrance's initial letter: "[W]e were astonished at your interference in matters which fall purely under the responsibility of the Ecumenical Patriarchate and were, at the same time, very sorry for your judgment concerning the person and theological work of the Most Sacred Metropolitan of Pergamum Mgr John, a Hierarch who enjoys the esteem and confidence of our Church and who also possesses a high prestige." See the letter from the Patriarch to Torrance dated March 8th 1988 in Box 170. The Archbishop of Canterbury's office responded: "From an Anglican perspective, it would now be quite improper to intervene in what is strictly an Orthodox decision. If you have any influence with Archbishop Methodios my private counsel would be to encourage him to accept this decision, even though I know how unhappy he feels about it." See the letter from the Rev. Canon Christopher Hill, the Archbishop of Canterbury's Secretary for Ecumenical

dox Church in Great Britain grew to the third largest in membership in the country and, according to Torrance in a letter dated 1984, it "grows so rapidly he has great difficulty getting enough Churches to cope with them."[46] It was in his capacity as Archbishop in Great Britain, however, that Methodios Fouyas would co-lead the Orthodox-Reformed Dialogue with Torrance, although he would later be removed from his episcopal and ecumenical positions in Great Britain (and replaced in the latter by John Zizioulas) due to, indeed, Byzantine intrigue, if the correspondence preserved in the Princeton Archives is any indication. It was as Archbishop and Moderator, then, that Fouyas and Torrance, respectively, began, in Dragas' words, "the period of the Official Orthodox-Reformed Dialogue."[47]

Ultimately, the approach of Torrance and Methodios (and Reformed and Orthodox) was one of deep mutual respect and appreciation for one another's traditions. Thus, the Orthodox-Reformed Dialogue began due to a personal and official relationship and appreciation between Torrance and Fouyas; and it proceeded through a shared commitment to the Christological and Trinitarian approach of the Greek fathers which they shared.

THE RELATIONSHIP BETWEEN TORRANCE AND FOUYAS

The relationship between Torrance and Fouyas during the 1970s provided the seedbed for the flowering of the Orthodox-Reformed Dialogue which

---

Affairs dated March 30th 1988 in Box 170. Torrance said in a letter February 8th 1988 in Box 172 that "[Zizioulas's] views, in my judgment, are not centrally Orthodox." Torrance seems to think he is more of an existentializing dialectician than a theologian. For more personal concerns, see Torrance's draft letter to the Ecumenical Patriarchate where he apologizes for seeming to interfere in Orthodox affairs but reiterates his personal concern for the replacement of Fouyas with Zizioulas and his strong sense of responsibility of the need to warn them because "it was I who brought John Zizoiulas to Edinburgh and thus introduced him to our Church and theological life in Great Britain" (dated March 17th 1988) and, in his letter to the Ecumenical Patriarchate, where he states he "helped to make his career as an academic theologian" (dated March 22nd 1988). Regardless, the newspaper articles and correspondence indicate that the dismissal of Fouyas and his replacement in the form of Zizioulas in ecumenical dialogue concerned Torrance primarily on a theological level as a poor representation of true Eastern Orthodox theology.

46. See Torrance's letter nominating Fouyas for a Templeton Prize, date 1984, in The Thomas F. Torrance Manuscript Collection. Special Collections, Princeton Theological Seminary Library. Box 172.

47. See Baker and Dragas, "Interview," 10.

would begin by the early 1980s. Throughout the 1970s and 1980s Torrance and Fouyas collaborated academically in various journals and lectures.[48] In 1970, says Torrance, formal contact was then made between the Patriarchate of Alexandria and the Church of Scotland and shortly thereafter, in 1973, Torrance was invited to give a series of lectures in Alexandria in commemoration of Athanasius who died in 373,[49] an event which ultimately led to his ordination by Methodios Fouyas as "Honorary Protopresbyter" in the Greek Orthodox Patriarchate of Alexandria. Torrance even received a pectoral cross to prove it![50] In correspondence with Florovsky dated June 12th 1973 contained in the St Vladimir's Seminary Georges Florovsky Library archive, Torrance recounts this experience: "The Greek Orthodox Church make [sic.] me a Protopresbyter within the Alexandrian Patriarchate, which astonished me! This is an act of ecumenical union, on the ground of patristic theology, which I appreciate greatly."[51] Whilst the office of "Honorary Protopresbyter" is perhaps unusual, this did not stop Archbishop Methodios from promoting Torrance, no doubt this time with a wink in his eye, to the office of "Patriarch of Scotland" during tea years later in the Edinburgh moderatorial office, according to George Dragas.[52] When Torrance was elected Moderator of the Church of Scotland in 1977, one of his first visits as Moderator was to the Patriarchate of Alexandria. Torrance, following

---

48. Ibid., 9. Fouyas edited and founded many journals including *Ekklesiastikos Pharos, Abba Salama, Texts and Studies,* and *Church and Theology*. He clearly had an ecumenical interest and published books such as *Orthodoxy, Roman Catholicism, and Anglicanism*.

49. Torrance, "Introduction" to *Theological Dialogue between Orthodox and Reformed Churches*, 1:x.

50. See Baker and Dragas, "Interview," 9. Torrance was given a pectoral cross worn by Orthodox presbyters. Dragas states: "[T]his unprecedented and unusual event caused some controversy among the Orthodox at the time. It was officially explained, however, that this honor was an *ad hoc* event, and did not in any sense establish a precedent. It was, rather, a spontaneous act of honoring a person who had made such incredible contributions to the understanding of the legacy of the Church of Alexandria, as well as to the rapprochement of Reformed Christians to Orthodoxy." See ibid., 9. Nevertheless, it was in 1973 that Torrance, already a Church of Scotland minister, was ordained Priest in the Orthodox diocese of Alexandria. This "honorary ordination" was certainly not without controversy; as it is put in notes contained in the Torrance Archives for a presentation given to The Fellowship of Saint Andrew (a Scottish Group for Fellowship with Orthodox Christians): "TFT—Protopresbyter—Protest!!" See The Thomas F. Torrance Manuscript Collection. Special Collections, Princeton Theological Seminary Library. Box 40.

51. Baker, "Correspondence between Torrance and Florovsky," 319.

52. Baker and Dragas, "Interview," 10.

Part 1: A Critical Appreciation of the Orthodox-Reformed Theological Dialogue

Moderators before him, began a tour of visitation in his new official capacity of other Reformed churches throughout the world. He included in his visit of Reformed churches many Orthodox churches. As Dragas states, this was "an unprecedented event; he was the first Reformed Moderator to visit in his term of office Orthodox Churches along with sister Churches of the Reformed tradition."[53] It was through his friendship with Fouyas that he was able to make these official visitations, during which he began sowing the seeds that would grow into the Orthodox-Reformed Dialogue beginning less than a decade later.

Fouyas' admiration of Torrance that led to his ordination as "honorary protopresbyter" was only matched by Torrance's great love of Fouyas. Torrance nominated Fouyas for The Templeton Foundation Prize for Progress for Religion in 1984, reasoning:

> Methodios Fouyas is one of the most remarkable, dynamic Christians of our time, and the most outstanding leader and personality in the Orthodox Churches today. He is an extremely learned scholar . . . leader of astonishing charisma among Hellenic peoples all over the world, and a redoubtable champion of human freedom in society and politics . . . in Great Britain he stands out as the most robust, dynamic, and colourful Church leader who combines theological, ecclesiastical and human interests in an unparalleled way . . .[54]

In his speech on Fouyas' receipt of the Gold Medal and Diploma of Honor from the Rotary Club of Athens, Torrance compares Fouyas to King David's "mighty men of valor."[55] Torrance says of Methodios: he is a "Churchman of remarkable gifts and vigour who stood head and shoulders above others, and was clearly marked about by God for the Episcopate." Torrance says:

> Methodios is a completely dedicated man of God. The zeal of God's House eats him up. Everything in his life, whether small or great, whether work or leisure, is made to serve the supreme end for which he has been ordained Presbyter and consecrated Bishop. He has finally no other ambition but to use the gifts and resources God has given him and the high office that has been

---

53. Ibid., 9.

54. See Torrance's nomination letter, date 1984, in The Thomas F. Torrance Manuscript Collection. Special Collections, Princeton Theological Seminary Library. Box 172.

55. For this and subsequent references to this document, see Torrance's speech in The Thomas F. Torrance Manuscript Collection. Special Collections, Princeton Theological Seminary Library. Box 172.

thrust upon him to the mission of the Gospel and the growth of Christ's Church.

Ultimately, Torrance concludes his speech by stating that "Methodios is essentially an 'apostolical man.'" The many high personal and professional praises Torrance has for Methodios are ultimately circled around a key theme in Torrance's speech: Archbishop Methodios' Christian statesmanship and zeal for Orthodoxy, both of which Fouyas harnesses to, according to Torrance, to great success in the Ecumenical movement during their time.

As Torrance concludes concerning the importance of his friendship with Fouyas for the Dialogue,

> since, apart from personal friendships that had grown up over the years, these contacts had been brought about and continued to be sustained by profound theological accord, it seemed right that an attempt should be made to engage in formal theological consultations with the Ecumenical Patriarchate with a view to clarifying together the classical bases of Orthodox and of Reformed theology and in the hope of reaching the same kind of profound accord with respect to the 'theological axis' of Athanasian/Cyrilline theology, to which the Reformed Church has looked as having a regulative force in its understanding of Christian doctrine hardly less than the Greek Orthodox Church.[56]

The Orthodox-Reformed Dialogue was thus initiated on the basis of a friendship that focused upon these shared commitments to the Trinitarian and Christocentric theology of the Greek fathers.

THE PROFOUND ACCORD: A CHRISTOCENTRIC AND TRINITARIAN APPROACH TO TRADITION

Torrance and Fouyas' profound accord and shared commitment provided fertile ground for the Orthodox and Reformed to begin their dialogue. Once the Dialogue began, two main elements emerged as shared commitments but with difference emphases, namely, (1) the shared Christocentric and Trinitarian approach and (2) the commitment to tradition. These two shared commitments emerge in the published writings of the

---

56. Torrance, "Introduction" to *Theological Dialogue between Orthodox and Reformed Churches*, 1:x.

Orthodox-Reformed Dialogue as well as the discussions following the papers as highlighted in the Official Minutes.

The Shared Christocentric and Trinitarian approach

Once the Dialogue began, the Reformed and Orthodox agreed upon a commitment to a Trinitarian and Christocentric approach, driven by Torrance and Fouyas' shared commitment.[57] For example, Torrance argues that they must remain focused upon the Nicene *homoousion* inasmuch as it is the "king-pin" of the Nicene-Constantinopolitan Creed, which expresses the core evangelical belief that in Jesus Christ humanity is confronted with the very self-giving and self-revealing of God as he is in himself.[58] As such, at the Dialogue Torrance proposes a return in the Orthodox-Reformed Dialogue to the Athanasian-Cyrilline axis of theology; a commitment to which the Orthodox agreed wholeheartedly.[59]

The Shared Commitment to Tradition

On the basis of the Trinitarian and Christocentric conversation and in light of their shared commitment to the Greek fathers the Reformed and Orthodox came to realize they had a shared commitment to the catholic tradition but that they had some important differences which, in large part, stemmed from different ways of appropriating the fathers. In short, the Reformed approach to tradition at the Orthodox-Reformed Dialogue was a Word-based and Christocentric approach whereas the Orthodox approach was a Church-based and synthetic approach. According Reformed and Orthodox, therefore, seemed to have figures they emphasized at the Dialogue. Overall, in the discussion the Reformed emphasize an ongoing consensus of *doctrine* whereas the Orthodox emphasize an ongoing consensus of *figures*. The Reformed approach reveals a commitment to a Word-based and Christocentric appropriation of the Greek fathers and a turn to their consensus of doctrine. For example, Torrance states: "here we must be aware of the apostolic nature of the church, and the obedience of the Church to

---

57. Torrance, "Memoranda on Orthodox/Reformed Relations," 11.

58. See, e.g., Torrance, *The Incarnation*, xi–xv. The Orthodox indeed agreed with the Reformed that this is a lynchpin. See ibid., 1–15.

59. Torrance, "The Triunity of God," 3–13.

the truth of the Apostles. That is why the fathers were not infrequently criticized and corrected by the Councils. We have to note the magisterial authority of the Councils vis-à-vis the Fathers."[60] In contrast, the Orthodox approach to the fathers in the Dialogue highlights a more synthetic understanding of tradition. In response to Torrance's focus on Athanasius, the Orthodox state "of course the fathers could be cited in this direction but one must attempt to grasp the totality of the consensus patrum"[61] and "Is not Torrance in danger of over-absolutizing Athanasius in relation to the Cappadocians?"[62] Rather than pitting one Father against another, the Orthodox offer a more synthetic approach whereby theology is done by means of the whole tradition. Along these lines the Orthodox mention the importance of the "line of continuity" for the *Consensus Patrum*, for, they state, "There is a magisterial element in the weight of tradition."[63]

In light of these shared commitments with different approaches to the theological tradition, three figures in particular come under heavy critique at the Orthodox-Reformed Dialogue: Basil the Great, Augustine, and Gregory Palamas. First, Torrance consistently urges for a return to the "Athanasius-Cyril axis" and bifurcates this from the Cappadocians. Torrance contends that the Cappadocians departed from a more Athanasian and dynamic conception of the doctrine of the Trinity. The Cappadocians are constantly pitted against Athanasius and Cyril by Torrance, on the doctrine of the Trinity in particular. For Torrance, the Cappadocians, especially Basil, divide God's Being from God's Persons in a way that Athanasius and Cyril and their conception of God's Being as dynamically Trinitarian do not.[64] Second, Gregory Palamas is critiqued for holding to a theological dualism which divides God's Acts from God's Being.[65] Torrance un-

---

60. See the Minutes from the 1981 meeting contained in The Thomas F. Torrance Manuscript Collection. Special Collections, Princeton Theological Seminary Library. Box 170.

61. See ibid.

62. See ibid.

63. See ibid.

64. See, e.g., Torrance's comments in the 1981 Minutes in The Thomas F. Torrance Manuscript Collection. Special Collections, Princeton Theological Seminary Library. Box 170. He states: "Athanasius did not so separate [οὐσία and ἐνέργεια] as in the Cappadocians and what later became characteristic of much Byzantine theology."

65. See, e.g., the Thomas F. Torrance Manuscript Collection. Special Collections, Princeton Theological Seminary Library. Box 170. Torrance believes that the Essence/Energies distinction makes God unknowable in himself.

derstands this to undermine the basic theological point, preserved by the Nicene *homoousion*, that what God is to us he really is in himself. Torrance sees in Gregory Palamas an unhappy distinction, as well, between God's Essence and Energies.[66] In the Dialogue Torrance depicts Athanasius and Palamas as intrinsically opposed to one another in basic theology on this point.[67] Third, at the Dialogue Torrance accuses Augustine of neoplatonic dualism.[68] Augustine and Augustinianism were not discussed in great detail in the Dialogue; after all, they were returning to the classical theology of Athanasius and Cyril, but nevertheless, Augustinian theology is generally used negatively in the Dialogue.[69]

CONCLUSION

Throughout the Dialogue, the Orthodox argue for a synthetic reading of the tradition. As highlighted above, Torrance and the Reformed are accused of emphasizing "select theologians" over others. This critique is surely valid and Torrance is open about his emphasis upon the "Athanasius-Cyril axis of classical theology"[70] and Athanasius, "the foundation of classical theology."[71] Indeed, Torrance probably could have been more synthetic in his reading of theological history. Perhaps the Orthodox were equally as selective in their reading of theological history. Throughout the Dialogue, they read Athanasius and Cyril through the lens of the Cappadocians and, even more so, through the lens of Gregory Palamas.[72]

---

66. See Torrance, *Trinitarian Faith*, 38–39, esp. 38n69. See also *Theology in Reconciliation*, 252.

67. Torrance, "Memoranda on Orthodox/Reformed Relations," 11. The Orthodox suggest that Torrance over-absolutizes Athanasius against the Cappadocians. See the 1981 Minutes in The Thomas F. Torrance Manuscript Collection. Special Collections, Princeton Theological Seminary Library. Box 170.

68. See, e.g., Torrance's comments in the 1983 Minutes contained in The Thomas F. Torrance Manuscript Collection. Special Collections, Princeton Theological Seminary Library, Box 170.

69. See ibid. Torrance calls the Palamite Essence/Energies distinction an "eastern Augustinianism." See the Conclusion of this book for engagement with the fairness of this accusation.

70. Torrance, *Theology in Reconciliation*, 14.

71. Ibid., 215–66.

72. This is generally consistent with the larger Orthodox approach to reading the fathers. See, e.g., Florovsky's essay: "Gregory Palamas and the Tradition of the Fathers," in *Bible, Church, Tradition*. See also *Augustine and Orthodoxy* for a collection of essays

The shared commitment between Orthodox and Reformed at the Dialogue, exhibited most clearly through the personal and indeed theological friendship between Torrance and Fouyas, however, certainly produced much fruit. The Orthodox-Reformed Dialogue began in 1979 emerging out of the 1970s when Torrance and Fouyas were official leaders in their respective churches, Fouyas Archbishop of Great Britain and Torrance as Moderator of the Church of Scotland or, as Fouyas put it, "Patriarch of Scotland." A direct fruit of this theological relationship, the Orthodox-Reformed Dialogue officially began in 1979 and lasted until 1992, producing real agreement on the doctrine of the Trinity exhibited by "The Agreed Statement on the Holy Trinity." Thus, it is to these two topics that this book now turns. The next chapter will explore the history of the Dialogue, focusing upon the Five official gatherings which developed "The Agreed Statement on the Holy Trinity," and the subsequent chapter will examine "The Agreed Statement on the Holy Trinity" itself, exploring its nature as a Third-Wave Trinitarian document that deserves more attention today.

---

by Orthodox theologians. Often, Augustine is critiqued for not holding to the Essence/Energies distinction of Gregory Palamas.

CHAPTER 3

The Five Consultations
Toward an Agreed Statement on the Holy Trinity

The desire and the turning to the East since the time of Calvin and Zwingli up to the present is historically witnessed.

His All-Holiness The Ecumenical Patriarch Dimitrios I[1]

The Reformed have historically felt very close to the Orthodox, because of your concern and our concern for the Apostolic Faith.

President James I. McCord[2]

INTRODUCTION

As explored in the previous chapter, the Orthodox-Reformed Dialogue grew out of a common and ecumenical commitment to the Trinitarian and Christocentric theology of the Greek fathers exhibited by the deep theological friendship between Torrance and Methodios, yet they also had

---

1. Address by His All-Holiness The Ecumenical Patriarch Dimitrios I to the Delegation of the World Alliance of Reformed Churches, Istanbul, 1979. See the 1979 Minutes in The Thomas F. Torrance Manuscript Collection. Special Collections, Princeton Theological Seminary Library, Box 170.

2. McCord, Address to the Ecumenical Patriarchate, July 26, 1979 recorded in Torrance, "Introduction" to *Theological Dialogue between Orthodox and Reformed Churches*, 1:xvi.

many differences in theological approach to the tradition of the church fathers. The friendship and theological collaboration between Torrance and Methodios provided much of the initial impetus for the Orthodox-Reformed Dialogue. However, once the Orthodox-Reformed Dialogue began, Torrance and Methodios, while remaining important, became a part of a much bigger movement.

Scope of the Chapter

The present chapter offers an history of the Orthodox-Reformed Dialogue. In this chapter the contours of the history of the Dialogue will be explored, with a focus on the development of the Trinitarian theology at the Dialogue which led to "The Agreed Statement on the Holy Trinity." Ultimately, this chapter will argue that the Trinitarian *homoousion*-centered theology of Athanasius as seen by Torrance provides the grounds for developing "The Agreed Statement on the Holy Trinity," a Third-Wave Trinitarianism before its time.

OVERVIEW OF THE ORTHODOX-REFORMED ECUMENICAL DIALOGUE

The Orthodox-Reformed Dialogue, occurring in the 1980s and 1990s, was a movement of great ecumenical and theological import borne out of deep friendships between Reformed and Orthodox in Great Britain, particularly Torrance and Fouyas, as explored in the previous chapter of this book. The Orthodox-Reformed Dialogue itself officially took place in five sessions 1981, 1983, 1988, and 1990, with a concluding session in 1992. The goal was to clarify "together the classical bases of Orthodox and of Reformed theology and in the hope of reaching the same kind of profound accord with respect to the 'theological axis' of Athanasian/Cyrilline theology, to which the Reformed Church has looked as having regulative force in its understanding of Christian doctrine hardly less than the Greek Orthodox Church."[3] Thus it was through the friendship and "theological rapport" between Torrance and Fouyas that the Orthodox-Reformed Dialogued began.

3. Ibid.

Part 1: A Critical Appreciation of the Orthodox-Reformed Theological Dialogue

The stated goal was to explore the common roots between the two churches on the basis of Apostolic faith and order as explicated in classical Christianity. The doctrines of Triadology and Christology, therefore, conditioned their conversation throughout. Indeed, Torrance notes how he developed the view, while Moderator, that Orthodox-Reformed Dialogue should start with the doctrine of the Trinity.[4]

The Dialogue indeed began here, and proceeded with five consultations, three unofficial, two official, and one concluding. Each of the consultations was concerned with a different topic. In short, the first dealt with the catholicity of the church, the second with the role of authority in the church, and the third began, from the basis of catholicity and authority, to begin to discuss the doctrine of the Trinity. It was, however, not until the following two official consultations that the doctrine of the Trinity would be considered in full by the Dialogue. The first official consultation examined the doctrine of the Trinity and explored common roots and the second official consultation centered itself around the construction of and discussion of "The Agreed Statement" on the Holy Trinity. The concluding consultation finalized and affirmed "The Agreed Statement on the Holy Trinity" which was considered the official output of the Dialogue and hailed as the culmination and the fruit of the five consultations. This chapter will proceed by unpacking the theological developments of each of the consultations inasmuch as they paved the way for the important "Agreed Statement."

THE FIRST THREE PREPARATORY CONSULTATIONS

The early Orthodox-Reformed Dialogue, taking place in 1979 in Istanbul (the formal beginning of the Dialogue), in 1981 in Geneva, and in 1983 also in Geneva,[5] and the subsequent publication *Theological Dialogue Between Reformed and Orthodox Churches Volume 1* included papers given by Torrance,[6] Emilianos Timiadis,[7] Hans-Helmut Esser,[8] and Chrysostomos

---

4. See ibid. In "Memorandum A," Torrance says he proposed beginning with the doctrine of the Trinity and from there move to the doctrines of Christology and Pneumatology and then from there to the Eucharist, Church, and Ministry. See p. 10.

5. These were "later regarded as preparatory consultations." See Torrance, "Preface," vii.

6. Torrance, "Memoranda on Orthodox/Reformed Relations," 3–22.

7. Timiadis, "God's Immutability and Communicability," 23–49.

8. Esser, "The Authority of the Church and Authority in the Church according to the

Konstantinidis.⁹ These were figures of key importance in the Reformed and Orthodox worlds at the time. James McCord (President of Princeton Seminary), Archbishop of Constantinople Dimitrios I, Chrysostomos Konstantinidis (Metropolitan of Myra), Vasil Istravridis (Orthodox Bishop of Germany), Prof Jan Lochman (Reformed, Switzerland), Torrance, Emilianos Timiadis (Metropolitan of Selybria), Prof Hans Esser (Reformed, Germany), Richmond Smith (Theological Secretary of the W.A.R.C.), Prof Joe McLelland (Reformed, Canada), Damaskinos Papandreaou (Metropolitan of Tranoupolis), Gennadios Limouris (Orthodox Priest, France), Lukas Vischer (Chairman of the Department of Theology of the W.A.R.C.), Prof Istvan Juhasz (Reformed, Romania), Dr Edmund Perret (General Secretary of the W.A.R.C.), and John Breck (Orthodox Priest, France), who were key in the discussion as recorded in the Official Minutes, were all leaders in their respective churches and contributed greatly to the Dialogue.[10]

The First Consultation: Istanbul, 1979

The First Consultation took place in Istanbul in 1979 and was marked by a warm sense of catholicity between the Orthodox and the Reformed, although real theological issues were of course heartily discussed. The Istanbul consultation consisted initially of the Reformed, led by Torrance and James McCord, presenting their "Memoranda on Orthodox/Reformed Relations" to the Orthodox Patriarchate at Phanar in Istanbul.

George Dragas recalls Torrance first sharing the draft of the Memoranda with him in Dragas' hotel room during an interlude in the *Academie des Science Religieuses* prior to presenting at the 1979 consultation. According to Dragas:

> It was detailed, and in the heart of it there was a specific proposal that the theological dialogue should start with the doctrine of the Trinity according to the Nicene theology of Athanasius and Cyril and not that of the Cappadocian fathers. He justified this by pointing out certain serious problems that Orthodox theology had developed over the years by over-reliance on the Cappadocians to

---

Reformed Tradition," 50–57.

9. Konstantinidis, "Authority in the Orthodox Church," 58–78.

10. See the Official Minutes for the consultations in 1979, 1981, and 1983 contained in The Thomas F. Torrance Manuscript Collection. Special Collections, Princeton Theological Seminary Library. Box 170.

the neglect of the Alexandrians and more or less suggested that the dialogue with the Reformed theologians would supply the answers to the problems of the Orthodox![11]

Dragas says he responded to Torrance by saying:

> Professor Tom, this will not fly. Let me go through it and explain why . . . No Orthodox would approve of this opposition between the Alexandrians and the Cappadocians—we do not see the Fathers this way. Likewise, when you first go to approach an Orthodox Patriarch to ask him for a dialogue, you should not come with criticisms about his Orthodox theologians and their theological tradition. Rather, you should first present your credentials as Christians and state that in faithful obedience to the will of Christ you approach the Orthodox with a wish to be reconciled. You need first to explain to them who you are, what you believe and practice as Reformed Christians, that you have ordained clergy and sacraments, synods and so forth, and what all these mean to you.[12]

According to Dragas, Torrance responded: "George, can I ask you a favor? Can you write a memorandum as if you were the Reformed, requesting a dialogue with the Orthodox?"[13] Dragas then states:

> On his insistence I did so and sent it to him a little later. He revised it and used it for his memorandum to the Ecumenical Patriarch. After he returned from his visit to the Phanar in July 1979, he wrote me a letter and thanked me for my help with the memorandum. He said that he presented both memoranda, the one that I wrote and the one that he wrote and I did not agree with! And, he added, Patriarch Demetrios was delighted with both![14]

Thus, the Orthodox-Reformed Dialogue began with great collaboration between Torrance and his former student George Dragas, a collaboration which would continue throughout the Dialogue, ultimately leading to the construction of "The Agreed Statement on the Holy Trinity." Both Memoranda are included in *Theological Dialogue Between Orthodox and Reformed Churches* as well as in Part Two of this book.

---

11. Baker and Dragas, "Interview," 11. Memoranda A is, presumably, the first draft written by Torrance and Memoranda B is the second, written by Dragas.
12. Ibid., 11–12.
13. Ibid., 12.
14. Ibid.

The Official Minutes record that the initial discussion was "marked by warm cordiality between Orthodox and Reformed.[15] Dimitrius I, the Orthodox Patriarch, "a gentle, benign man" according to George Dragas,[16] delivered the initial address (in Greek), "a warm and appreciative welcome in which the Reformed delegation was assured of the personal desire of the Ecumenical Patriarch that the dialogue between Orthodox and Reformed should proceed 'with good will, with courage and with hope in our Lord.'"[17] The Orthodox Patriarch viewed this "turning east" as a monumental event in the history of the Reformed tradition, stating, "to the great dates of your uniting movement of the last hundred years, i.e., the years 1875,[18] 1891[19] and 1970,[20] we think that you are adding with your visit and with your proposal the present year 1979 also. This will remain reciprocally as a historical point in the relations of our churches."[21] President McCord then presented a gift to the Patriarch, and subsequent addresses were delivered by Metropolitan Chrysostomos and President McCord.[22]

The Official Minutes from the initial consultation in Istanbul highlight a number of key methodological similarities and differences that came to light during this first conversation between the Reformed and Orthodox. The similarities—and as Patriarch Dimitrios I says in his opening address (recorded in the Official Minutes), "there are many common points"[23]—largely pertain to shared commitments to the content of the Christian faith (the Trinitarian and Christocentric theology of the Greek fathers) and differences largely pertain to distinctions in forms of expression of the Chris-

15. See the Official Minutes, 1979. In The Thomas F. Torrance Manuscript Collection. Special Collections, Princeton Theological Seminary Library. Box 170.

16. Baker and Dragas, "Interview," 12.

17. The Thomas F. Torrance Manuscript Collection. Special Collections, Princeton Theological Seminary Library. Box 170.

18. The formation of an alliance of Reformed presbyterian churches.

19. The formation of an alliance of Reformed congregational churches.

20. The formation of an alliance between the already existing alliance of Reformed presbyterian churches and the already existing alliance of Reformed congregational churches, called "The World Alliance of Reformed Churches."

21. See the 1979 Official Minutes contained in The Thomas F. Torrance Manuscript Collection. Special Collections, Princeton Theological Seminary Library. Box 170.

22. See ibid.

23. See "The Address by His All-Holiness The Ecumenical Patriarch Dimitrios I to the Delegation of the World Alliance of Reformed Churches," Istanbul, 1979 contained in The Official Minutes, 1979, Box 170, as well as Torrance, "Introduction" to *Theological Dialogue between Orthodox and Reformed Churches*, 1:xvii.

tian faith (worship, revelation, church government). The Official Minutes from the 1979 consultation suggest the discussion following the various papers saw the Reformed delegation arguing these differences exist on the Reformed side (e.g. identifying Holy Scripture with revelation, simplicity in worship and in churches, identification of two sacraments rather than seven, and even Presbyterian church government) not as core to the content of Reformed theology—nor even representative of "classical Reformed theology" and form, but rather as "Calvinist" or "Puritan" or "Renaissance" developments. Thus, the sense The Official Minutes give of the dialogue following Torrance's initial paper on Orthodox Reformed relations is that the Reformed are making intentional efforts to show the Orthodox they are like them. Indeed, both groups seemed to desire irenic relations and seemed open to relegating a number of beliefs and practices to the realm of secondary importance.

In his opening address to the Orthodox, the President of the World Alliance of Reformed Churches, James McCord, articulates that the Reformed have "historically felt very close to the Orthodox, because of [their] concern for the Apostolic Faith."[24] Torrance states great appreciation for the approach offered by the Orthodox. Metropolitan Chrysostomos of Myra states that the Orthodox have also considered the Reformation as a "protest against the Western Establishment and as part of the schism of the Western Church."[25] Metropolitan Chrysostomos also articulates in this opening address the Orthodox appreciation for the "Reformed concern for the truth and witness of the Early Church."[26] Thus the Orthodox and Reformed Dialogue began with a strong shared commitment to and emphasis upon the theology and life of the early church; the Orthodox clearly understood themselves as consistently faithful to the patristic church and the Reformed clearly understood themselves in their protest against medieval Roman Catholicism returning to the patristic church and so the two delegations proceeded upon this important and essential common ground of self-understanding.

However, notes Torrance, "at that first meeting in Istanbul considerable attention was given to problems of method and the underlying assumptions

---

24. That is, Protestants protest against the same things the Orthodox are against in the West. Torrance, "Introduction" to *Theological Dialogue between Orthodox and Reformed Churches*, 1:xvi.

25. Torrance, "Introduction" to *Theological Dialogue between Orthodox and Reformed Churches*, 1:xix.

26. Ibid..

that gave rise to divergence in doctrinal formulation and in the structure of the ministry in the historical developments of Catholic and Evangelical Churches."[27] The Official Minutes record that after the initial papers, discussion focused precisely upon the issues of distinctives. Four issues are listed as arising from the Orthodox delegation: (1) a wish to emphasize grace over predestination, (2) a desire to get beyond seeming anthropocentric tendencies in Reformed interpretation, the relationship of revelation to Scripture and Tradition, (3) the Sacraments and ordination, and (4) the significance of the difference in forms of worship.[28] Interestingly, the Reformed comments in the Minutes seem to be direct defenses against the issues raised by the Orthodox. In particular, the Reformed delegation seems to want to articulate to the Orthodox that the issues highlighted are not core to who they are as Reformed, nor even representative of "classical Reformed theology." Indeed, the Reformed delegation says in their responses that (1) they wish to emphasize the sovereignty and grace of God over predestination and the will of God, (2) the anthropocentric individualism is a product of the Renaissance rather than the Reformation and is considered heresy by the Reformed, (3) they believe in two sacraments because this is dominical, but they agree with Calvin that the other five are "sacramental," and (4) the distinctively simple nature of Reformed worship is Puritan, not classically Reformed.[29] Ultimately, the Official Minutes indicate, the issues that make the Reformed different from the Orthodox are a result of historical development on the European continent during the Reformation and subsequent later additions, but the core of classical Reformed faith and order is based upon the Triune God of grace, just like the Orthodox. In other words, the Reformed delegation seems to be saying any differences do not *need* to continue to exist! Both Orthodox and Reformed agreed they should focus on agreement and start with the substantial undergirding of an exploration of the doctrine of the Trinity.

As Joseph Small puts it,

> Torrance's outline for the future of "Orthodox/Reformed Conversations" was both cautious and bold. Because substantive contact between Orthodox and Reformed had been virtually nonexistent, formal dialogue was premature. The more circumspect

27. Ibid., xxi.
28. See The Official Minutes, 1979. In The Thomas F. Torrance Manuscript Collection. Special Collections, Princeton Theological Seminary Library. Box 170.
29. See ibid.

"conversation" and "consultation" provided a free space for both Orthodox and Reformed to explore possibilities without committing themselves to the constraints of a formal ecclesial dialogue. Yet Torrance was also bold, for he proposed that the series of consultations focused on the doctrine of the Trinity.[30]

The proposal was met with enthusiasm. Thus, the Reformed-Orthodox Dialogue began with mutual appreciation, commitment to the Trinitarian and Christocentric theology of the Greek fathers, and an agreement that they should begin with an exploration of the doctrine of the Trinity.

The Second Consultation: Geneva, 1981

The initial consultation in Istanbul in 1979 provided an excellent grounding for the rest of the Orthodox-Reformed Dialogue over the subsequent decade and a half. The Orthodox and Reformed developed good rapport and exhibited truly mutual admiration for one another. The initial consultation also highlighted the many core similarities and core differences in approach to church life and thought in the Orthodox tradition and the Reformed tradition.

The initial consultation in Istanbul in 1979 ended optimistically and the warm sense of catholicity continued. As Joseph Smalls puts it, "while the first consultation explored areas of substantial theological coherence, it became clear that the relative authority of the conversation partners presented difficulties that had to be addressed."[31] At the second initial consultation, taking place in 1981, the topic of authority, revelation, and theological epistemology were therefore the main issues discussed.

The first paper, "God's Immutability and Communicability"[32] delivered by Emilianos Timiadis from the Orthodox argues for a synthetic church-focused patristic tradition in which God makes himself knowable as he is through his energies. The second paper, "The Authority of the Church and Authority in the Church According to the Reformed Tradition,"[33] by

---

30. Small, "Orthodox and Reformed in Dialogue," 110–11. As a minor historical point, it was in fact the Orthodox, not Torrance, who proposed a series of "consultations." See the 1979 Minutes in In The Thomas F. Torrance Manuscript Collection. Special Collections, Princeton Theological Seminary Library. Box 170.

31. Ibid., 111.

32. Timiadis, "God's Immutability and Communicability," 23–49.

33. Esser, "The Authority of the Church and Authority in the Church according to

Hans-Helmut Esser, from the Reformed, argues for a more Christocentric approach to knowledge of God, emphasizing an essential openness to the church "always reforming." Central to Esser's argument was the point that ecclesiology—and by extension any understanding of historical church authority—is ultimately derived from Christology.[34] The third paper, "Authority in the Orthodox Church,"[35] delivered by Chrysostomos S. Konstantinidis from the Orthodox side argues for a Christocentric and synthetic understanding of tradition, with a recognition of divergences between east and west but ultimately a suggestion to focus upon the consensus. He asks a question of the Reformed concerning how they understand authority exercised without episcopal oversight.[36]

The second consultation dealt with issues of interpreting tradition and understanding authority in the Reformed and Orthodox traditions. The Minutes bring to light conversations behind the scenes, notably: (1) can one church father be authoritative over another?, (2) can the ecumenical councils be authoritative over the fathers? and (3) is church tradition synthetic or thematic? In the discussion, the Reformed emphasize an ongoing consensus of *doctrine* whereas the Orthodox emphasize an ongoing consensus of *figures*. However, they both exhibit a Christocentric approach. Torrance states:

> Here we must be aware of the apostolic nature of the church, and the obedience of the Church to the truth of the Apostles. That is why the Fathers were not infrequently criticized and corrected by the Councils. We have to note the magisterial authority of the Councils vis-à-vis the Fathers.[37]

Accordingly, throughout the Minutes Torrance insists upon a return to the Christocentric theology of Athanasius. In contrast, the Orthodox approach to the fathers in the Dialogue highlights a more synthetic or, perhaps, syncretistic theology. In response to Torrance's critiques by means of a utilization of the theology of Athanasius in the paper's thrust, Chrysostomos (of the Orthodox) states: "of course the Fathers could be cited in this direction but one must attempt to grasp the totality of the consensus

---

the Reformed Tradition," 50–58.

34. Ibid., 50.

35. Konstantinidis, "Authority in the Orthodox Church," 58–75.

36. Ibid., 74.

37. See the 1981 Minutes. In The Thomas F. Torrance Manuscript Collection. Special Collections, Princeton Theological Seminary Library. Box 170.

patrum"[38] and Emilianos states: "Is not Torrance in danger of over-absolutizing Athanasius in relation to the Cappadocians?"[39] Rather than pitting one Father against another, the Orthodox suggest a more synthetic approach whereby theology is done by means of the whole combination of figures. Along these lines the Orthodox mention the importance of the "line of continuity" for the *Consensus Patrum*. As Chrysostomos states: "There is a magisterial element in the weight of tradition."[40]

At the end of the Second Consultation, Torrance proposes that the group "adopt a study programme . . . centred on the doctrine of the Trinity . . . taking the Nicene-Constantinopolitan Creed as a basic text"[41] and suggests "The Trinitarian Foundation and Character of Faith and of Authority in the Church (as exhibited in the Nicene-Constantinopolitan Creed)" as the subject of the upcoming Third Consultation. Chrysostomos agrees, but notes that an official approval of this route would need to be solicited from the Ecumenical Patriarch prior to any plans being made. The group agreed nonetheless to proceed on this basis. Ultimately, those in the discussion decided the next step was to discuss the doctrine of the Trinity and to place further questions of church and authority within an explicitly Trinitarian framework.[42]

The Third Consultation: Chambésy, 1983

The Third Consultation began steering the conversation toward a discussion of the doctrine of the Trinity and its relevance for the rest of theology and ministry. The focus was on two papers on the Trinitarian nature of the church and authority, one by Torrance and one by Metropolitan Emilianos Timiadis of Selybria. The papers ultimately moved towards a discussion of the doctrine of the Trinity and the discussion concluded with an agreement to open the Official Consultations whose aim would be to work toward an agreement on the doctrine of the Trinity.

In Torrance's paper, entitled "The Trinitarian Foundation and Character of Faith and of Authority in the Church,"[43] he argues for a unity of es-

38. See ibid.
39. See ibid.
40. See ibid.
41. See ibid.
42. See further Small, "Orthodox and Reformed in Dialogue," 113.
43. Torrance, "The Trinitarian Foundation and Character of Faith and of Authority

sence focused upon the *ousia* of the Trinity. At the Dialogue the Reformed and Orthodox embraced the Cappadocian formula of *mia ousia, treis hypostases*.[44] However, throughout the Dialogue Torrance urged them to utilize the phrase in what he saw as a more Athanasian sense with an insistence on the unity of Persons or in his words the "perfect equality of the Father, Son and Holy Spirit, in each of whom the Godhead is complete," rather than an emphasis on the threeness of the Persons.[45] For, Torrance argues in his paper, "we must take care that the natural images and analogies which this human language carries are not read back into God but are critically controlled by the self-revelation of God which they are employed to articulate."[46] Torrance insists that the focus must be on the Nicene *homoousion*, "the ontological substructure upon which the meaning of the New Testament message about Jesus Christ rested and through which its different writings and statements concerning Christ and the Gospel could be integrated in accordance with their essential import."[47]

Similarly to Torrance's other texts on the doctrine of the Trinity (such as *The Trinitarian Faith*[48] and *The Christian Doctrine of God*[49]), Torrance is concerned here by what he sees as the Cappadocian and Byzantine division of God's *ousia* and *hypostaseis* and God's *ousia* and *energia*[50] (Energy), which he sees in nascence in the Cappadocians, only emerging in full force in the later Byzantine tradition, Gregory Palamas in particular.[51] These approaches, they believed, read the "natural analogies" back into God without allowing revelation to reshape them. Here, as Small aptly states, "in charac-

---

in the Church," 79–120.

44. Greek: μία οὐσια, τρεῖς ὑπόστασεις" (one Being, three Persons). See Torrance, "The Trinitarian Foundation and Character of Faith and of Authority in the Church," 79.

45. Torrance, "The Trinitarian Foundation and Character of Faith and of Authority in the Church," 87.

46. Ibid., 79.

47. Ibid., 101.

48. Torrance, *The Trinitarian Faith*.

49. Torrance, *The Christian Doctrine of God*.

50. Greek: ἐνέργια.

51. Cf. Torrance, *Trinitarian Faith*, 38–39. Interestingly, in the conversation at the Dialogue following his paper Torrance clarifies that he thinks that "the ousia/dynameis distinction . . . [is] taken too seriously today perhaps because of Lossky's interpretation (injecting ideas from Boehme and Eckhart into patristic exegesis . . . a kind of Augustinianism of the East . . . the Neo-Platonism is evident and leads to similar problems." See the 1983 Minutes in The Thomas F. Torrance Manuscript Collection. Special Collections, Princeton Seminary. Box 170.

teristic Reformed fashion, Torrance insisted that theological language must be governed by revelation."[52] According to Torrance, the Dialogue should, therefore, focus upon Athanasius' conception of the procession of the Holy Spirit from the *ousia*[53] of the Father inasmuch as it cuts behind divisions between East and West[54] in its important emphasis upon the dynamic unity of the three Persons of the Godhead rather than the unity or the Trinity only[55] and the problem of the *filioque*, as Torrance argues elsewhere, "simply falls away."[56]

Torrance then extends his understanding of the relationship of revelation to theological language into the realm of epistemology and authority. Here Torrance argues for a Christological and Trinitarian understanding of authority as rooted in Christ.[57] Ultimately, Torrance concludes, in the words of Small, "since truth and authority are one in Christ, embodied authority is not exercised in judicial relations, but only through union and communion with Christ."[58] The distinction between a judicial/legalistic understanding of authority and tradition versus a Christocentric understanding would be drawn out further in the discussion following the Dialogue.[59]

Emilianos Timiadis responded with a paper entitled "The Trinitarian Structure of the Church and Its Authority."[60] Similarly to Torrance, Timiadis grounds his understanding of ecclesiastical authority in the doctrine of the Trinity and in Christology, albeit more sacramentally via God's

---

52. Small, "Orthodox and Reformed in Dialogue," 113. There is a need, Torrance states in the Official Minutes, "to protect our terminology from becoming sacrosanct." The Thomas F. Torrance Manuscript Collection. Special Collections, Princeton Seminary. Box 170.

53. Greek: οὐσία translated "being," "essence," or "nature."

54. Torrance, "Introduction" to *Theological Dialogue between Orthodox and Reformed Churches*, 1:xi.

55. Torrance, *Trinitarian Perspectives*, 13–20.

56. Torrance, "My Interaction with Karl Barth," 132.

57. Torrance, "The Trinitarian Foundation and Character of Faith and of Authority in the Church," 91–120.

58. Small, "Orthodox and Reformed in Dialogue," 114.

59. According to the 1983 Minutes, Torrance states: "[T]he Reformation broke from the forensic notion of the medieval church i.e. canon law determining how doctrine can be formulated . . . perhaps similarly we can now, together, cut behind our differences (whether substantive or cultural and terminological) by giving the doctrine of the Trinity the absolute place at every level." The Thomas F. Torrance Manuscript Collection. Special Collections, Princeton Seminary. Box 170.

60. Timiadis, "The Trinitarian Structure of the Church and Its Authority," 121–56.

energies.[61] According to Timiadis, for the Orthodox, the Trinitarian and Christocentric authority of the church is thus exhibited most clearly by Christians synthetically inasmuch as "God is never alone . . . bound to his people . . . the Church is divine and human . . . [and] once we accept the permanent indwelling and active present of the Holy Trinity in the saving mission of the Church, we can easily conclude that she possesses the authority to discern sound doctrine from false."[62] Thus, whilst his articulation of authority is certainly as Trinitarian and Christocentric as Torrance's, Timiadis nevertheless proposed a more Church-based approach.

According to the Official Minutes, Torrance raised some questions regarding Timiadis' paper. First, Torrance wondered how this "embodied authority" functions in the church.[63] Second, Torrance raised a concern that the approach of embodied authority via God's energies along the lines of, e.g., Pseudo-Dionysius is a sort of Thomism of the East in which God cannot really be known.[64] However, notably, the focus of the conversation had largely to do with the implications of a pluralistic or unitarian focus in the doctrine of the Trinity, i.e. whether a focus on the threeness led to a more hierarchical understanding of the episcopacy and whether a focus on the oneness led to a more collegiate understanding.[65]

As Small elucidates, it is important to see that both Timiadis and Torrance ground authority in truth, and ground truth in Christ, so that truth and authority are one. Reformed and Orthodox distinctives are displayed in the different ways that Timiadis and Torrance articulated shared convictions."[66] Indeed, both Timiadis and Torrance argue for the same kind of authority: a Trinitarian and Christocentric authority exhibited in the patristic tradition. In the conversation after the papers, Torrance argues that the similarity between the two traditions goes even further: "as to 'identity', the Reformed Church is closer to Orthodoxy than any other Church . . . inasmuch as identity for us is tied up in theology."[67]

61. See, e.g., Timiadis, "The Trinitarian Structure of the Church and Its Authority," 122–24. Timiadis states: "[B]elievers participate in the fullness of the life of Christ, experienced by receiving his body and blood. See 123–24.

62. Timiadis, "The Trinitarian Structure of the Church and Its Authority," 151.

63. The Thomas F. Torrance Manuscript Collection. Special Collections, Princeton Seminary. Box 170.

64. Ibid.

65. Ibid.

66. Small, "Orthodox and Reformed in Dialogue," 115.

67. See the Official Minutes. The Thomas F. Torrance Manuscript Collection. Special

For Torrance and the Reformed, the church fathers witness to this truth and authority whereas for Timiadis and the Orthodox, this truth and authority is embedded within the church fathers. Another notable difference between the Reformed and Orthodox at this point of the Dialogue is their different emphases in terms of sources. Whereas Torrance and the Reformed focus upon fourth- and fifth-century church fathers such as Gregory Nazianzen,[68] Emilianos, and the Orthodox focus upon Maximus, Gregory Palamas, and *The Divine Liturgy of John Chrysostom*.[69] This difference in figures in turn causes something of a difference in emphasis in terms of the doctrine of the Trinity itself. Torrance focuses upon unity of essence and Emilianos focuses upon the order of the Trinity.

In the "Concluding Affirmation," included in *Theological Dialogue Between Orthodox and Reformed Churches* the Dialogue so far is summed up as envisaging

> making the doctrine of the Trinity the starting point and the controlling theme for all further consultation in a way that could cut behind traditional divergences, not only between the Orthodox and the Reformed, but between the Eastern and Western Church, the Evangelical and Catholic Churches, and even between the historical contrapositions of Antiochian and Alexandrian, Chalcedonian and non-Chalcedonian approaches to Christology and Soteriology, not least the problems that gave rise to the disunion of East and West on the *filioque* clause.[70]

This proposal for Dialogue by the Reformed was "received with much satisfaction and was endorsed by the Orthodox Representatives . . . "[71] The Dialogue thus moved forward with a common ground for the basis of their conversation. According to the Minutes, the group agreed to proceed by examining Athanasius, *Letters on the Spirit*, Basil, *On the Holy Spirit*, Gregory

---

Collections, Princeton Seminary. Box 170.

68. Torrance, "The Trinitarian Foundation and Character of Faith and of Authority in the Church," 79–120. According to the Official Minutes, Torrance "explained that he had attempted to take into account chiefly, those Fathers such as Athanasius and Cyril, and also Nazianzus, who reflect creedal and conciliar authority with particular reference to Athanasius' model of the flexibility of terminology in which terms reflect the (Trinitarian) realities to which they refer and on which they are based." See The Thomas F. Torrance Manuscript Collection. Special Collections, Princeton Seminary. Box 170.

69. Timiadis "The Trinitarian Structure of the Church and its Authority," 121–56.

70. Torrance, "Concluding Affirmation," 157.

71. Ibid., 158.

Nazianzen, *Theological Orations* (especially on the Holy Spirit), Calvin, the doctrine of the Holy Spirit in the *Institutes,* and Karl Barth's doctrine of the Holy Spirit in *Church Dogmatics* I/1.[72]

THE TWO OFFICIAL CONSULTATIONS AND THE CONCLUDING SESSION

It was in the Two Official Consultations, occurring in 1988 and 1990 as well as the Concluding Session in 1992 that the real discussion about the doctrine of the Trinity developed. At these later Official Consultations, the output of which was published in *Theological Dialogue Between Orthodox and Reformed Churches Volume 2,* many of the same figures were involved, plus a number of newcomers. The second volume of publications has papers (which were originally delivered at the consultations) given by Torrance,[73] George Dragas (Lecturer in Patristics at Durham, associated at the time with the Ecumenical Patriarchate),[74] Totju Koev (Professor, part of the Bulgarian Church),[75] Lukas Vischer (Switzerland, Reformed),[76] Christos Voulgaris (Orthodox),[77] Christopher Kaiser (Reformed, USA),[78] Archbishop Simon of Riazon (Orthodox),[79] and Bruce Rigdon (Reformed, USA).[80] Most regrettably, the Official Minutes and Schedules from the later consultations do not contain details concerning comments by participants, but rather contain brief summaries of what happened.[81]

Throughout the Dialogue, the Reformed and Orthodox note there are historical and ecclesiological differences and divisions that must be

---

72. The Thomas F. Torrance Manuscript Collection. Special Collections, Princeton Seminary. Box 170.

73. Torrance, "The Triunity of God," 3–37; "Working Paper on the Holy Trinity," 109–21.

74. Dragas, "St Athanasius on the Holy Spirit and the Trinity," 38–60.

75. Koev, "The Teaching about the Holy Trinity on the basis of the Nicene-Constantinopolitan Symbol of Faith," 61–85.

76. Vischer, "The Holy Spirit," 86–108.

77. Voulgaris, "The Biblical and Patristic Doctrine of the Trinity," 122–60.

78. Kaiser, "The Biblical and Patristic Doctrine of the Trinity," 161–92.

79. Archbishop Simon, "The Trinity and Prayer," 193–210.

80. Rigdon, "Worship and the Trinity in the Reformed Tradition," 211–18.

81. See Box 170 for the Official Minutes from the First Official Theological Consultation in Leunberg in 1988 and Box 171 for programs/schedules for the Second Official Theological Consultation in Minsk in 1990.

acknowledged, for example the Orthodox emphasize the undivided church until the eleventh century whereas the Reformed respond to medieval scholasticism.[82] However, they ultimately agreed that at the core, each group's understanding of the doctrine of the Trinity is in agreement.[83] Torrance's *foreword* to his collection of essays published as *Theology in Reconciliation: Essays Towards Evangelical and Catholic Unity in East and West*[84] offers a plea to Roman Catholics, Eastern Orthodox, and Protestants to return to this Trinitarian foundation found in the Athanasius-Cyril axis and leave behind their cultural additions (while at the same time keeping their distinctive pietistic differences), embracing the "patristic foundation" of their common faith.[85] The Reformed and Orthodox made the important commitment at these Official Consultations to avoid discussion of the *filioque* itself, and the Reformed even stated:

> As regards the 'Filioque' clause, the Reformed members stated the prevailing position among the Reformed Churches, according to which the above clause should be removed from use since it did not belong to the original version, but that the theological issues relating to the "Filioque' controversy should be discussed with a view to reaching a common mind.[86]

Dragas elucidates on the commitment stating:

> The critical question of the *filioque* was never actually discussed in the dialogue: in fact it was strategically left for later—and that was on my advice to Tom, because I said, "If you start with the *filioque* we will never get anywhere."[87]

---

82. Torrance, "Introduction" to *Theological Dialogue between Orthodox and Reformed Churches*, 2:xi.

83. Ibid., xxi.

84. Torrance, *Theology in Reconciliation*, 7–14.

85. See ibid., 14.

86. Torrance, "Introduction" to *Theological Dialogue between Orthodox and Reformed Churches*, 2:xii.

87. Baker and Dragas, "Interview," 13–15. Fouyas, as well, notes this when he states in a letter to Torrance regarding "The Agreed Statement," which is dated December 5th, 1992: "I notice that you omit the *filioque* and you extend the patristic evidence up to John of Damascus which is very important so that your teaching is sound and catholic." See The Thomas F. Torrance Manuscript Collection. Special Collections, Princeton Theological Seminary Library, Box 172.

Thus, the Official Consultations of the Orthodox-Reformed Dialogue began with discussion of the issues surrounding the *filioque* but avoiding the explicit issue itself, a move of great ecumenical importance.[88]

The First Official Consultation: Leuenberg, 1988

Four main papers were read at the First Official Consultation. Torrance delivered a paper entitled "The Triunity of God: Athanasius, Basil, the Gregories, and Didymus, Epiphanius and the Council of Constantinople."[89] George Dragas Delivered a paper entitled "St Athanasius on the Holy Spirit and the Trinity."[90] Totju Koev delivered a paper entitled "The Teaching about the Holy Trinity on the basis of the Nicene-Constantinopolitan Symbol of Faith."[91] Lukas Vischer delivered a paper entitled "The Holy Spirit—Source of Sanctification, Reflections on Basil the Great's Treatise on the Holy Spirit."[92] As Small notes, the papers from this session were theologically dense, but they were necessary "in shaping the emerging conviction that the Orthodox and Reformed Churches were in broad agreement on the essential elements of the doctrine of the Trinity."[93]

In the Orthodox-Reformed Dialogue, Reformed and Orthodox agreed upon a commitment to a Trinitarian and Christocentric approach to theology. In his paper, Torrance urges for a focus upon Athanasius and Cyril, especially their emphasis on the Nicene doctrine of *homoousion* contra the Cappadocian-Byzantine trajectory.[94] Torrance emphasizes the importance of approaching the doctrine of the Trinity from this *homoousion*-focused

---

88. Siecienski's chapter in Habets's recent edited volume is about the modern attempts of ecumenical dialogues to resolve the issue (omitting the Orthodox-Reformed Dialogue), traces largely unsuccessful attempts, arguably rooted in their beginning with the issue itself (which the Orthodox-Reformed Dialogue, as argued, avoids). For example, Weinandy's proposal of a *filioque* and *spiritque* to solve the problem. See Siecienski, *The Filioque*, 193–213. See p. 204 for the Weinandy account. See also Weinandy, *The Father's Spirit of Sonship*, 34, cited by Siecienski. So, it seems this approach is now being followed more widely.

89. Torrance, "The Triunity of God," 3–37.

90. Dragas, "St Athanasius on the Holy Spirit and the Trinity," 39–60.

91. Koev, "The Teaching about the Holy Trinity on the basis of the Nicene-Constantinopolitan Symbol of Faith." 61–85.

92. Vischer, "The Holy Spirit," 87–106.

93. Small, "Orthodox and Reformed in Dialogue," 116.

94. Torrance, "The Triunity of God," 5.

standpoint. In his paper, Dragas offers a substantially similar approach.[95] From the outset of the Dialogue, Torrance had contended that the best method for discussion and the best approach for agreement is on the basis of Athanasian-Cyrilline theology[96] and the common roots of Alexandrian and Cappadocian theology, as well as the Conciliar Statements which these important church fathers informed so greatly.[97] Torrance argues elsewhere that theology must remain focused upon the Nicene *homoousion* inasmuch as it is the "king-pin" of the Nicene-Constantinopolitan Creed, which Torrance believes expresses the core evangelical belief that in Jesus Christ humanity is confronted with the very self-giving and self-revealing of God as he is in himself.[98] Torrance recalls that in the discussions following the papers presented at the earlier meetings, everyone "kept returning to the need for a dynamic understanding of the living Triune God in the inseparability of his Being and Act."[99] Via this focus, Torrance believed that the Reformed and Orthodox traditions would be able to return to their common fount and "cut behind" the theological dualism which problematically informed later developments in the Byzantine East and Augustinian West.[100] Torrance argues that this would bring about theological agreement and ecumenical rapprochement between Chalcedonians and non-Chalcedonians, Orthodox and Reformed, and Roman Catholics and Evangelicals.[101] Torrance argues that both the Reformed and Orthodox need to return to their core fulcrum of the Athanasius-Cyril axis of classical theology.[102]

The Official Minutes note that general discussion following Torrance and Dragas' papers aimed at clarifying their arguments concerning the

---

95. See Small, "Orthodox and Reformed in Dialogue," 116, for helpful comparison of the two papers.

96. According to the Official Minutes, in the discussion, Emilianos states: "Is not Torrance in danger of over-absolutizing Athanasius in relation to the Cappadocians?" See The Thomas F. Torrance Manuscript Collection. Special Collections, Princeton Theological Seminary Library. Box 170.

97. Torrance, "Memoranda on Orthodox/Reformed Relations," 11.

98. Thomas F. Torrance, *The Incarnation*, xi–xv. The Orthodox indeed agreed that this is a lynchpin. See 1–15 of the same book.

99. Torrance, "Introduction to *Theological Dialogue Between Orthodox and Reformed Churches Volume 1*," xxiii.

100. Torrance, "Memoranda on Orthodox/Reformed Relations," 11.

101. Ibid., 10–11.

102. Torrance, "The Triunity of God," 3–13.

patristic developments leading to the First Ecumenical Council.[103] During the conversation, a telegram from The Ecumenical Patriarch Dimitrios arrived stating: "We congratulate you on the inaguration of your work. We pray for the success of the dialogue as a contribution to the promotion of the sacred task of Christian unity."[104] As Small notes, "while the papers of Torrance and Dragas cohered in approach and substance, a clear difference in tone was evident in the papers of Koev and Vischer. While both affirmed the absolute centrality of the Trinity, there was a marked disparity in the character of their deference to the Nicene Creed."[105] The main difference that began to emerge was the distinction between the Reformed as "always reforming" and the Orthodox as tethered to the ancient creeds and statements of faith as dogma.[106] As Torrance notes in his introduction to the published volume, "it became clear throughout the discussions that historical/ecclesiological considerations were unavoidable."[107] However, the participants aimed to remain focused upon the doctrine of the Trinity and, as Torrance says, "a broad agreement was reached about the essential elements of the doctrine of the Holy Trinity."[108] Torrance and Dragas were ultimately given the task of drafting a paper on the Holy Trinity to serve as the basis of the next Official Consultation to be held in Minsk in 1990.[109] Accordingly, the Orthodox-Reformed Dialogue was moving towards real and substantial agreement on the doctrine of the Trinity.

The Second Official Consultation: Minsk, 1990

In addition to Torrance presenting the "Working Paper on the Trinity," drafted by him and Dragas (a document that would ultimately developed into "The Agreed Statement"), four papers were presented at the Second Official Consultation. Christos Voulgaris delivered a paper entitled "The

---

103. The Thomas F. Torrance Manuscript Collection. Special Collections, Princeton Seminary. Box 170.

104. Ibid.

105. Small, "Orthodox and Reformed in Dialogue," 116.

106. See further ibid., 116–17.

107. Torrance, "Introduction" to *Theological Dialogue between Orthodox and Reformed Churches*, 2:xi.

108. Ibid., xii.

109. Ibid., xiii.

Biblical and Patristic Doctrine of the Trinity."[110] Christopher Kaiser delivered a paper entitled "Biblical and Patristic Doctrine of the Trinity. In what ways can their relationship be established?"[111] Archbishop Simon of Ryazan and Kasimov delivered a paper entitled "The Trinity and Prayer."[112] Bruce Rigdon delivered a paper entitled "Worship and the Trinity in the Reformed Tradition."[113] The focus at this final Official Consultation was on the "Working Paper on the Holy Trinity" which, through this discussion, was revised and developed into a draft version of "The Agreed Statement on the Holy Trinity."[114] As Small puts it, "the working paper was intended to provide the basis for fulfilling the hope of the dialogue, and it accomplished its purpose."[115] Towards the end of this consultation, the participants agreed that the document needed "to be tidied up in respect to some minor linguistic points."[116] Here Torrance was also asked to write a short text outlining the key points of "The Agreed Statement."[117]

The Concluding Session: Kappel, 1992

According to Torrance, after working through the doctrine of the Trinity together for the first two Official Consultations, the Reformed and Orthodox concluded at the Dialogue that they agreed "on the content of the doctrine [of the Trinity]"[118] and produced as their fruit, "The Agreed Statement"[119] to express their substantial agreement. Torrance and his former student

---

110. Voulgaris, "The Biblical and Patristic Doctrine of the Trinity," 123–60.

111. Kaiser, "Biblical and Patristic Doctrine of the Trinity," 161–92.

112. Archbishop Simon, "The Trinity and Prayer," 193–210.

113. Rigdon, "Worship and the Trinity in the Reformed Tradition," 211–18.

114. Torrance, "Introduction" to *Theological Dialogue between Orthodox and Reformed Churches*, 2:xxii.

115. Small, "Orthodox and Reformed in Dialogue," 118.

116. Torrance, "Introduction" to *Theological Dialogue between Orthodox and Reformed Churches*, 2:xxiii.

117. Ibid.

118. Ibid., xxi.

119. Contained in ibid., 1:219–26; Torrance, *Trinitarian Perspectives*, 115–22.

George Dragas,[120] drafted this important text.[121] After examining and reflecting upon key texts such as Athanasius' *Ad Serapionem*, Basil's *On the Holy Spirit*, Gregory Nazianzen's *Theological Orations*, Calvin's *Institutes* and Karl Barth's *Church Dogmatics*,[122] as well as the papers presented at the dialogues, the Reformed and Orthodox produced "The Agreed Statement on the Holy Trinity." The document represents a major achievement in ecumenical theology inasmuch as it presents a doctrine of the Trinity which preserves both Greek and Latin commitments to the Trinity of Persons (Greek) and unity of Being (Latin) in God the Holy Trinity.[123]

THE AGREED STATEMENT ON THE HOLY TRINITY: THIRD-WAVE TRINITARIANISM IN PRACTICE

The outcome of the Orthodox-Reformed Dialogue was "The Agreed Statement on the Holy Trinity," an important text which exhibits Third-Wave Trinitarianism before there was such an entity. The significance of "The Agreed Statement" is all the more evident when correspondence surrounding its construction is used to shed light on the document's development as stemming from core agreement between Eastern and Western theologians (and the church fathers they were using), with a difference only in language and, perhaps, emphasis. Correspondence strongly indicates that Dragas and Torrance drove the construction of "The Agreed Statement on the Holy Trinity" which was the product of these two Official Theological Consultations.[124]

Drafted in 1989, revised at a meeting in Geneva in 1991, the document was not completed until 1992 at the Concluding Session. Torrance wrote

---

120. In a letter recommending George Dragas for the Chair in Church History at the University of Aberdeen, Torrance sings Dragas' praises with enthusiasm. See the letter in The Thomas F. Torrance Manuscript Collection. Special Collections, Princeton Theological Seminary Library. Box 178.

121. The Torrance Manuscript Collection in Princeton contains some fascinating correspondence between Torrance and Dragas as they worked to complete "The Agreed Statement." See Box 170.

122. Torrance, "Introduction" to *Theological Dialogue between Orthodox and Reformed Churches*, 1:xxvii.

123. See Torrance, *Trinitarian Perspectives* for the most accessible version of "The Agreed Statement" and Torrance's reflections on its significance.

124. See the 1989–1990 folder in The Thomas F. Torrance Manuscript Collection. Special Collections, Princeton Theological Seminary Library. Box 170.

the initial draft but Dragas recounts that when Torrance brought it to him he was concerned "that his draft of the statement was much too Reformed and 'Torrancian.' There was terminology there which, while claiming to be patristic and Athanasian, was in fact full of neologisms, which would be unfamiliar to the Orthodox."[125] That is, Torrance's initial version was too dominated by a theological reconstruction of the fathers. Torrance and Dragas corresponded with one another for the next two years regarding "The Agreed Statement" and would meet at Torrance's home in Edinburgh, on which occasions Dragas would stay over and Torrance would have breakfast ready in the morning to fuel a day of Trinitarian conversation.[126] In a letter to Torrance Dragas writes: "I have made a few comments on our text which are not difficult to deal with. The one I particularly find difficult is the point on page 7 that Monas is identical to Trias."[127] Dragas suggests that they leave the statement out completely. Correspondence with Fouyas (by this point removed from his position in British ecumenical work in an official capacity) indicates a similar sentiment. Fouyas states in a letter that he finds Torrance's early draft of "The Agreed Statement" to express "in contemporary formulation an Athanasian statement."[128] Fouyas, however, suggests Torrance remove language referring to time and magnitude such as "prior" and "greater" in the statement; advice Torrance indeed follows. Fouyas also suggests Torrance clearly distinguish between the Being of God and Person of the Father so as to avoid any confusion. Similarly, in his letter Fouyas urges Torrance to make sure he distinguishes between the particular roles of each person of the Trinity in God's actions: through the Son and by the Holy Spirit.[129] Through collaboration with Dragas and Fouyas, Torrance removes his more Reformed and Torrancian language and, as he states in a Church of Scotland pamphlet, "though steps have been taken to clarify trinitarian language, the focus of attention throughout ["The Agreed Statement"] is on the reality of faith in the Trinity rather than specific theological terminology, which naturally must vary in different communions with different languages."[130] In doing so, "The Agreed Statement" offers an

---

125. Baker and Dragas, "Interview," 13–15.

126. Ibid., 14.

127. The Thomas F. Torrance Manuscript Collection. Special Collections, Princeton Theological Seminary Library. Box 170.

128. Ibid.

129. Ibid.

130. Torrance, "Another 'Wall' Comes Down."

ecumenical document which claims to do what the current Trinitarian conversation is doing.

CONCLUSION

This chapter has traced the history of the Orthodox-Reformed Dialogue. In particular, the chapter has focused upon the development of "The Agreed Statement" but the Dialogue. "The Agreed Statement" was created by Torrance with the help and revision of Dragas and was thus a truly Orthodox-Reformed document. The document is relevant inasmuch as, in it, Orthodox and Reformed confess together (the document begins with "we confess") a doctrine of the Trinity that truly gets behind the *filioque* and offers a patristically-grounded and Christologically oriented doctrine of the Trinity in which East and West truly do speak with one voice.

In his reflection on "The Agreed Statement" in *Trinitarian Perspectives*, Torrance raves about the relevance of the document, particularly that it "cuts across mistaken polarised views of the doctrine of the Holy Trinity according to which Latin theology moves from the Oneness of God to the three Persons of the Father, the Son and the Holy Spirit, while Greek theology moves from the three Persons of the Father, the Son and the Holy Spirit to the Oneness of God."[131] As such, the document is relevant as an example of what Third Wave Trinitarians aim to do: show that there is no substantive difference between East and West on the doctrine of the Trinity. If Torrance is right, therefore, this document has much relevance for Trinitarian theology today. Therefore, it is to "The Agreed Statement on the Holy Trinity" itself that this book now turns, focusing in particular on its theological content and its relevance for Third-Wave Trinitarianism.

---

131. Torrance, "Significant Features, a Common Reflection on the Agreed Statement on the Holy Trinity," 232.

CHAPTER 4

The Agreed Statement on the Holy Trinity
A Trinitarian Theology Ahead of Its Time

> [The Agreed Statement] cuts across mistaken polarised views of the doctrine of the Holy Trinity according to which Latin theology moves from the Oneness of God to the three Persons of the Father, the Son and the Holy Spirit, while Greek theology moved from the three Persons of the Father, the Son and the Holy Spirit to the Oneness of God. What is provided by the Agreed Statement of the Orthodox Reformed theologians in the East and the Reformed theologians in the West is preeminently a Statement on the Triunity of God as Trinity in Unity and Unity in Trinity.
>
> Thomas F. Torrance[1]

INTRODUCTION

ANDY GOODLIFF STATES "It seems to me that the doctrine of the Trinity can either become something so complicated in nuance that it becomes almost impossible to talk about or it can be so simplified and asked to become so practical a doctrine that we think of God in too human-like terms."[2] Goodliff's summary of western and eastern doctrines of the Trinity

---

1. Torrance, "Significant Features, A Common Reflection on the Agreed Statement," 232.
2. Goodliff, Review of *The Holy Trinity Revisited*, 26.

as focusing on abstract unity versus immanent practicality, as traditionally bifurcated, is all to accurate and, as Tom Noble states, "Torrance's Trinitarian theology holds out the best hope of combining the concerns for divine Unity with the concerns of the social Trinitarians."[3] Torrance and the Orthodox-Reformed Dialogue (particularly the document they create, "The Agreed Statement on the Holy Trinity") successfully offer a doctrine of the Trinity that avoids these two poles: it is neither the extremely bifurcated approach of Second-Wave and de Régnon Trinitarians nor the flattened out simplification of the Third-Wave Trinitarians; fitting somewhere in the middle, the Orthodox-Reformed Dialogue is arguably a better, more nuanced, and less oversimplified version of Third-Wave Trinitarianism. "The Agreed Statement," according to Torrance, "cuts across mistaken polarised views of the doctrine of the Holy Trinity according to which Latin theology moves from the Oneness of God to the three Persons of the Father, the Son and the Holy Spirit, while Greek theology moves from the three Persons of the Father, the Son and the Holy Spirit to the Oneness of God. What is provided by the Agreed Statement of the Orthodox theologians in the East and the Reformed theologians in the West is preeminently a Statement on the Triunity of God as Trinity in Unity and Unity in Trinity."[4] Torrance's claim sounds very much like what Third-Wave Trinitarian theologians are claiming to do in their rereading of Nicaea and the patristic era. If this is true, "The Agreed Statement" offers a Third-Wave Trinitarianism during the era of Second-Wave Trinitarianism. Torrance argues that the core of "The Agreed Statement" is that only through God can God be known[5] or, in other words, God really is in himself as he is to us, and it is through this lens that Torrance and the Dialogue present a Third-Wave Trinitarianism before there was such a thing, yet Torrance and the Dialogue are almost entirely unutilized in the movement.[6]

---

3. Ibid., 215n41.

4. Torrance, "Significant Features, a Common Reflection on the Agreed Statement," 232.

5. Ibid., 229.

6. This is problematic for, as Ziegler puts it, "no honest account of [the resurgence of the doctrine of the Trinity in the late 20th century] could be narrated that did not view T. F. Torrance's contribution as fundamental." See Ziegler, *Trinitarian Grace and Participation*, xxvii. See also Habets and Tolliday, eds., *Trinitarian Theology after Barth*.

Part 1: A Critical Appreciation of the Orthodox-Reformed Theological Dialogue

Scope of the Chapter

Having explored the core similarities and differences in theological approach for the Orthodox and the Reformed as they appeared in the Orthodox-Reformed Dialogue, particularly at the initial consultation in Istanbul in 1979, this chapter now turns to the basis of the Orthodox-Reformed Dialogue, namely, a shared commitment to the Greek fathers (especially Athanasius and Cyril of Alexandria and, to some extent, the Cappadocian fathers) and their theology (especially a dynamic doctrine of the Trinity as undergirding all theology). The chapter utilizes the published (*Theological Dialogue Volumes 1 and 2*) and unpublished (*Torrance Manuscript Collection*) material as well as patristic texts which were key in the Dialogue (e.g. Basil, *De Spiritu Sancti*, Athanasius, *Ad Serapionem*, Karl Barth, *Church Dogmatics*). In particular this chapter emphasizes the commitment to a dynamic doctrine of the Trinity (as captured especially in "The Agreed Statement on the Trinity") of God as Unity in Trinity and Trinity in Unity, bypassing traditional Orthodox-Reformed, Protestant-Orthodox, Catholic-Orthodox, and indeed Western-Eastern distinctions in emphases.

The main emphasis of this chapter, therefore, is on the doctrine of the Trinity (especially the theology of "The Agreed Statement on the Trinity"). The doctrine of the Trinity discussed and agreed upon in the Dialogue will be examined and constructively engaged in light of contemporary discussions in Systematic Theology on the doctrine of the Trinity, in which conversation Torrance is seriously underutilized and usually entirely unutilized as has been argued elsewhere.[7] The present chapter will proceed by examining "The Agreed Statement on the Holy Trinity" in light of Third-Wave Trinitarianism. Through a case-study of the document, this chapter will argue that Third-Wave Trinitarianism itself has some shortcomings to which "The Agreed Statement," a Third-Wave Trinitarian document before there was such a movement, offers an answer. Thus, it is to an exploration of "The Agreed Statement" as a better and more nuanced Third-Wave Trinitarianism that this book now turns.

---

7. For example, "T. F. Torrance and the Patristic Consensus on the Doctrine of the Trinity"; and "T. F. Torrance in Light of Stephen Holmes's Critique of Contemporary Trinitarian Thought," 21–38.

THIRD-WAVE TRINITARIANISM AND "THE AGREED STATEMENT"

Sarah Coakley's Third-Wave Trinitarians are a relatively varied group including Patrologists, Church Historians, and Theologians. However there are two major commitments they all share: (1) the de Régnon thesis is erroneous because East and West really spoke with one voice and (2) Social Trinitarianism, the hallmark of Second-Wave Trinitarianism, is problematic because the church fathers held above all else to the absolute simplicity of God.

First, the theme that East and West spoke with "one voice" is core to Third-Wave Trinitarianism.[8] The "one voice" of Eastern and Western patristic theology on the doctrine of the Trinity is, in short, a combination of Augustine (as traditionally viewed) whereby we must start with God's essential unity and of the Cappadocians (as traditionally viewed) whereby the distinctiveness of the three persons are distinguished only by their relation to each other. Third-Wave Trinitarians insist that traditional categories of Nicene, Cappadocian, etc., are far more fluid than traditionally understood.[9] For example, one Third-Waver, Stephen Holmes concludes that "neither position on the filioque does violence to the received orthodox and catholic tradition."[10]

Second, according to Third-Wave Trinitarians, the crux of the view shared by East and West on the doctrine of the Trinity is a commitment to the simplicity of God. Holmes outlines Patristic Trinitarianism in eight points, the first of which is "the divine nature is simple, incomposite, and ineffable."[11] Another Third-Waver, Lewis Ayres, states: "within the simple Godhead, the distinct Word possesses the fullness of the indivisible Godhead."[12] Their commitment to the simplicity of God is to an extent

---

8. See, e.g., Holmes, *The Holy Trinity,* 144. Holmes asserts a seamless garment, a "one voice," of the classical and truly ecumenical Christian tradition on the doctrine of the Trinity spanning East and West, Greek and Latin. See Holmes, *The Holy Trinity,* 144–46. See also Ayres, "The Fundamental Grammar of Augustine's Trinitarian Theology," 51–76; "Remember that you are Catholic (serm 52.2): Augustine on the Unity of the Triune God," 39–82; Barnes, "Rereading Augustine's Theology of the Trinity," 145–76; "Augustine in Contemporary Trinitarian Theology," 237–50; "De Régnon Reconsidered," 51–79.

9. See, e.g., Parvis, *Marcellus of Ancyra and the Lost Years of the Arian Controversy* 325–345.

10. Holmes, *The Holy Trinity,* 164.

11. Ibid., 199.

12. Ayres, *Nicaea and Its Legacy,* 295–96.

that they deem social Trinitarianism unfaithful to the patristic tradition. As Holmes says, "we [of Second-Wave Trinitariansm] called what we were doing a 'Trinitarian Revival'; future historians might want to ask us why."[13]

The Agreed Statement on the Holy Trinity

When viewed in light of these two Third-Wave commitments, Torrance, the Dialogue, and "The Agreed Statement" come to light as highly relevant for the current conversation as a more nuanced and much more constructive version of Third-Wave Trinitarianism. "The Agreed Statement" offers a real agreement between East and West that is focused on the church fathers without bulldozing differences.[14] As Small states, the document "is an extraordinary theological and ecumenical achievement."[15] "The Agreed Statement" offers a way around the *filioque* problem. When viewed in this light, arguably the strongest contribution of "The Agreed Statement" comes to light, namely, it is theologically constructive whereas the approach of Third-Wave Trinitarianism is largely historical.[16] "The Agreed Statement" is structured around key points from the Dialogue which are: (1) The centrality of God's revelation of himself as Trinity; (2) the distinctiveness of the three Trinitarian hypostases; (3) the view that the order of hypostases in the Trinity begins with the Father who has monarchia; (4) yet the Godhead is undivided and One; (5) the perichoretic mutual indwelling of all members of the Trinity; (6) the affirmation of the formula *mia ousia, treis hypostaseis*, and; (7) the assertion that the doctrine of the Trinity is true and actual and indeed the core of the Apostolic and Catholic Faith.[17] An examination of "The Agreed Statement" highlights a number of contributions in light of Third-Wave Trinitarianism.

---

13. Holmes, *The Holy Trinity*, 200.

14. Third-Wave Trinitarianism tends to flatten out differences. See, e.g., Holmes, "In Praise of Being Criticized," 149: "[T]he Cappadocians look very like Augustine on Trinitarian theology." See also Ayres, *Nicaea and Its Legacy*, 188–221; 365–83.

15. Small, "Orthodox and Reformed in Dialogue," 122.

16. Illustrative of this point is Holmes, *The Holy Trinity*; and Ayres, *Nicaea and Its Legacy*.

17. See further discussion on this in Radcliff, "T. F. Torrance in light of Stephen Holmes's critique of contemporary Trinitarian thought"; Radcliff, "T. F. Torrance and the Patristic Consensus on the Doctrine of the Trinity"; Radcliff, "Thomas F. Torrance's Conception of the *Consensus Patrum* on the Doctrine of Pneumatology."

The Self-Revelation of God as Father, Son and Holy Spirit[18]

The beginning of "The Agreed Statement" consists of the insistence that God as Trinity is more than accidental or peripheral to the Christian faith. Thus, "The Agreed Statement" begins by stating "according to the Holy Gospel God has revealed himself in the Father, the Son and the Holy Spirit."[19] The Reformed and Orthodox wished through this to express two aspects of their Dialogue: (1) the fact that Trinitarian theology is central and (2) the connection between who God is to us is the same as who God is in himself. Citing John of Damascus[20] and Athanasius,[21] "The Agreed Statement" says "to believe in the Unity of God apart from the Trinity is to limit the truth of divine Revelation."[22] Part of the emphasis here is the insistence on the connection between the immanent and the economic Trinity.

Three Divine Persons

"The Agreed Statement" then articulates the Unity in Trinity and Trinity in Unity of God through a discussion of the three Persons of the Trinity. Emphasizing both the distinctiveness of Persons and the Unity of Being, "The Agreed Statement" argues that the Persons at the core work together for, as it states, "what God the Father is toward us in Christ and in the Spirit he is inherently and eternally in himself, and what he is inherently and eternally in himself he is toward us in the Incarnation of his Son and in the Mission of the Spirit."[23] This section of "The Agreed Statement" utilizes Gregory Nazianzen,[24] to uphold the equality of Divine Persons in greatness, divinity, and order, and Athanasius, to preserve the *perichoresis*[25] or mutual

---

18. The wording of the headings here and through the rest of the direct exposition of "The Agreed Statement" are taken from the document itself.
19. "The Agreed Statement on the Holy Trinity," 219.
20. They cite *De fide orthodoxa* 1.1.
21. They cite *Contra Arianos* 1.18.
22. "The Agreed Statement on the Holy Trinity," 220.
23. Ibid., 221.
24. They cite *Oration* 31.14; 40.43.
25. Greek: περιχώρησις.

indwelling of the three Persons[26] and thus their unity, preserving the connection of the immanent and economic Trinity.[27]

Eternal Relations in God

Whilst avoiding explicit and direct discussion of the *filioque* itself, "The Agreed Statement" does articulate a viewpoint concerning the eternal relations within God, stating "the Son is eternally begotten of the Father and the Spirit eternally proceeds from the Father and abides in the Son."[28] However, "The Agreed Statement" argues that "the generation of the Son and the procession of the Spirit are unknowable mysteries which cannot be explained by recourse to human or creaturely images"[29] and any procession and any abiding is "beyond all time (ἀχρόνως), beyond all origin (ἀνάρχως), and beyond all cause (ἀναιτίως)."[30] Referring to Athanasius,[31] Cyril of Jerusalem,[32] Gregory Nazianzen,[33] Basil the Great,[34] Didymus the Blind,[35] and Cyril of Alexandria,[36] this portion of "The Agreed Statement" emphasizes the essential Unity of the three Persons, particularly in their economic activity initiated by the Father, effected by the Son, and perfected by the Holy Spirit.[37]

The Order of Divine Persons in the Trinity

"The Agreed Statement" argues that there is an order within the Trinity that places the Father first, the Son second, and the Holy Spirit third, however this priority, or Monarchy, of the Father only exists in relation,

---

26. They cite *In. ill. om.*, 6.
27. They cite *Ad Serapionem*, 3.7; 4.6; *De Synodis* 52; *Contra Arianos* 3.16.
28. "The Agreed Statement on the Holy Trinity," 222.
29. Ibid., 222.
30. Ibid.
31. They cite *Contra Arianos* 2.36.
32. They cite *Catecheses* 11.11.
33. They cite *Orations* 31.14; 16.
34. They cite *De Spiritu Sancto* 16.38.
35. They cite *De Trinitate* 2.36.
36. They cite *On John* 15.1.
37. "The Agreed Statement on the Holy Trinity," 222.

that is, it is a Monarchy of relation.[38] Referencing Gregory Nazianzen[39] and Athanasius,[40] this portion of "The Agreed Statement" emphasizes the equality of Persons in the Holy Trinity, but with a Monarchy of the Father within the order of the Trinity.

Trinity in Unity and Unity in Trinity, the One Monarchy

"The Agreed Statement" offers a creative and unique version of the Monarchy[41] of the Father. It states the *arche*[42] or "Monarchy of the Father within the Trinity is not exclusive to the Monarchy of the whole undivided Trinity,"[43] or, in other words, to say that God the Father is the fount, foundation, beginning, source of the Trinity does not mean that the Son and the Spirit do not share the Monarchy. Here, after a slew of patristic quotations from Gregory Nazianzen[44] and one from Epiphanius of Salamis,[45] "The Agreed Statement" articulates a version of the Monarchy of the Father that immediately insists that this Monarchy is inseparable from the other three Persons inasmuch as the Unity (Μονάς) of God is inseparable from his Trinity (Τριάς) due to their shared essence/being.[46]

Perichoresis: The Mutual Indwelling of Father, Son, and Holy Spirit

In its articulation of perichoresis, "The Agreed Statement" suggests a new answer to the *filioque* debate. It says: "The Holy Spirit proceeds from the Father, but because of the unity of the Godhead in which each Person is perfectly and wholly God, he proceeds from the Father through the Son for the Spirit belongs to and is inseparable from the Being of the Father and of

---

38. Ibid., 223.
39. They cite *Oration* 36.15.
40. They cite *Letters to Serapion* 1.33.
41. Greek: μοναρχία. It means "beginning" or "source of action."
42. Greek: ἀρχή.
43. "The Agreed Statement on the Holy Trinity," 224.
44. They cite *Oration* 29.2; 39.11; 40.11.
45. They cite *Heresies* 62.3.
46. "The Agreed Statement on the Holy Trinity," 224.

the Son."⁴⁷ Quoting Hilary of Poitiers, "The Agreed Statement" says each Person contains, envelops, and is enveloped by each of the other Persons.⁴⁸

One Being, Three Persons

Thus, "The Agreed Statement" says any articulation of the Holy Trinity must begin with the confession of the Synod of Alexandria when it says "One Being (οὐσια), Three Persons" but the Being of God must be understood in a dynamic rather than abstract sense.⁴⁹ Citing Athanasius,⁵⁰ "The Agreed Statement" argues that the Being of God, which all three Persons share, is ever-living and dynamic, not an abstract Being.⁵¹

The Apostolic and Catholic Faith

Ultimately then, citing Athanasius,⁵² "The Agreed Statement" says that the belief in God the Trinity as Unity in Trinity and Trinity in Unity is the apostolic and catholic faith. Thus, "The Agreed Statement" frames itself as a truly catholic document seeking to emphasize a truly ecumenical statement of the doctrine of the Trinity. It is this ecumenical nature of the document which highlights its many contributions to the current conversation regarding the doctrine of the Trinity emerge, namely (1) offering a more nuanced account of East and West, (2) offering a dynamic understanding of God's oneness that bridges a gap between the largely polarized views of Social/Second-Wave Trinitarians and the emphasis on Divine Simplicity by the Third-Wave, and (3) offering a constructive theology in a largely historical Third-Wave movement.

---

47. Ibid.

48. They cite *On the Trinity* 3.1.

49. "The Agreed Statement on the Holy Trinity," 225. Thus, the Dialogue does not emphasize the simplicity of God in the way that Third-Wave Trinitarians do.

50. They cite *Contra Arianos* 3.6; 4.1; *De Synodis* 34–36; *De Decretis* 22.

51. "The Agreed Statement on the Holy Trinity," 225.

52. They cite *Letters to Serapion* 1.28.

Contribution #1: The Agreed Statement Offers A Nuanced View of East and West

"The Agreed Statement" begins with an important phrase: "we confess." Here, Reformed and Orthodox, East and West, Patriarch of Constantinople and President of Princeton Seminary state together with one voice: "we confess together the evangelical and ancient Faith of the Catholic Church in '*the uncreated, consubstantial and coeternal Trinity*', promulgated by the Councils of Nicaea (AD 325) and Constantinople (AD 381)." As Torrance writes in his notes/outline of "The Agreed Statement" prior to writing it, "the textbook distinction [of de Régnon on the doctrine of the Trinity] is invalid" and the Orthodox-Reformed Dialogue provide the "end of the filioque problem" exhibiting "basic agreement [between] Catholic and Evangelical [and] East and West.[53] The Third-Wave Trinitarian connection of Eastern and Western patristic theology on the doctrine of the Trinity is, in some senses, a sentiment with which Torrance and the Orthodox-Reformed Dialogue wholeheartedly agree.[54] Despite the widespread assumption of the strict distinction between East and West on the Trinity, Torrance sees Augustine as basically Greek in his doctrine of the Trinity,[55] ranking Augustine's *De Trinitate* as, in his words, "a supremely great work in Christian theology" alongside Karl Barth's *Church Dogmatics* II (Torrance's favorite of the series), Athanasius' *Contra Arianos*, Thomas Aquinas' *Summa,* and Calvin's *Institutes*.[56] Torrance asserts that John Calvin adopted his doctrine of the Trinity from Augustine, who despite a lack of knowledge of the Greek language, was steeped in Greek patristic theology due to the influence of Hilary on his theology. Augustine does not play an explicit role in "The Agreed Statement" but he was clearly active behind the scenes, at least in Torrance's mind, and Torrance wrote as such in *Trinitarian Perspectives*.[57] Torrance is often misrepresented as painting Augustine as, to use the words of Habets, "tarred with every brush of Western heresy."[58] In the

---

53. See his notes in The Thomas F. Torrance Manuscript Collection. Special Collections, Princeton Theological Seminary Library. Box 170.

54. As Holmes caricatures the Second-Wave claims about Augustine: "Augustine's doctrine of the Trinity . . . was basically an exercise in metaphysics." See Holmes, "In Praise of Being Criticized," 147–48.

55. See Torrance, *Trinitarian Perspectives*, 22.

56. Torrance, "My Interaction with Karl Barth," 124.

57. Torrance, *Trinitarian Perspectives*, 22.

58. Habets, "Getting Beyond the *Filioque* with Third Article Theology," 222n22.

Dialogue Torrance does indeed accuse Augustine of neoplatonic dualism,[59] a sentiment many of the Orthodox would no doubt have agreed with[60] considering some Orthodox theologians hold Augustine responsible for "most of what went wrong with the west in the middle ages . . . ."[61]

Torrance certainly accused Augustine of the Latin Heresy in, for example, "Karl Barth and the Latin Heresy"—and even accused him of being an ancient version of Schleiermacher[62]—however, Torrance critiques Barth for the "elements of 'subordinationism' in his doctrine of the Trinity"[63] and one certainly could not accuse Torrance of wishing to depart entirely from Barth! However, rather than proposing a return to Augustine—or any other western fathers or theologians—Torrance suggests at the Dialogue that they return to the truly ecumenical, catholic, and thus pre-East/West divine church fathers like Athanasius and Cyril. If theologians do this, argues Torrance, "the *filioque* clause . . . simply falls away."[64] There may have been inconsistencies here in terms of Torrance's use of Augustine, but overall he seems to wish to depart from him as a focus rather than reject him completely.

Herein, Torrance and the Dialogue were ahead of their time considering the prevalence of the so called "de Régnon thesis" at the time. "The Agreed Statement" references eastern fathers such as John of Damascus[65] and Basil the Great[66] and western fathers such as Hilary of Poitiers,[67] however the main figures, quotations and references are church fathers Torrance

---

59. See, e.g., Torrance's comments in the 1983 Minutes in The Thomas F. Torrance Manuscript Collection. Special Collections, Princeton Theological Seminary Library, Box 170.

60. See, e.g. Romanides, *The Ancestral Sin; Franks, Romans, Feudalism, and Doctrine*; Yannaras, *Elements of Faith*; *Orthodox and the West*.

61. See Papanikolaou and Demacopoulos, "Augustine and the Orthodox: 'The West' in the East," 33.

62. Torrance, "My Interaction with Karl Barth," 122.

63. Ibid., 131.

64. Torrance, *Trinitarian Faith*, 237.

65. "The Agreed Statement on the Holy Trinity," 220.

66. Ibid., 222.

67. Ibid., 224.

The Agreed Statement on the Holy Trinity

views as catholic and ecumenical, standing somewhere between East and West like Athanasius,[68] Cyril,[69] Gregory Nazianzen,[70] and Epiphanius.[71]

As Torrance puts it in his "Common Reflection on the Agreed Statement" (which Dragas says was entirely written and presented by Torrance at the concluding session),[72] "the account of the Trinity given by the Statement . . . [is arrived at] through guidance taken mostly from Athanasius and Gregory the Theologian."[73] As such Torrance and "The Agreed Statement" offer a more nuanced view of the substantial similarity between East and West on the doctrine of the Trinity, however, they avoid bulldozing over the real differences. As Torrance says of "The Agreed Statement," "it cuts across mistaken polarised views"[74] and while "both the Orthodox and the Reformed readily acknowledged that they have different emphases in their approaches to the doctrine of the Holy Trinity . . . they insisted that they agree on the content of the doctrine."[75]

Torrance and the Dialogue acknowledged that differences do exist. For example, Torrance does take issue with overly strong emphases on either the unity or plurality of the Trinity, clearly wishing to depart from an overly Western or overly Eastern approach as traditionally understood. Any divergence means for Torrance a subtraction from the central patristic assertion that due to the *homoousion* humankind has knowledge of God *in himself* and is truly united to God and saved. In general, he sees these departures as falling into some sort of theological dualism/Arianism which cuts off knowledge of and union with God *in himself* and thus as unfaithful to the meaning of the Nicene *homoousion*. These overly strong Eastern or Western emphases need to be "unknown" because they are historical developments that should be reshaped theologically, i.e. Christologically, around the *homoousion*.[76] Accordingly, Torrance is critical of overly-Augustinian

68. Ibid., 221; 222; 223; 225; 226.
69. Ibid., 222.
70. Ibid., 220; 223.
71. Ibid., 224.
72. Baker and Dragas, "Interview," 15.
73. Torrance, "Significant Features, a Common Reflection on the Agreed Statement of the Holy Trinity," 232.
74. Ibid.
75. Torrance, "Introduction" to *Theological Dialogue between Orthodox and Reformed Churches*, 2:xxi. Notably, Barth agreed with this concerning East and West. See *Church Dogmatics*, 1/1:477.
76. Torrance, "Memoranda on Orthodox/Reformed Relations," 5.

or Cappadocian approaches to the doctrine of the Trinity and critiques them often throughout his writings.

Torrance criticizes overly Augustinian approaches as too focused on the abstract oneness of God. This is an approach shared by other Second-Wave Trinitarians, for example Karl Rahner.[77] Torrance also criticizes overly Cappadocian approaches as too focused on the plurality of the persons in the Trinity and the implied causality and subordination contained therein. Torrance's primary problem with the Cappadocians is their understanding of *ousia* as referring to the general and of *hypostasis* referring to the particular in God and the related locating of the *monarchy* in the *hypostasis* of the Father. The main problem in his mind is that this suggests subordination in the Being of God. However, more deeply Torrance takes issue with what he sees as inherent theological dualism in the move. For Torrance this move divides God's economy from God's ontology.[78]

Contribution #2: The Agreed Statement Offers a Dynamic View of the Oneness of God

The doctrine of the Trinity agreed upon at the Orthodox-Reformed Dialogue departs from the traditional western acceptance of the *filioque*, yet, it does not simply return to the eastern rejection of the doctrine. Rather, the doctrine of the Trinity that arose from the Dialogue is a Reformed version of the classical eastern patristic viewpoint and, as such, offers a *via media* of ecumenical importance. According to Torrance, it is only through the Nicene *homoousion* that one is able to approach the doctrine of the Trinity.

At the Dialogue Torrance contends that the fathers, especially Athanasius, did not adhere to a general/abstract notion of *ousia*, like the Cappadocians did. "The Agreed Statement" articulates this conviction in a few ways. First, it states that despite the Trinity consisting of three Persons, as Gregory Nazianzen says, "One is not more or less God, nor is One before and after Another . . . for there is no greater or less in respect of the Being

---

77. For example, Rahner, *The Trinity*. Rahner proposes a departure from the Augustinian Trinitarian approach of his own Catholic tradition for he argued that, following Augustine and Aquinas, Western theology has separated the one God *(De Deo Uno)* from the Triune God *(De Deo Trino)* (see pages 9–48). Torrance greatly appreciates Rahner's work here, and lauds him in *Trinitarian Perspectives*. See pp. 81–84.

78. Torrance, "The Triunity of God," 32; "Working Paper on the Holy Trinity," 119.

of the consubstantial Persons."[79] Elsewhere, Torrance, following Athanasius, argues that the term *ousia* has "an intensely personal and concrete meaning."[80] Here Torrance wants to preserve the dynamic nature of the *ousia* because he sees the term as personal as opposed to abstract and static, which he contends is Athanasian.[81] "The Agreed Statement" therefore articulates that there is only one *Arche* or *Monarchia* of the Godhead, and roots it in the Father, but notably not the Person of the Father, but, at least as Torrance understood it, the Being of the Father.[82] As such, the monarchy of the Father is on the one hand particular to the Father and at the very same time shared by the other Persons of the Trinity by nature of their sharing the same Being.[83] As McDowell puts it, "[Torrance holds to] a Triune conception of divine monarchy."[84] It is here that Torrance and the Dialogue's critics often misunderstand "The Agreed Statement" and Torrance. Benjamin Dean, for example, argues that the move "effectively denies" the role of the monarchy of the Person of the Father.[85] It is true that "The Agreed Statement" roots the monarchy in the Being of the Father, but this includes the Person of the Father; it, however, is not limited to the Person of the Father because of the unity of the Persons. This is due both to the perichoresis of the three Persons[86] but also—and perhaps even more so—to the insistence of the Dialogue and "The Agreed Statement" that the Being of God is not an "abstract essence" but the "I am" of God, a dynamic Being/Essence that is revealed by the Father, through the Son, and in the Holy Spirit.[87] Here is

---

79. "The Agreed Statement on the Holy Trinity," 220.

80. Torrance, *The Christian Doctrine of God*, 129, citing Athanasius, *De Decretis* 16ff, 22ff; *Ad Episcopos* 17–18; *Contra Arianos* 1.16, 28; 2,33; 3.1ff; *Ad Afros* 4–5. See *The Christian Doctrine of God*, 125–29, for the full discussion. Put otherwise, "the gift and the Giver are the same." See Torrance, *Trinitarian Perspectives*, 9. See also 218–19 where Torrance cited Athanasius, *Contra Arianos* 2:2, 38, referring to Athanasius's conception of ἐνούσιος ἐνέργεια (Energy inherent to Being).

81. Torrance, *The Christian Doctrine of God*, 104.

82. Ibid., 223–24. As Molnar puts it "Torrance notes that the Council of Nicaea referred to the Son as proceeding from the being of the Father and not the Person of the Father." See Molnar, "Introduction," xix.

83. "The Agreed Statement on the Holy Trinity," 223; "Significant Features, a Common Reflection on the Agreed Statement on the Holy Trinity," 231.

84. McDowell, "On Not Being Spirited Away," 170.

85. Dean, "Person and Being," 72. See Molnar, "Theological Issues Involved in the Filioque," 37–38, for a successful debunking of Dean's argument.

86. "The Agreed Statement on the Holy Trinity," 224.

87. Ibid., 225. See also Torrance's "Commentary on the Agreed Statement" in

Part 1: A Critical Appreciation of the Orthodox-Reformed Theological Dialogue

the real genius of Torrance and the Dialogue's move. By rooting the monarchy—and by extension the procession of the Holy Spirit—in the Father, they utilize classically Greek patristic thought. However, by rooting it in the Being of the Father they also utilize classical Latin patristic thought. They arrive at this agreement via a reconstruction of both positions around the *homoousion* or, as Torrance puts it, by orienting themselves around "the fact that it is only through God that God may be known."[88] Starting with the self-revelation of God, i.e. the *homoousion*, allows Reformed and Orthodox to successfully bypass the *filioque* debate altogether. As Ellis says, "the filioque is an ultimately unsuccessful attempt to secure what the homoousion (rightly understood) successfully accomplished."[89] Indeed, discussion of the *filioque* was, according to Dragas, "strategically left for later."[90] As Torrance says, "a further study in depth of this procession might help us to find ways of cutting behind the division between the East and the West over the so-called *filioque*, for it does not allow of any idea of the procession of the Spirit from two ultimate principles or ἀρχαι."[91]

In many ways, the conclusions of Torrance and the Dialogue on the dynamic nature of God's Being is something which Third-Wave Trinitarians would appreciate. They certainly emphasize God's oneness and seem to suggest that the church fathers from both East and West agreed God is, at the core, one and of a simple nature. For example, Holmes states: "the divine nature is simple, incomposite, and ineffable."[92] However, the one Being of the Trinity discussed in "The Agreed Statement" is not the abstract, simple Being discussed by, at least Holmes, if not the other Third-Wave Trinitarians. The dynamic Being discussed in "The Agreed Statement" is understood in a more nuanced and dynamic fashion, largely due to their constructive-theological approach as opposed to an historical-theological approach.

Torrance, *Trinitarian Perspectives*, 142. This approach offers a helpful nuance to the simplicity of God emphasis seen in Third-Wave Trinitarianism.

88. Torrance, "Significant Features, a Common Reflection on the Agreed Statement on the Holy Trinity," 229.

89. Ellis, "The Spirit From the Father, Of Himself God," 94.

90. Baker and Dragas, "Interview," 15.

91. Torrance, "Significant Features, a Common Reflection on the Agreed Statement on the Holy Trinity," 231.

92. Holmes, *The Holy Trinity*, 199.

Contribution #3: The Agreed Statement is Constructive Theology

Torrance's many connections and reconstructions in exploration of the connections between Greek patristic and Reformed evangelical theology raise the question as to whether he is fair to the fathers at the Dialogue. Afterall, reading contemporary theological issues back into the church fathers is a key critique that Third-Wave Trinitarians have of Second-Wavers.[93] Dragas certainly suggests something like this when he says the original draft of "The Agreed Statement" was "too Reformed and 'Torrancian.'"[94] Furthermore, as Fairbairn says, "Torrance rarely quotes his sources."[95] One might reasonably ask, then, whether the *homoousion* of Torrance's patristic consensus is indeed the same as the Nicene *homoousion*. Connected, one might ask whether Torrance's understanding of the procession of the Spirit from the Being of the Father is really what Gregory and Athanasius would have understood. Georges Florovsky warns of the danger of a "Western captivity" of the Fathers when their theology is forced into categories foreign to them.[96] Is Torrance open to this accusation? Is the Nicene *homoousion* which Torrance emphasizes so heartily really just western (or even Barthian) theological concepts in the Greek language? Some critique Torrance accordingly. Foremost in the critiques is that Torrance's reading of the fathers, primarily Athanasius and the *homoousion*, sounds too Barthian.[97] Gunton puts a related critique forward of Torrance when he argues that Torrance's reading of the *homoousion* is too western and sounds more Augustinian than Athanasian.[98]

---

93. See, e.g., ibid., 1–32, and 182–200 for scathing critiques of Second-Wave Trinitarianism, ending with the question "we called what we were doing a 'Trinitarian Revival'; future historians might want to ask us why." See p. 200.

94. Baker and Dragas, "Interview," 13.

95. That is, he only references them. See Fairbairn, "Review of Thomas F. Torrance and the Church Fathers," 117. However, it should be noted that *The Agreed Statement* is full of quotations from the church fathers, especially Athanasius.

96. See Meyendorff, *Byzantine Theology*, 128.

97. Ernest, *The Bible in Athanasius of Alexandria*, 17. Cf. Molnar, *Thomas F. Torrance*, 325.

98. Gunton, *Father, Son, and Holy Spirit*, 44–52. Gunton wonders whether "the immense stress on the ὁμοούσιον does not run the risk of flattening out the particularities, so that the divine *being* tends to be stressed at the expense of the divine *persons*." He suggests that Torrance's reading of the Greek Fathers was perhaps more western, Latin, and Augustinian than Greek patristic.

Part 1: A Critical Appreciation of the Orthodox-Reformed Theological Dialogue

It is certainly true that Athanasius' use of the *homoousion* is not exactly the same as Torrance's[99] It is indeed then possible to level an historical critique at Torrance;[100] and it is notable that the critiques that Third-Wavers have of Second-Wavers is often historical. Holmes ends his book criticizing Second-Wave Trinitarianism with the question: "we called what we were doing a 'Trinitarian Revival'; future historians might want to ask us why," ultimately arguing that the problem with Second-Wave Trinitarianism is that they are not faithful to the patristic sources.[101] Similarly, Lewis Ayres' book *Nicaea and Its Legacy* is largely an historical account of the development of fourth- and fifth-century Trinitarian Theology, albeit with an eye to current theological conversations and development.[102] Third-Wave Trinitarianism is largely, then, concerned with questions of historicity. However, Torrance and the Orthodox-Reformed Dialogue do not place their work in the field of history; rather, it is constructive systematic theology, which ultimately makes it a tenable possibility. Indeed, they agree that there are historical developments that they need to "unknow." Torrance and the Orthodox-Reformed Dialogue are not aiming to be historical; their project is constructive and theological.[103] Torrance and the Orthodox-Reformed

---

99. Torrance applies the *homoousion* and other patristic terms much more broadly than the fathers did themselves by combining it with his own Reformed commitments. Holmes, for example, does take this route when he argues that Athanasius and the Nicene fathers used the word *homoousion* simply as a word with which Arius would not agree. Holmes argues that the bishops at Nicaea would have had variegated understandings of what the word actually meant and certainly they would not have agreed (and, perhaps, not even Athanasius would have thought) that it meant what Torrance says it means. See Holmes, "Response: In Praise of Being Criticized," 152.

100. See, e.g., Ernest, "*The Bible in Athanasius of Alexandria,* 13.

101. Holmes, *The Holy Trinity,* 200.

102. For example, Ayres argues against the idea that the word *homoousion* carried the theological weight for Athanasius and the pro-Nicene bishops that later interpreters would argue it did. See Ayres, *Nicaea and Its Legacy,* 90–98.

103. The constructive approach is not something the Third-Wave generally does, but they would not necessarily disagree with it. As Holmes says: "[If Augustine and the Cappadocians are basically the same on Trinitarian theology] this still does not make social Trinitarianism wrong—it merely makes it innovative. The degree to which this conclusion is found to be worrying will vary according to the ecclesiology of the writer; for John Zizioulas, an Orthodox bishop, a claim that his theology is an innovation unknown to, or even opposed to, the tradition would be unacceptable . . . for a Schleiermachian (or perhaps, a certain sort of contemporary feminist theologian) the same claim might well be worn as a badge of honour." See Holmes, "Response: In Praise of Being Criticized," 149. Notably, John Behr praises the constructive yet Christological type of approach in his critique of most patrology today being more of an historical study of late antiquity

Dialogue's emphasis on the *homoousion* provides fresh insight into the Fathers by paring away patristic theology that did not focus on it and highlighting the classical theology that did. Third-Wave Trinitarianism, in its more historical emphasis, misses the important constructive move made by the Orthodox-Reformed Dialogue.[104] In short, Torrance and the Dialogue offer a way of approaching the tradition that avoids a staticity of tradition which says the fathers must be read at face value and, on the other pole, an idiosyncraticism that says the fathers can be reshaped any way one likes.[105] Torrance and the Dialogue sit at the feet of the church fathers and theologize with them about God as he has revealed himself in Jesus Christ.[106]

CONCLUSION

Third-Wave Trinitarians have shown that the long-held "de Régnon thesis" which sharply distinguishes between Latin (Augustinian) and Greek (Cappadocian) doctrines of the Trinity is currently falling out of fashion with patristics scholars[107] and current scholarship is moving toward seeing Augustine and Latin Triadology in line with Greek (both Athanasian and Cappadocian) Triadology.[108] Torrance, though still falling into some now outdated categories (such as Cappadocian vs. Nicene) is at the same time a pioneer in his time inasmuch as he sees Augustine in line with Greek Trinitarian thought.[109] Furthermore, Torrance and the Orthodox-Reformed

than anything else. See Behr, *The Mystery of Christ*, 18.

104. Third-Wave Trinitarianism is self-aware of its historical focus. See, e.g., Holmes, "Response: In Praise of Being Criticized," 148: "I considered only the historical claims."

105. That is, they avoid the extreme reshaping done by the Second-Wave and the extreme historicity of the Third-Wave.

106. It is worth noting that Holmes says "Torrance offers a doctrine of the Trinity that is in visible continuity with the classical doctrine . . . ." See Holmes, "Response: In Praise of Being Criticized," 152.

107. Therein, Gunton's categories (and critiques of Torrance) are somewhat out of date.

108. Or, they at least see them as not necessarily contradictory to one another. See Ayres, *Nicaea and Its Legacy*; Ayres, *Augustine and the Trinity*; Barnes, "Rereading Augustine's Theology of the Trinity." Even the Orthodox, though still somewhat critical of Augustine on the Trinity, are beginning to see more similarities than they once did. See Papanikolaou and Demacopoulos, eds., *Orthodox Readings of Augustine*, for a collection of essays from a conference exploring this subject.

109. Noble makes a similar connection, pointing to Augustine as not necessarily absolutely opposed to the eastern fathers. See Noble, *Holy Trinity, Holy People*, 215–17.

Part 1: A Critical Appreciation of the Orthodox-Reformed Theological Dialogue

Dialogue, especially "The Agreed Statement on the Holy Trinity" help to show the essential unity of East and West on the Trinity. As such Torrance's scholarship in this area has much to offer the current Trinitarian conversation and he is seriously under-utilized by patristics scholars and theologians alike on this topic. As Noble states: "Torrance's Trinitarian theology holds out the best hope of combining the concerns for divine Unity with the concerns of the social Trinitarians."[110] The doctrine of the Trinity of the Dialogue is a resource for the current *via media* for the current Trinitarian debate with his dynamic conception of the Trinity consisting of three *hypostases* inhering in the one *ousia*. As Paul Molnar says,

> Torrance's thinking about the unity and Trinity of God is fully in line with classical doctrine of the Trinity espoused by Catholics, Orthodox, Anglicans, Lutherans, and Reformed. It is enshrined in the Orthodox and Reformed Agreement on the Trinity. And it allows Torrance himself to assert that all Christians can legitimately speak of the Spirit proceeding "from the Father through the Son" and "from the Father and the Son" as long as there is no confusion of the order of the persons with their unity of being; as long as there is no espousal of a concept of derived deity with respect to the Son and the Spirit.[111]

This type of theological agreement is—or at least should be—the goal of any Third-Wave Trinitarianism. Torrance, Fouyas, the Orthodox-Reformed Dialogue, and "The Agreed Statement" have reached this goal in their understanding of God as *mia ousia, treis hypostaseis* in a *homoousion*-focused, Christologically-oriented, Athanasius-centered statement of God as unity in Trinity and Trinity in Unity. This book therefore now turns to a concluding chapter where the many contributions of the Orthodox-Reformed Dialogue will be extended into suggestions for further ecumenical and theological conversation.

---

110. Ibid., 215n41.
111. Molnar, "Theological Issues Involved in the Filioque," 39.

Conclusion

A Proposed Way Forward from "The Agreed Statement"

> *What was proposed was not the usual kind of ecumenical dialogue concerned with comparative beliefs and ecclesiologies, but something far more basic, which could affect all Christendom, through a deep-ground clarification of the mind of the Church regarding the ultimate ground and structure of the faith on the doctrine of the Holy Trinity.*
>
> Concluding Affirmation[1]

INTRODUCTION

THE THEOLOGICAL AGREEMENT REACHED at the Orthodox-Reformed Dialogue, as encapsulated in "The Agreed Statement on the Holy Trinity" is truly monumental and unprecedented, offering an ecumenical Trinitarian theology ahead of its time, not least on the doctrine of the Trinity. Many points of application for the contemporary situation arise from exploration of the theology of the Dialogue. Thus, the conclusion offers a summary of the book and suggests further critical points regarding the way forward for Orthodox-Reformed and, perhaps, other relations between different traditions on the basis of the Trinitarian and Christocentric theology of the

---

1. "Concluding Affirmation: Agreed Understanding of the Theological Development and Eventual Direction of the Orthodox/Reformed Conversations Leading to Dialogue," 157.

Part 1: A Critical Appreciation of the Orthodox-Reformed Theological Dialogue

Greek fathers. By way of a case study of Torrance's "Common Reflection On The Agreed Statement," this concluding chapter will highlight practical ways forward from the Dialogue, ultimately arguing that it would be fruitful to use the good work of the Dialogue, particularly the theological approach of "The Agreed Statement," as a template for Trinitarian and ecumenical theology today.

SUMMARY OF THE BOOK

This book has explored the Orthodox-Reformed Dialogue, spearheaded by T. F. Torrance and brought about through his friendship and shared theological convictions with Archbishop Methodios Fouyas. After a brief Introduction highlighting the book's scope and argument, Chapter One offered a general overview of the Orthodox-Reformed Dialogue and its precedents, examining in particular the catholic and Greek patristic foundations of the Dialogue, suggesting ways in which Torrance's catholic reading of the church fathers would in many ways open the door to the Dialogue. Chapter Two explored more closely the friendship and shared theological commitments of Torrance and Archbishop Methodios, suggesting their "theological rapport" provided the basis for the Dialogue. Chapter Three examined the Five Consultations and the Concluding Session of the Orthodox-Reformed Dialogue. Focusing upon the discussions following the papers and the emerging agreement on the doctrine of the Trinity, this chapter offered an historical account of the Dialogue and traced the emergence of "The Agreed Statement on the Holy Trinity." Chapter Four focused on "The Agreed Statement" and, through a close study of the text, offered a critical examination which ultimately argued that "The Agreed Statement" is a more nuanced and more constructive version of Third-Wave Trinitarianism before there was even such a thing. The Conclusion now seeks to articulate some points of application and departure by drawing out the many positive qualities and suggesting ways some aspects might be left with the Dialogue.

APPLICATION #1: A DIALOGUE OF CONTENT OVER FORM

The Orthodox-Reformed Dialogue offers a helpful form of approach for ecumenical conversation and interaction. The focus of the Dialogue was, very sharply, on God's self-revelation in Jesus Christ. As Torrance states at the very beginning of his "Common Reflection," "the theological orientation of the Agreed Statement is governed by the fact that it is only through God that God may be known."[2] This orientation gave the Dialogue a shared focus and approach. In the Orthodox-Reformed Dialogue, Reformed and Orthodox agreed upon a commitment to a Trinitarian and Christocentric approach to theology. In his writing related to the Dialogue Torrance argues that they must remain focused upon the Nicene *homoousion* inasmuch as it is the "king-pin."[3] The Dialogue offers a return to the Athanasian-Cyrilline axis of theology.[4]

Ultimately, the approach of the Dialogue in discussing of content of the faith over form offers a solid template to follow. For example, Torrance states that both Reformed and Orthodox have elements of their traditions that are historical developments that they should unknow, exhibiting a humbleness of approach to his own tradition.[5] The Dialogue also relishes some of the historical developments and differences, while acknowledging the ultimate importance of the shared content of the faith. This approach provides an excellent template for ecumenical discussion: relishing certain historical differences, departing from others, and focusing on the common fount of all traditions, namely, Trinity and Christology. Torrance and the Dialogue have provided an excellent example for future ecumenical Dialogues to follow in their emphasis on the doctrine of the Trinity.

As Torrance draws out his "Commentary on The Agreed Statement," the content of the doctrine of the Trinity affects all other areas of church life. Torrance states that the work of the Orthodox-Reformed Dialogue was to not only get behind doctrinal divisions between East and West but also to see the doctrine of the Trinity "as it came to expressions in the θεοσέβειαία and θεολογία of the Early Church in the hope that it may help to unify the mind of the Church today."[6] For Torrance, part of the goal of coming to agreement on the doctrine of the Trinity was to extend this into the wider life of the church.

---

2. Torrance, "Significant Features, a Common Reflection on the Agreed Statement on the Holy Trinity," 229

3. Torrance, *The Incarnation*, xi–xv.

4. Torrance, "The Triunity of God," 3–13.

5. Torrance, "Memoranda on Orthodox/Reformed Relations," 5.

6. Torrance, "Commentary on the Agreed Statement," 127.

Part 1: A Critical Appreciation of the Orthodox-Reformed Theological Dialogue

Application #2: Trinitarian Language

A second contribution of the Orthodox-Reformed Dialogue drawn out in Torrance's "Common Reflection" is the role of Trinitarian language. As Torrance highlights, "The Agreed Statement" utilizes the Greek theological language of the church fathers but in no way wishes these terms to remain static. Rather, the Dialogue sought to use Trinitarian language in a dynamic way, allowing the reality of the Trinity to which the language witnesses to reform and reshape the language as necessary.[7] As Torrance's "Common Reflection" states, terms like οὐσία, ὑπόστασις, and φύσις are "borrowed by the Church from Greek are consistently handled in the new shape given to them as they are harnessed in the service of God's trinitarian self-revelation."[8] These words, Torrance continues, "must be understood in a wholly spiritual, personal yet genderless way."[9]

The trajectory of this approach of the Dialogue is that Trinitarian language, whilst helpful, should not be the focus nor should it be immovable. The Dialogue was very open to departing from Latin translations of Being and Essence as well as non-theological abstract understandings of οὐσία and ὑπόστασις in favor of more concrete interpretations of the Greek terms.[10] In doing so, both the Reformed and Orthodox at the Dialogue opened up their very expression of the doctrine of the Trinity for reform and reconstruction in light of the theology the terms seek to witness. For Torrance, as Molnar puts it, "we must use our creaturely terms in speaking about the triune God; but we must use them in their transformed sense."[11]

The ultimate reason for the Orthodox-Reformed Dialogue's understanding on the inherent dynamism of theological language is that they understood all ecclesiastical and theological language to ultimately rest upon God's self-revelation in Jesus Christ. As Torrance puts it in his "Commentary on the Agreed Statement," "it is upon faith in Jesus Christ as Lord and Saviour and upon his relation to the one God revealed in the Scriptures ... that everything finally pivots."[12]

---

7. See also ibid. 129–30.

8. Torrance, "Significant Features, a Common Reflection on the Agreed Statement on the Holy Trinity," 229.

9. Ibid. 230.

10. See ibid. 229–230.

11. Molnar, "Introduction," xxii.

12. Torrance, *Trinitarian Perspectives*, 128.

Application #3: The Monarchy

As Torrance states in his "Common Reflection on the Agreed Statement," "Of far-reaching importance is the stress laid upon the Monarchy of the Godhead in which all three divine Persons share, for the whole indivisible Being of God belongs to each of them as it belongs to all of them together."[13] Indeed, inasmuch as the Monarchy cannot be limited to one Person of the Trinity and because of the doctrine of *perichoresis*, the understanding of the Holy Spirit is that the Spirit proceeds from the Father through the Son and thus the *filioque* debate is essentially nullified; according to the approach of the Dialogue, one could hold to the *filioque* or reject it (i.e. using different Trinitarian language) so long as they understand the procession of the Spirit to be from the Father,[14] but not the Person of the Father.[15]

Torrance concludes that "a further study in depth of this procession might help us to find ways of cutting behind the so-called '*filioque*', for it does not allow of any idea of the procession of the Spirit from two ultimate principles . . . " As such, Torrance and the Orthodox-Reformed Dialogue provide a starting point for further ecumenical dialogue focused upon the Trinity: an exploration of the *filioque* from the groundwork already laid by "The Agreed Statement on the Holy Trinity." That is, how might one unknow the Trinitarian language concerning the *filioque* and remain focused upon the dynamic Being of God and the procession of the Holy Spirit from the Father, through the Son?

Application #4: Ecumenical Significance

Ultimately, Torrance concludes "the Statement on the Holy Trinity is thus of considerable ecumenical significance in offering an approach to the doctrine of the Trinity which is neither from the Three Persons to the One Being of God, nor from the One Being of God to the Three Persons."[16] Rather, says Torrance, it is "at one and the same time the Trinity and the

---

13. See Torrance, "Significant Features, a Common Reflection on the Agreed Statement on the Holy Trinity," 231.

14. By which Torrance clearly means the *ousia* of the Father. See Torrance, "Introduction" to *Theological Dialogue between Orthodox and Reformed Churches*, 1:xi. See also Torrance's "Commentary on the Agreed Statement" in *Trinitarian Perspectives*, 132–36.

15. See Torrance, "Significant Features, a Common Reflection on the Agreed Statement on the Holy Trinity," 231.

16. See ibid., 232.

Unity of God."[17] Therefore "it cuts across mistaken polarised views of the doctrine of the Holy Trinity."[18] Thus, the Orthodox-Reformed Dialogue reached an ecumenically significant[19] agreement on the Trinity which unifies churches and theological viewpoints as well as offers insight into the contemporary Trinitarian conversation.

WHAT TO LEAVE BEHIND?

This book has argued that the Orthodox-Reformed Dialogue was a largely successful endeavor and has much to offer the current ecumenical and theological conversation. However, as has become clear, some aspects and assumptions of the Dialogue have become outdated. The concluding section will thus proceed by considering some areas that perhaps ought to be left in the 1980s, or at least rethought today, and offering some suggestions concerning how to extend the Dialogue more generally today.

Is the "Cappadocian Distinction" Really a "Zizioulan Distinction"? The Dialogue's Critique of Second-Wave Trinitarianism

At the Dialogue, the Cappadocian Fathers (especially Basil the Great) come under heavy critique, at least by Torrance. Torrance urges for a return to the "Athanasius-Cyril axis" and bifurcates this from the Cappadocians, especially Basil, arguing that the Cappadocians departed from a more Athanasian and dynamic conception of the doctrine of the Trinity. Torrance suggests the Cappadocians held a dualistic view that separated God's Being from his Persons. John Zizioulas' emphasis upon the Cappadocians and their encapsulation of "social Trinitarianism," focusing upon the threeness of God's Persons, has been critiqued by Third-Wave Trinitarians as being more "Zizioulan" and existential than Cappadocian.[20] Third-Wave

---

17. See ibid. See also Torrance, *Trinitarian Perspectives*, 137–42.

18. See Torrance, "Significant Features, a Common Reflection on the Agreed Statement on the Holy Trinity," 232.

19. In Emilianos's words, they were seeking an "eirenic understanding." See the 1981 Official Minutes. They reached it. See The Thomas F. Torrance Manuscript Collection. Special Collections, Princeton Theological Seminary Library. Box 170.

20. See, e.g., Holmes, *Holy Trinity*, 12–16; 145–46. See also Radcliff, "Thomas F. Torrance's Conception of the *Consensus Patrum* on the Doctrine of Pneumatology," 431–32. Torrance accuses Zizioulas of an "existentialising interpretation of the Greek Fathers."

Trinitarians want to view the Cappadocians as focusing on the unity of God as much as his plurality, departing from the social Trinitarian model of Zizioulas. Contra Zizioulas and the Second-Wave, Ayres and Meredith, for example, argue that the Cappadocians insisted upon the essential unity of God, rejecting any notion of hierarchy or subordination.[21]

Torrance's critiques during the Orthodox-Reformed Dialogue of the Cappadocians, while not mentioning Zizioulas, are obvious critiques of Zizioulas' reading of the Cappadocians and thus are probably more about the 1980s than the 380s.[22] It is notable that Torrance's critique of the Cappadocians really only becomes prevalent in the 1980s, in particular in Torrance's *Trinitarian Faith*.[23] Torrance's published critiques in the Dialogue and elsewhere, while not mentioning Zizioulas, are clearly critiques of Zizioulas' reading of the Cappadocians.[24] In unpublished correspondence Torrance accuses Zizioulas of an "existentialising interpretation of the Greek Fathers."[25] Torrance's openness in the Dialogue (and elsewhere in

---

For this quote, see a Draft Letter from Torrance to Fenar dated March 17th, 1988 in The Thomas F. Torrance Manuscript Collection. Special Collections, Princeton Theological Seminary Library. Box 170.

21. See Ayres, *Nicaea and Its Legacy,* 195 and Meredith, "The Idea of God in Gregory of Nyssa," 133–34.

22. See Radcliff, "T. F. Torrance in light of Stephen Holmes's critique of contemporary Trinitarian thought," 32–33; and Radcliff, "T. F. Torrance and the Patristic Consensus on the Doctrine of the Trinity." Holmes agrees with this argument. See Holmes, "Response: In Praise of Being Criticized," 186.

23. Notably, Torrance considered this book to be directly relevant to the Reformed-Orthodox Dialogue. See Torrance's comments on this in a letter written to Demetrius I, the Ecumenical Patriarch dated 1988 contained in The Thomas F. Torrance Manuscript Collection. Special Collections, Princeton Theological Seminary Library. Box 172.

24. See Radcliff, "T. F. Torrance in light of Stephen Holmes's critique of contemporary Trinitarian thought," 32–33 and Radcliff, "T. F. Torrance and the Patristic Consensus on the Doctrine of the Trinity" for more on this point.

25. See the Draft Letter from Torrance to the center of the Ecumenical Patriarchate in Phanar, Istanbul dated March 17th, 1988 in The Thomas F. Torrance Manuscript Collection. Special Collections, Princeton Theological Seminary Library. Box 170. Torrance clearly felt theological responsibility for Zizioulas and thus took his existentialism personally. In a Draft Letter from Torrance to the center of the Ecumenical Patriarchate in Phanar (a term from the Greek φανάριον, which is the name of the neighborhood where the Patriarchate is located and used as shorthand for the Patriarchate), Istanbul dated March 17th, 1988 Torrance states that "it was I who brought John Zizioulas to Edinburgh and thus introduced him to our Church and theological life in Great Britain, and have supported him in every way I could." George Dragas even went so far as to call Torrance Zizioulas' "greatest benefactor" (for this see a letter from George Dragas written

Part 1: A Critical Appreciation of the Orthodox-Reformed Theological Dialogue

his published books) to many elements in the Cappadocians would suggest that he does not dismiss the Cappadocians entirely; rather Torrance is concerned by certain emphases in their theology which were being focused upon[26] during his own time by Zizioulas.[27]

Is Augustine or Medieval Latin Scholasticism the Problem?

At the Orthodox-Reformed Dialogue, Augustine falls under critique for his dualism and abstract understanding of God's Being.[28] However, current scholarship on Augustine now tends to avoid viewing Augustine in light of neoplatonism and in contrast with Greek patristic theology.[29] Scholarship is tending towards seeing Augustine and the Cappadocians and, indeed, more broadly the Greek Fathers and the Latin Fathers to be in line with one another theologically, particularly on the doctrine of the Trinity.[30] Scholars today do not consider Augustine to be a neoplatonist in his doctrine of the Trinity.[31] Indeed, Third-Wave Trinitarians such as Barnes see substantial overlap between Augustine and the Cappadocians on the doctrine of the Trinity, tracing many of Augustine's Trinitarian themes to the Cappadocians.[32]

---

to Torrance dated March 22nd, 1988 contained in The Thomas F. Torrance Manuscript Collection. Special Collections, Princeton Theological Seminary Library. Box 170.

26. Perhaps "over-absolutized" would be an even better term, to use the language of Emilianos.

27. See, e.g., Torrance, *Trinitarian Faith*, 218; *Theology in Reconstruction*, 217. Generally, however, it is not until his publications during the 1980s that Basil starts to come under critique. See Radcliff, *Thomas F. Torrance and the Church Fathers*, 134–41.

28. This is basically an accusation toward Augustine of neoplatonism. See, e.g., the 1983 Minutes in The Thomas F. Torrance Manuscript Collection. Special Collections, Princeton Theological Seminary Library. Box 170.

29. Holmes, *Holy Trinity*, especially 144–46. See, e.g., Ayres, *Nicaea and Its Legacy* and *Augustine and the Trinity*; Anatolios, *Retrieving Nicaea*; Rist, *Augustine*; Barnes, "Rereading Augustine's Theology of the Trinity," in *The Trinity: An Interdisciplinary Symposium on the Trinity*; Barnes, *Orthodox Readings of Augustine*.

30. See Noble, *Holy Trinity: Holy People*, 215–17. Connected, scholars today think the accusation towards Augustine of neoplatonism is unfair. See, e.g., Holmes, *Holy Trinity*, 144–46 and Ayres, *Augustine and the Trinity*. As Studer forcefully argues, Augustine began his doctrine of the Trinity with the Nicene formulations, not his neo-platonic psychological analogy. See Studer, *The Grace of Christ and the Grace of God in Augustine of Hippo*, 106.

31. See, e.g., Ayres, *Augustine and the Trinity*, 19–41.

32. See, e.g., Barnes, *The Power of God* and "One Nature, One Power," 205–23.

A Proposed Way Forward from "The Agreed Statement"

The critiques of Augustine at the Dialogue, however, come largely from the Reformed, mainly Torrance. When examined more deeply, it becomes clear that, once again, Torrance's critiques are not so much of Augustine but more so of Latin, Scholastic, and Westminster theology. At the Dialogue Torrance was mainly critical of "Augustinian thought" rather than Augustine himself.[33] Elsewhere, Torrance critiques Augustinian thought for dividing God from his Word and critiques the Latin tradition more generally for emphasizing the juridical aspect of the atonement dividing God from Christ.[34] Notably, Torrance critiques Roman Catholicism and Federal Calvinism for essentially the same thing,[35] and so it is reasonable to surmise that Torrance's critiques of Augustine are perhaps veiled critiques of Roman Catholicism and Westminster Calvinism, much like his critiques of Arius are veiled critiques of nineteenth-century liberalism when Athanasius becomes a fourth-century Barth. Perhaps, then, the Augustine of the Dialogue should not be swept away with critiques of Augustinianism. Both East and West, indeed Orthodox, Protestant, and Catholic are now returning to Augustine as a church father to be revered from whom much can be learned and whose doctrine of the Trinity is not unlike the Cappadocians and Athanasius.[36]

Is Palamas really a dualist or was it Lossky? The Dialogue's Critique of First-Wave Trinitarianism

In his published works, Torrance sees in Gregory Palamas a problematic and dualistic distinction between God's Essence and Energies, only interacting with the world by the latter thus cutting off God as he is himself from the world.[37] In the Dialogue Torrance depicts Athanasius and Palamas as

33. See, e.g., Torrance, *Gospel, Church, and Ministry*, 209; and Torrance, "Memoranda on Orthodox/Reformed Relations," 12.

34. See, e.g., "Karl Barth and the Latin Heresy," *Scottish Journal of Theology*, 470–79.

35. See, e.g., *Theology in Reconciliation*, 9–10; and Torrance's "Introduction to *The School of Faith,*," xvi–xxi.

36. Ayres's exposition and articulation of Augustine's doctrine of the Trinity as unity in Trinity and Trinity in unity makes a convincing case. See Ayres, *Augustine on the Trinity*, 177–272.

37. See Torrance, *Trinitarian Faith*, 38–39, esp. 38n69. See also *Theology in Reconciliation*, 252. The reading of Palamas as dualistic was the prevalent reading in Torrance's time. See, e.g., Wendebourg, "From the Cappadocian Fathers to Gregory Palamas, 194–99.

intrinsically opposed to one another in basic theology on this point.[38] The Minutes, however, highlight discussion which indicates that perhaps Torrance's problem was rather more with Vladimir Lossky (and his reading of Palamas in particular) than Gregory Palamas himself. In discussion in 1983, Torrance suggests that the Essence/Energies distinction, as understood at the time, seemed to him to be more "Losskian" than Palamite.[39] Notably, Torrance does not interact here or elsewhere with Palamas directly in his published texts but only, it seems, Lossky's version of Palamas.[40]

Departing from the Losskian Palamas, modern Palamite tends to understand Palamas' essence/energies distinction to contain an emphasis on God interacting with the world personally through his energies. For example, according to Rossum[41] and even Meyendorff,[42] Palamas' essence-energies distinction was actually an insistence that God really interacts with the world personally, which is precisely what Torrance wants to preserve.

Proposed Departure From Outdated Bifurcations

Ultimately, if Torrance and the Orthodox-Reformed Dialogue are able to be placed in a Second-Wave Trinitarian or critiqued by Third-Wave Trinitarianism, it is due to their distinctions and bifurcations at the Dialogue between East and West, Cappadocians and Athanasius, and Byzantine theology and Greek theology. In light of the recent Third-Wave scholarship, and building off the ground laid by the Dialogue, perhaps Reformed and Orthodox today ought to reconsider some of Torrance's bifurcations. Perhaps Athanasius, Cyril, the Cappadocians, and Augustine (and more broadly East and West, Greek and Latin) offer more complementary theological approaches, particularly on the doctrine of the Trinity. However, if

---

38. Torrance, "Memoranda on Orthodox/Reformed Relations," 11; *Trinitarian Faith*, 38–39; *Theology in Reconciliation*, 252. See also the 1981 Minutes in The Thomas F. Torrance Manuscript Collection. Special Collections, Princeton Theological Seminary Library. Box 170.

39. See The Thomas F. Torrance Manuscript Collection. Special Collections, Princeton Theological Seminary Library. Box 170. Torrance says that Lossky "injected ideas from Boehme and Eckhart into Palamas."

40. See also Baker, "The Place of St. Irenaeus of Lyons in Historical and Dogmatic Theology According to Thomas F. Torrance," 42.

41. Rossum, "Creation-Theology in Gregory Palamas and Theophanes of Nicaea, Compatible or Incompatible?," 373–78.

42. Meyendorff, *Introduction A l'étude de Grégoire Palamas*, 195–296; 279–310.

as argued above, the issues Torrance and the Dialogue had with the Cappadocians were really issues with Zizioulas, the issues Torrance and the Dialogue had with Augustine were really with Latin Scholasticism, and the issues Torrance and the Dialogue had with Palamas were really with Lossky, the Third-Wave Trinitarian nature of Torrance and the Dialogue become even clearer; indeed, Third-Wave Trinitarians have basically the same critiques!

Furthermore, one of the major contributions of the Orthodox-Reformed Dialogue is that it does not bulldoze the differences the way that Third-Wave Trinitarianism does sometimes. Robert Letham, similarly arguing against flattening out the differences between East and West on the doctrine of the Trinity, states that surely East and West had their differences, as seen most notably in the apophatic theology of Gregory Palamas.[43] Ultimately, Torrance and the Dialogue acknowledge differences in emphasis, but commitment to the core of the doctrine of the Trinity.

CONCLUSION

Torrance and the Orthodox-Reformed Dialogue have much from which contemporary ecumenical theology and Trinitarian scholarship can learn. The irenic and gracious approach of the Dialogue is notable as well as their commitment to the Trinitarian and Christocentric theology of the Greek fathers. There is much, therefore, from which contemporary ecumenical dialogue, Trinitarian Theology, and theology more generally can learn today.

Torrance, the Orthodox-Reformed Dialogue, and Theology Today

Torrance and the Orthodox-Reformed Dialogue are seriously underutilized in the current scholarly conversation on the doctrine of the Trinity. This book has argued that the current scholarly consensus, encapsulated in Third-Wave Trinitarianism, is to see East and West as complementary to one another on the doctrine of the Trinity. The Orthodox-Reformed Dialogue developed "The Agreed Statement," an ecumenical document which offers a dynamic combination of the doctrine of the Trinity in the

---

43. Letham, "Old and New, East and West, and a Missing Horse," 31. See also Hussey, "The Palamite Trinitarian Models," 83–89.

East as traditionally understood (emphasis on God's Persons) and the West as traditionally understood (emphasis on God's Being), as traditionally bifurcated by the "de Régnon thesis." This move is precisely the move that Third-Wave Trinitarianism is making today, and yet Torrance and the Dialogue are not a part of the conversation. As such, Torrance, the Orthodox-Reformed Dialogue, and, in particular, "The Agreed Statement on the Holy Trinity" should be much more widely used today. The Orthodox-Reformed Dialogue has already said much of what is being said by the contemporary conversation and "The Agreed Statement on the Holy Trinity" offers an accessible and brief document capturing many of the basic points current theological scholarship is currently making, but in a more nuanced fashion. In the contemporary discussion, Torrance and the Orthodox-Reformed Dialogue have much to offer as an example and contain much constructive theology. As such, their statement of God as "Trinity in Unity and Unity in Trinity," encapsulated in "The Agreed Statement," should be uplifted as a good example of the best constructive theology, the best ecumenical theology, and a Third-Wave Trinitarianism before there was such a thing.

The Relevance of the Trinitarian and Christocentric Approach of the Dialogue

As Paul Molnar puts it,

> Torrance's understanding of the expression that, what God is toward us in history he is eternally in himself, led him to express the classical doctrine of the Trinity in a way that makes his ideas valuable, necessary and even revolutionary for twenty-first century theologians as they reflect on the implications of the Nicene faith today.[44]

The many contributions of the Orthodox-Reformed Dialogue regarding the doctrine of the Trinity notwithstanding, it might be argued that the ultimate "fruit" of the Dialogue was its exhibition of a theological method for ecumenical dialogue and, indeed, ecumenical theology. Their aim as two radically different expressions of Christianity was to unknow, or at least not emphasize, their external distinctions but to focus upon their shared commitment to the Trinitarian and Christocentric theology of the Greek

---

44. Molnar, "Introduction" to the Torrance, *The Christian Doctrine of God: One Being, Three Persons,*" 2nd ed., xxiv.

fathers and, from this common foundation, rebuild or to use Torrance's language "reconstruct" together.

In his Memoranda written at the beginning of the Orthodox-Reformed Dialogue, Torrance proposes that the Dialogue begin with the doctrine of the Trinity and from that basis, the doctrine of Christology and Pneumatology from which basis he proposed they explore the Eucharist, Church, and Ministry.[45] This initial proposal by Torrance provides a helpful template for proceeding. Indeed, Orthodox and Reformed continued along these lines and, as Small helpfully traces in his essay on the Orthodox-Reformed Dialogue, the Dialogue on the Trinity developed naturally into the Dialogue on Christology, the latter of which produced "The Agreed Statement on Christology."[46] However, Small suggests that, while certainly containing many notable contributions to ecumenical Christology, "The Agreed Statement" fell short of the high water mark left by "The Agreed Statement on the Holy Trinity" inasmuch as it departs from the truly one voice of the "we confess" which starts the statement on the Trinity, replacing it with statements of compromise rather than agreement[47] and, eventually, "comparative ecclesiology" with Orthodox and Reformed views in alternating paragraphs.[48] For Small, "The Agreed Statement on the Holy Trinity" exhibits the Orthodox and Reformed speaking together about a true agreement and, he argues, this makes the text truly unique amongst previous, and indeed subsequent, ecumenical dialogues which typically "agree to disagree" on certain aspects of theology, coming to a compromise perhaps, but not the one voice of "we confess."[49] Small concludes with an incisive

---

45. Torrance, "Memoranda," 10.

46. Small, "Orthodox and Reformed in Dialogue," 124.

47. See ibid., 118–26, esp. 124–25.

48. Small, "Orthodox and Reformed in Dialogue," 125. Small lists the "Common (not agreed) statements on 'The Church as the Body of Christ' (1998), 'Membership and Incorporation into the Body of Christ' (2000), 'The Holiness of the Church' (2003), and 'The Catholicity and Mission of the Church' (2005)."

49. Small notes that in "The Agreed Statement on Christology," Orthodox *theosis* and Reformed *sanctification* are compared and the "we confess" of "The Agreed Statement on the Holy Trinity" is replaced with "Orthodox and Reformed confess," "is normative for both the Orthodox and Reformed traditions," and "both Orthodox and Reformed recognize." Small finds this disheartening inasmuch as the Orthodox and Reformed cease speaking with one voice. See Small, "Orthodox and Reformed in Dialogue," 124. The subsequent (and continuing) dialogues certainly contribute much to theology, but it seems Torrance's direct involvement in the Dialogue on the Trinity drove its trajectory and outcome in a way that was lacking in the later conversations post-1992. With the loss

point: "a dramatic difference between the Agreed Statement on the Holy Trinity and all subsequent statements is the absence of patristic references ...."[50] If subsequent theology has departed from the "we confess" of "The Agreed Statement" due to a lack of patristic, Trinitarian, and Christocentric grounding, the question arises as to what areas of theology might benefit from an application of the methods of the Orthodox-Reformed Dialogue? As Torrance states:

> It is my plea to the Orthodox that they should resist the temptation to take their main stand today, somewhat one-sidedly, on the Cappadocian development from Athanasius, but reconsider the centrality of the Athanasius-Cyril axis on which there can be deep agreement ... it is my plea to Roman Catholics that a rapprochement be made with Greek patristic understanding of the Trinity and the vicarious humanity of Christ ... My plea to Protestants is that they learn to look behind the pluralist society and the fragmented patterns of the Reformation Churches to the 'wholeness' that belongs to the apostolic foundation of the Church in Christ.[51]

If theology listens to Torrance and the Orthodox-Reformed Dialogue and returns to the Christocentric and Trinitarian theology of Athanasius and Cyril, what might it learn?

The homoousion

First, Torrance and the Orthodox-Reformed Dialogue's use of the Nicene *homoousion* continues to be unutilized today. The *homoousion* drives all of Torrance's theology, not least his creative reconstruction of the church fathers around it.[52] As Holmes says, "Torrance makes the *homoousion to Patri* do the work that divine simplicity did for the Cappadocians,"[53] arguing that Torrance's *homoousion* is, in other words, a different way of stating "Rahner's Rule" that God really is in himself as he is to us.[54] Similarly, Ellis says that "the filioque is an ultimately unsuccessful attempt to secure

---

of Torrance's personal influence, it seems the later dialogues lost the sense of urgency and passion involved in the conversations in the 1980s.

50. Small, "Orthodox and Reformed in Dialogue," 125.
51. *Theology in Reconciliation*, 9–10.
52. See further Radcliff, *Thomas F. Torrance and the Church Fathers*, esp. chap. 3.
53. Holmes, "Response: In Praise of Being Criticized," 152.
54. Ibid., 153.

what the homoousion (rightly understood) successfully accomplished."[55] In the current Third-Wave Trinitarian conversations, Torrance and the Orthodox-Reformed Dialogue's utilization of the Nicene *homoousion,* despite no doubt offering a reconstruction of the term, deserves a more prevalent place. Indeed, the term does what many Third-Wavers wish to do in the rereading of patristic Trinitarian theology.

Christology

Second, the patristic, Trinitarian, and Christocentric "we confess" might be applied to an ecumenical discussion about the vicarious humanity of Christ. As Baker states,

> Torrance's notion of the vicarious humanity of Christ, moreover, must be regarded as a major restatement of the Irenaean doctrine of recapitulation, from which Orthodox theologians today can learn much—particularly in relation to twentieth century uses of St. Gregory Palamas, which all too often failed to relate adequately the doctrine of grace as uncreated *energeia* to the humanity of Christ in anything more than an instrumental way.[56]

There is much concerning the role of the vicarious humanity of Christ that Orthodox and Reformed could discuss and agree upon, but one key issue concerns the question of Christ's assumption of fallen or unfallen humanity.[57]

Similarly, Torrance brings up the possibility of discussion on the doctrine of the Virgin Mary when he states that there is a

> need to rethink at a much deeper level the *doctrine of the Virgin Mary.* As I understand it this would involve a deep-seated reconsideration of the relation between Christians and Jews in the one Church in which both Jews and Christians have access to God the Father, through the Son and in the Holy Spirit . . . this is an area of Christian theology and tradition in which Roman Catholics, Lutherans, and Reformed have had to do a lot of thinking, but in which the Orthodox Church has so far done very little . . . Mary has to be related to the 'vicarious' mission of Israel in the mediating of

---

55. Ellis, "The Spirit From the Father, Of Himself God," 94.
56. Baker, "The Place of Irenaeus in Theology According to Torrance," 42.
57. See Radcliff, *Thomas F. Torrance and the Church Fathers,* 104–11.

divine revelation to mankind, and becomes misunderstood when detached from it.[58]

Exploring further the vicarious humanity of Christ and Mary's relationship to it might bear much fruit in not only ecumenical and theological but even interreligious dialogue. Perhaps a Trinitarian, Christocentric, and Patristic "we confess" concerning the vicarious humanity of Christ and the connection of this to the Virgin Mary would bear ecumenical fruit. In particular, certain figures and bifurcations from the Orthodox-Reformed Dialogue who were rejected by Torrance for their lack of emphasis on the vicarious humanity of Christ due to their focus upon God's energies such as Basil the Great and Gregory Palamas might be reconsidered.[59] Revisiting the key issue from the Orthodox-Reformed Dialogue concerning their divergence of figures might bring about further ecumenical rapprochement. Indeed, the bridge between the Orthodox focus upon the undivided church and the Reformed response to the medieval church might be bridged by a study of Byzantine figures from the era of Palamas. Furthermore, a "we confess" might bridge the gap between Protestant and Roman Catholic/Eastern Orthodox positions on Mariology.

Worship and the Sacraments

Third, a Trinitarian, Christocentric, and Patristic "we confess" might bear much fruit in ecumenical understandings of worship and the sacraments. Here, Torrance's "The Problem of Apollinarianism in the Liturgy" is an incredibly important essay. Gunton reflects that Torrance's essay "The Problem of Apollinarianism in the Liturgy" is one of his works that needs to be extended into contemporary scholarship.[60] The essay's Cyrilline understanding of worship and the sacraments as rooted entirely in the humanity of Christ, the Great High Priest, has much to offer today's more individualist understanding. For Torrance, baptism,[61] worship, and Eucharist[62] are all rooted in the vicarious humanity of Christ and must be viewed in a

---

58. Torrance, "The Orthodox Church in Great Britain," 331. David W. Torrance, T. F. Torrance's brother, has done much work in this area. See, e.g., *The Witness of the Jews to God*.

59. See Radcliff, *Thomas F. Torrance and the Church Fathers*, 143–44.

60. Gunton, "T. F. Torrance's Doctrine of God," 54.

61. See Torrance, "The One Baptism Common to Christ and His Church," 82–105.

62. See Torrance, "Introduction to *The Mystery of the Lord's Supper*, 13–36.

A Proposed Way Forward from "The Agreed Statement"

Trinitarian way. This approach is all the more relevant today because, as Roger Newell puts it,

> Whether in corporate or individualistic forms, the effect on worship is the same—to eclipse Christ's humanity with our own. For example, a Eucharistic celebration may be ornately decorated with "smells and bells" or rival the formality of a White House lawn ceremony. Or the priest, pastor, or worship leader may invest the presiding role with drama and grand stage presence. Either approach can lead the community to focus on the rite itself, which implicitly becomes a substitute for the agency of Christ.[63]

When a Christocentric focus is absent, worship and the sacraments tend to be understood in a unitarian, rather than Trinitarian fashion, to use the language of James Torrance.[64]

Perhaps a Trinitarian, Christocentric, and Patristic "we confess" concerning worship and the Sacraments might bear ecumenical and theological fruit. In particular, bridging the pietistic differences acknowledged early in the Orthodox-Reformed Dialogue and, indeed, bridging the many differences between Roman Catholic, Orthodox, and the many Protestant varieties of worship and churchmanship might begin through a return to the axis of the vicariously human Great High Priest, Jesus Christ, and his role in Trinitarian worship, steering all traditions away from the unitarian and individualistic worship so common today.

Ordination and Ethics

Lastly, a Trinitarian, Christocentric, and Patristic "we confess" concerning ordination, marriage, and ethics might bear much fruit today, particularly concerning the issue of the ordination and marriage of homosexuals. Torrance holds that the one true Priest/Minister is Jesus Great, the Great High Priest.[65] During Torrance's time, the ecumenically hot issues were the question of presbyterian structure versus episcopal structure and the question of the ordination of women. Torrance, without hesitation, supported

---

63. Newell, "Apollinarianism in Worship Revisited," 51–52.
64. See James Torrance, *Worship, Community, and the Triune God of Grace*.
65. See, e.g., Torrance, *The Ministry and the Sacraments of the Gospel*, 137, 145; and also Torrance, *Royal Priesthood*.

a hybrid presbyterian-episcopal structure[66] and women being ordained,[67] both rooted in Christ as the one Great vicarious High Priest. He forcefully argues, in particular, contra the typical argument of conservatives which states that because Christ was a man—and the minister is an image of Christ—the minister must be a man,[68] that the one true Minister is Jesus Christ in whose priestly ministry the ordained minister shares and thus the gender of the person representing Christ does not matter.[69]

Torrance's argument cuts into the heart of the two polarized approaches to the issue of the ordination of practicing homosexuals and also homosexual marriage. Torrance's intense Christocentric lens magnifies the problem with the typical approaches, both of which are unitarian and focused on the human person ministering or person marrying, rather than Christ the Great High Priest and the Church his Bride.[70] The approach of the Orthodox-Reformed Dialogue, namely their insisting that terms and theology be dynamic and open to reformation and reconstruction by the divine realities that they, in human language, signify, offers a new basis for the conversation. What if the debate about homosexual marriage and homosexual ordination were removed from the context of sexual ethics and placed rather into the context of the doctrines of Trinity and Christology and, from that basis, into the context of the sacraments (or "sacramental things" if one holds to only two)? At the Dialogue, traditional Eastern and Western understandings of the doctrine of the Trinity—and the theological language used to express this—were reshaped by the realities to which they witness.[71] As Dragas recollects, Torrance took this commitment seriously and even invented new Greek-Patristic words to express theology.[72]

---

66. See, e.g., Torrance, *Royal Priesthood*.

67. See Torrance, "The Ministry of Women," 201–19.

68. See, e.g., C. S. Lewis, "Priestesses in the Church?"

69. See Torrance, "The Ministry of Women," 201–19.

70. See, e.g., Radcliff, "Does the Church in Scotland Still Need Theology?," for a critique of the liberal approach that essentially projects the cultural experience onto God and for a "Reformed Asceticism" that attempts to rectify aspects of this via the Trinitarian, christocentric, and patristic understanding of asceticism, as opposed to a strict biblicism or fundamentalism.

71. Torrance states: "human language when applied to God is inevitably and rightly stretched beyond its ordinary or conventional sense if it is to serve the purpose intended." See "Significant Features, A Common Reflection on the Agreed Statement," 229.

72. See Baker and Dragas, "Interview," 13.

A Proposed Way Forward from "The Agreed Statement"

Torrance does the same with his understanding of the ordination of women; he reshapes his understanding of ministry in light of the reality, Christ the Great High Priest, to which human ordained ministry witnesses. As Torrance puts it,

> the idea that only a man, or a male, can represent Christ or be an *ikon* of Christ at the Eucharist, conflicts with basic elements in the doctrines of: the incarnation and the new order of creation, the virgin birth, which sets aside male sovereignty and judges it as sinful, the hypostatic union of divine and human nature in the one Person of Jesus Christ who is of the same uncreated genderless being as God the Father and God the Holy Spirit, the redemptive and healing assumption of complete human nature in Christ, and the atoning sacrifice of Christ which he has offered once for all on our behalf, in our place, in our stead. And therefore it conflicts also with the essential nature of the Holy Eucharist and the communion in the body and blood of Christ given to us by him.[73]

Torrance concludes that "Through the Incarnation, death, and resurrection of the Lord Jesus Christ, humanity has thus been set upon an entirely new basis of divine grace, in which there is no respect of persons, and women share equally with men in all the grace-gifts or *charismata* of the Holy Spirit, including gifts for ministry in the church."[74] Radically, Torrance uses the classic doctrines of Trinity and Christology (and the church fathers who informed the doctrines) to reshape his understanding of women's ordination, ultimately concluding that, theologically, there is no reason why women cannot be ordained. One rarely sees this theological, Trinitarian, Christocentric, and patristic approach today in relation to the issue of homosexual ordination. Nor does one see this approach in relation to the issue of homosexual marriage.

To be clear, this is not to suggest anything about whether homosexuality is right or wrong, but is rather more of a critique of the traditional Liberal ("humanity writ large")[75] vs. Biblicist ("rigid framework of beliefs")[76] di-

---

73. Torrance, "The Ministry of Women," 218.

74. Ibid., citing Justin Martyr, *Dialogue with Trypho* 88.

75. See, e.g., Karl Barth, "Preface," for a critique of this approach. Basically, the "liberal approach" is culture projected onto God, i.e., if culture arrives somewhere, that must dictate a theological understanding. Alisdair Heron convincingly argues this was essentially the Arian approach as well. See Heron, "Homoousios with the Father," 58–87.

76. See, e.g., Torrance, *Reality and Evangelical Theology*, 16–17, for a critique of this approach. Basically, the "Biblicist approach" says, in a fundamentalist fashion, if the Bible

chotomy in approaching the issue of homosexual ordination and marriage within the realm of theological ethics. Obviously, the arguments for and against women's ordination in Torrance's day were different from the arguments for and against the ordination and marriage of homosexuals today. No one reasonably considers being a woman a sin; the homosexual issue is due to the divide on whether it is a sin or not. However, that is precisely the point. Similarly to how the Reformed and Orthodox of Torrance's day differed on their approach to the *filioque* and therefore avoided the issue directly altogether, intentionally deciding rather to start from their shared commitment to the Trinitarian and Christocentric theology of the Greek fathers and from that common ground, work outwards towards an agreed doctrine of the Trinity which in the end bypassed their very disagreements on the *filioque*, the work of Torrance and the Dialogue could be extended to suggest that the issue of homosexual ordination might be removed from the ethics discussion where of course those who are for homosexual ordination and those who are against differ and placed into a Trinitarian and Christocentric framework for discussion, building off common ground and shared understanding of a Trinitarian and Christocentric understanding of ordination itself. Too often, the two polarized sides on the issue begin either from a Biblicist or cultural framework, rather than a Trinitarian one. Therefore, the question here is really: how might we remove the issue of the ordination and marriage of homosexuals from this false dichotomy that is presented when the issue is viewed as an ethical one and place it in the realm of a Trinitarian, Christocentric, and patristic theology, answering it not from the basis of a cultural or Biblicist framework, but from the basis of God's economy and self-revelation in Jesus Christ as particularized in the vicarious humanity of Christ, the Great High Priest? A Trinitarian and Christocentric attempt at an answer to the issue might explore ordination and marriage as Sacraments or at least sacramental and start the discussion from an exploration of the Trinitarian and Christocentric understanding of ordination and marriage and build from there. That is to say, as Dragas said to Torrance about the *filioque* (but replacing "filioque" with "homosexual issue"): if you start with the homosexual issue, you won't get anywhere! But, if the discussion is begun with an exploration of the Trinitarian and Christocentric understanding of ordination and marriage as seen in the Greek fathers, perhaps, from there, a fruitful discussion might develop.

---

says something it must be taken at face value at all times (i.e., a proof-text).

The Orthodox-Reformed Dialogue here provides an inspirational framework.[77] An attempt at answering this question in such a way might include an exploration of Christ as vicarious Great High Priest in the writings of Cyril of Alexandria (regarding ordination) and the writings of Augustine against the Donatists (concerning the sacraments and by extension the sacramental nature of marriage) and John Chrysostom's writings on marriage symbolizing Christ and his Bride, the church. The Trinitarian and Christocentric sacramental approach to the issue might think about Torrance's critiques of the Roman Catholic dogma of the immaculate conception and the Protestant doctrine of inerrancy as both falling into the error of believing that the Word of God cannot come to the world except via a sinless medium.[78] If ordination and marriage are Trinitarian and Christocentric sacramental realities, can a possibly sinful and imperfect sacrament witness just as well to the grace of God in Jesus Christ? When the homosexual issue that divides churches so often today is explored from within this shared Trinitarian and theological framework (and, indeed, personal experience within mainline Protestantism, especially the PCUSA and TECUSA, would suggest to me that this framework is still shared), perhaps something closer to the "we confess" of the Orthodox-Reformed Dialogue might begin to take shape, rather than the many divisions in Christianity today on the issue.

---

77. The framework is essentially and most broadly: move away from looking at ethics *qua* ethics but rather look at ethics as *theological ethics*. Todd Speidell has written, most recently, a very helpful theological framing of ethics in *Fully Human in Christ* and David Torrance and Jock Stein in their edited volume *Embracing Truth*, Murray Rae and Graham Redding in their edited volume *More Than a Single Issue* (especially Alan Torrance's article), and Gary Deddo in his article "Why We're Gendered Beings" have each attempted more specifically to explore the ethics of homosexuality from a theological perspective (Speidell does this as well in parts of his book). Each of these works aims to move the discussion away from ethics and place it back into a theological framework. However, the suggestion here is that they have not gone far enough. If the framework of Torrance and the Orthodox-Reformed Dialogue of (a) the Trinitarian and Christocentric theology of the Greek fathers and (b) avoiding discussion of the issue (in the case of the Dialogue, the "filioque" and in the case of the issue here, "homosexuality") explicitly. That is to say, the above mentioned books do well, but they do not follow the example of the Orthodox-Reformed Dialogue inasmuch as they actually discuss homosexuality. Perhaps discussing "a theology of ordination," rather than "ordination of homosexuals" and discussion "a theology of marriage" rather than "marriage of homosexuals" would produce more agreement on the right grounds. The Theological Forum from the Church of Scotland General Assembly in 2017, notably spearheaded by Iain Torrance, drew similar theological conclusions to what I am proposing.

78. See Torrance, *The Mediation of Christ*, 40.

Final Considerations

One final question is really begged of an exploration of Thomas F. Torrance and the Orthodox-Reformed Dialogue, namely, how representative is Torrance of the Reformed or even Protestant tradition in his approach? As Nesteruk says, "Thomas Torrance knew Greek Patristics well and in his personal contacts with the present author he clearly indicated that in his perception of Christianity he was an orthodox with a capital "O."[79] Torrance viewed the Greek fathers and the Ecumenical Councils as normative for theology, he heavily critiqued Calvinism, he visited the Greek Orthodox Diocese of Alexandria, rather than Reformed churches as was traditional, during his Moderatorial visits, and he was honorarily ordained proto-presbyter in the Orthodox Church. Furthermore, exhibited in "Memorandum A," Torrance's ecclesiological understanding of the Reformed tradition as a Greek patristic tradition in relation to the western church as a movement of reform within it, rather than distinct from it, oozes of Torrancian commitments. Finally, the subsequent Orthodox-Reformed Dialogues did not carry the same sense of urgency that the "we confess" of the Dialogue on the Trinity carried. So, it must be admitted that in many ways the Orthodox-Reformed Dialogue is very Torrancian. Yet, therein lies its importance. Torrance spearheaded the Dialogue and trail-blazed his way to Constantinople, sure of his own Reformed and evangelical theological convictions, sure of the importance of the Reformation, but equally sure that the division between Reformed and Orthodox in matters of tradition did not detract from the substantial similarity they have in doctrine. Rallying other Reformed and Orthodox behind them, Torrance, Fouyas, and Dragas offer an example of what great movements and agreements can flower from a "deep theological rapport"[80] over the Trinitarian and Christocentric theology of the Greek fathers. If Torrance is not representative of the Reformed and Protestant traditions, well, he should be! Torrance is here doing the Reformation right and there is much to learn from him, Fouyas, Dragas, and the Orthodox-Reformed Dialogue.

The Trinitarian, Christocentric, and patristic "we confess" framework of ecumenical theology has much to offer the church today. It is the hope of this book that the study contained herein points to Torrance, Fouyas,

---

79. See "Universe, Incarnation, and Humanity," 214.

80. Torrance, "Introduction" to *Theological Dialogue between Orthodox and Reformed Churches*, 1:x.

and the Orthodox-Reformed Dialogue of the 1970s, 1980s, and 1990s as a profoundly positive example. Hopefully this book has pointed—and will continue to point—to the Orthodox-Reformed Dialogue and "The Agreed Statement on the Holy Trinity" as an excellent example in both content and method of the Trinitarian, Christocentric, and Patristic "we confess" of the truly ecumenical One, Holy, Catholic, and Apostolic Church.

PART 2

Primary Sources from the Orthodox-Reformed Theological Dialogue

Chapter 1

Address by President Dr James I. McCord, W.A.R.C. President to his All-Holiness the Ecumenical Patriarch, Dimitrios I, Istanbul, July 26, 1979

Your All-Holiness,

First of all, we, Reformed, are grateful for the Ecumenical leadership of the Orthodox Church. It is now more than 50 years since the call came from this historic Throne to Christians to unite. And one of the great blessings that has come to me in 30 years with the Ecumenical Movement has been working with Orthodox colleagues. One of thoses my neighbour and colleague, who is under Your jurisdiction, Professor Georges Florovsky.

The second thing I want to say is very close to the Orthodox, because of your concern and our concern for the Apostolic Faith. We think of you as the Church of the Holy Spirit, and John Calvin, one of our ancestors, has been called the theologian of the Holy Spirit.

And the third thing is the family that we represent the Reformed and the Presbyterian is the most international of all Protestant families. We go by different names in different parts of the world. On the continent of Europe, we are called Reformed, because in the sixteenth-century Reformation, the dominant issue was the faith. Our Church was then called first in France the Church of Jesus Christ Reformed according to the Word of God. In the British Isles, the problem tended to be one of polity or government, and, therefore, the name Presbyterian was given to us. We now represent nearly 150 autocephalous Churches around the world. Because of the commitment of the Reformed family to the whole Oikumene, we look forward to these days with You and Your Commission in Istanbul and to the opportunity to discuss with You the historic Apostolic Faith.

We pray for the blessing of the Holy Spirit on our discussion. We pray for the continued blessing of the Holy Spirit on You and Your people. You are very much in the thoughts and prayers of the Reformed world.

And we are grateful to God for Your heroic leadership of the faithful from this historic Patriarchate.

CHAPTER 2

Address by his All-Holiness the Ecumenical Patriarch Dimitrios I to the Delegation of the World Alliance of Reformed Churches, Istanbul, July 26, 1979

REVEREND AND HONOURABLE SIRS, The President, The General Secretary and representatives of the World Alliance of Reformed Churches,

Welcome to this city and to this historical Throne, which is the First of Eastern Orthodoxy. It is the first in the general structure of the Orthodox Church. It is especially so in the diaconia of the other Churches, and in its contribution to strengthening "the unity of the spirit in the bond of peace" (Eph.) among the Churches and among all men of good will.

We greet you in love and we receive you with great honour. You represent in the most official way the large and well-respected world of the Reformed Churches. You came here with the sacred and concrete purpose of making the official proposal for the opening of the Theological Dialogue with Orthodoxy. We shall favourably study this proposal and we shall forward it properly to all other Orthodox Churches in the spirit of service to the great cause of unity.

You have the great responsibility of representing the highest Body of the Reformed Churches, which is the World Alliance. You hold different posts, the most significant in the administration and in the theological thought of this Body. At this moment the two great families, of the Presbyterians and of the Congregationalists, and the more than 140 Reformed Churches and Confessions, from Europe, from North and Latin America, from Asia, from Africa and Australasia, have turned attention to this important visit of their Representatives.

To the great dates of your uniting movement of the last hundred years, i.e., the years 1875, 1891, and 1970, we think that you are adding with your visit and with your proposal the present year 1979 also. This will remain reciprocally as a historical point in the relations of our Churches.

The millions of your faithful are waiting for a positive response to their wholehearted wish and desire for the meeting, cooperation and growing-together in Dialogue with Orthodoxy.

If between you and us in questions of faith, practice, tradition and worship there are no common points of agreement—and definitely there are—yet on the other hand there are many common points which the two sides will underline and will evaluate through the contacts and dialogue.

The desire and the turning to the East since the time of Calvin and Zwingli up to the present is historically witnessed.

On our side the wish and prayer for rapprochement and the "unity of all" has always been constant.

We must proceed to the Dialogue with good will, with courage, with hope in our Lord. "The hope maketh not ashamed" (Rom. 5,5). And the Lord never belies those expectations put upon Him.

Addressing you again with a warm welcome, we assure you that we shall look forward with interest and trust to the fruits of the conversations which you will have in these days with our Synodical Commission on Inter-Christian Affairs.

Let the Lord be your help and inspirer in your common efforts.

So be it!

Chapter 3

Memoranda on Orthodox/Reformed Relations

—Thomas F. Torrance

MEMORANDUM A

'The Reformed Church' does not set out to be a new or another Church but to be a movement of reform within the One Holy Catholic and Apostolic Church of Jesus Christ, in obedience to its Apostolic foundation in him, and, through constant renewing of the Holy Spirit, seeks throughout its mission on earth steadily to be conformed to Christ as his Body, constantly presenting itself before God through him as a living sacrifice, solely to the glory of God, Father, Son and Holy Spirit. Thus while through the exigencies of history and changing cultures 'Reformed Churches' have arisen, and have taken on an 'autocephalous' character, similar to that of the Orthodox Churches, they are intrinsically committed to the unity of the One Church as the undivided Body of Christ, and continue to seek the realisation of that unity in space and time on the basis of the Apostolic Faith and Practice, which our Lord himself established with the saving economy of his life, death, resurrection and ascension, and with the gift of the Paraclete Spirit who was sent by the Father through him, and by him from the Father, to abide with and to guide the Apostolic Church throughout its earthly mission until he comes again.

The Reformed Church claims to be both 'Apostolic' and "Catholic' for it does not look to any other foundation than that of the Apostolic Church in what it received from Christ and in his One Spirit and handed on to the world through the Holy Scriptures and through a Ministry dependent on it. The Reformed Church interprets this Apostolic Tradition in agreement with and on the basis of the Catholic theology of the Ecumenical Councils of the undivided Church. The Apostles' Creed and the Nicene-Constantinopolitan Creed have preeminent place in its own faith and doctrine, but in the dogmatic understanding and appropriation of this the Reformed Churches have constantly taken their guidance from the classical Greek Theology, especially as taught by the great Alexandrian and Cappadocian theologians. The Churches which constitute the World Alliance of Reformed Churches have, through their historical and cultural ties in Western Christendom also been deeply influenced by the Augustinian tradition, which is most evident in its understanding of grace opposition to Pelagianism, in its doctrine of the Church as the Communion of the Elect, and in its conception of Sacrament; but in the doctrine of the Holy Trinity, in Christology, Soteriology and Eschatology they have, with John Calvin, taken their main orientation from the Greek Fathers, and those 'Western' Fathers, Irenaeus and Hilary, who belonged to this Greek tradition.

This orientation marks certain deep differences between the Reformed Churches and the Latin Churches, in Trinitarian theology, in the emphasis upon the Resurrection (the 'caput fidei' as Calvin in called it), and in the recovery of the *Epiclesis*, in an understanding of the Church as the Body of Christ, of Baptismal incorporation into him, and of Eucharistic union and communion with him. This is probably most evident in that epicletic dimension lifts the life, worship and communion of the Reformed ChurCh out of the hard causal and juridical structures of the Latin development which have so deeply characterised Western forms of thought in dogma, law and ecclesiastical institutions. Thus, for example, the Reformed understanding of the 'real presence' is much closer to that of Greek than that of Latin theology. In many respects the Reformed Church stands closest to the Anglican Church in the West, but differs from it in respect of the *Epiclesis* and its bearing upon history, and in that it has always insisted that the order of the Church is basically a *de fide* matter, at which point the 'non-episcopal' character of most Reformed Churches is to be understood. All non-Roman Churches in the West, and especially the Churches in the new world, have been deeply influenced by the notions of 'democracy' that have come out of the 'Protestant' centuries, and not least the nineteenth century, which have affected Church life and practice in a wide way. Yet into this the Reformed Church more than any other Church in the West has constantly asserted the belief that the Church is above all the Body of Christ united to him through his Spirit, that is, in Karl Barth's words, 'Christ's own earthly-historical form of existence, one Holy Catholic and Apostolic Church', so that throughout history the Church on earth is the provisional representation of the whole world of humanity, called, justified and sanctified in Christ. Moreover, against a democratic understanding of the Ministry, the Reformed Church has always insisted that the ministry is to be understood 'above and not from below', as deriving from Christ himself the Lord and Head of the Church and not from the membership of the Church.

The Reformed Church honours the Greek Orthodox Church for its faithfulness to Apostolic Faith and Practice, and to the Catholic theology of the Greek Fathers to which the whole Church of Christ in East and West is so deeply indebted. The Reformed Church also acknowledges that the Orthodox Church has developed a rich Church tradition of worship, life and activity, which transcend the historical and cultural milieu of the Byzantine empire and subsequent developments. It recognizes that during this long period forms of piety, personal and monastic, which are distinctive manifestations of the Christian faith, have grown up to become inalienable aspects of ecclesiastical life and essential to the tradition of Orthodox liturgical worship and witness. Some of these forms of piety are strange to the life and witness of the Reformed Churches which have developed in a different cultural and historical milieu and have come to emphasize the word rather than the icon, but Reformed Churches do not regard these differences in forms of piety as entering into the substance of the faith, or as ruling out genuine koinonia between them and the Orthodox Churches. On the other hand, the Reformed Churches appreciate the theological foundations of Orthodox worship and share with the Orthodox the conviction that all earthly forms of worship in the Church are a participation through the Spirit in the ongoing worship which the risen and enthroned Christ, the Lamb of God, who is both 'Offerer and Offering', constitutes in his own high Priestly self-presentation before the Father on behalf of all those whom he has redeemed and consecrated in union with himself. They believe that this sharing in the worship of the Father, which Christ himself is, is the heart of the Church's Eucharistic worship and communion, and that it is from that centre that the life and the activity of the church on earth are nourished and directed.

The Reformed Churches would not wish to enter into discussion with the Orthodox Church Without frank admission that there are elements in their own tradition which they must learn to 'unknow'(to borrow a term from the Pseudo-Dionysius), not least in their commitment to unity with other Churches in the One Holy Catholic and Apostolic Church. They believe that it is in ecumenical dialogue and fellowship that this 'unknowing' may take place, as deeper and deeper mutual koinonia in the Mystery of Christ takes place. Hence they enter into discussion ready for critical questions directed at them which may help them to be what they profess to be in their commitment to constant renewal and reformation. With a view to this, it may help at the outset to set out briefly the basic position of the Reformed Churches in respect of the Apostolic Faith in Practice.

The Apostolic Faith

Since the Reformed Churches believe that Apostolicity constitutes the criterion for its understanding of the Oneness, Holiness and Catholicity of the Church, they are committed to the Apostolic Canon of Holy Scripture and to the rule of faith and life which it provides for the church in all ages. They acknowledge the creeds of the ancient Church, received and formulated by the Nicene Fathers, and accept the doctrinal 'limits' of the great conciliar statements after Nicaea and Constantinople, especially of Ephesus and Chalcedon. While the Reformed Churches in the sixteenth and seventeenth centuries produced catechetical and confessional formulations for the guidance of their life, teaching and proclamation of the Gospel, these were and are held only a 'secondary standards' subordinate to the Apostolic Faith as mediated through the New Testament, and to the Catholic doctrine as defined by the Apostles' and Nicene-Constantinopolitan Creeds.

Thus the Reformed Churches believe in the Trinity and Unity of the Father, Son and Holy Spirit (the *mia ousia*, the *homoousia*, and *treis hypostaseis*). They are aware of the differing approaches in East and West and of different interpretations of the Unity in relation to the Trinity and of the Trinity in relation to the Unity of God, but do not regard any one of them as an explanation of the Mystery of God's Triunity which is more to be adored that expressed. But they believe that the Trinity and Unity of God is given to us in the Mystery of God's self-communication to his church in the Incarnation of his Son and of the Holy Spirit.

The Reformed Churches believe in Christ the eternal Son of God who became for us and our salvation, one undivided Person in two natures. They accept the dogmatic Christological confessions of the Orthodox Ecumenical Councils, and emphasize the vicarious Person and work of Jesus Christ in his birth, life, death, resurrection and ascension, and look for his coming again in great glory to judge and renew the whole creation.

The Reformed Churches believe that the Holy Spirit is God of God, no less than the Father and the Son, and that he proceeds from the Godhead through the Son. While the Reformed Church has traditionally accepted to *Filioque* clause of the Western Creed, by this is not meant that it holds that there are two Sources of the Spirit, or that the *Filioque* explains the hypostatic *idioma* of the Spirit. Rather it is intended to say that the Spirit proceeds from the Father through the Son, and leads us through the Son to the Father, yet in such a way that everything we say of the Father we say the Son and of the Spirit except 'Father', for the Spirit is not subordinated to the Sather or the son but is of equal honour and being with the Father and the Son in the one indivisible *homoousia*. They believe that the Holy Spirit is at work in the whole creation, sanctifying and bringing it to its *telos* in God, but that he dwells in the Church in a distinctive way, uniting us to Christ and making us participate in his saving reality, and leading an empowering the Church in the mission on which it has been sent by Christ the Saviour of the world.

Apostolic Practice

The Reformed Church believes that the pattern of its life in mission derives from the pattern which Jesus Christ constituted as the Incarnate son of God's love in our human existence and nature, and the pattern is exhibited through the Apostles as the rule of life. That pattern is indivisibly bound up with the Apostolic Ministry which derived immediately from Christ himself, and with the Holy Ministry which the Apostles themselves launched in dependence on their own Apostleship from Christ. The Reformed Church believes that the Holy Ministry thus mediated through the Apostles is the gift of Christ to and for his Church. While the Apostles were the earthly and historical instruments of that mediation, the gift of the Holy Ministry comes in and with the Gift of the Holy Spirit sent upon the Church from the Father, yet in such a way that the gift of the Ministry took its historical shape and order through the practice and ordinances of the Apostles whom Christ set at the head of his Church as its wise 'Masterbuilders'.

The Reformed Church believes that there is only one Priesthood, the Royal Priesthood of Jesus Christ himself, but that through the Spirit the Church as Christ's Body participates in that Priesthood in a distinctive way through serving it in the ministry of Word and Sacrament, and that within the Priesthood of the Church some members are set apart to participate in that priestly service in a particular authoritative way, preaching and acting in Christ's Name and place, in such a way that through their service of him, it is he himself who acts in and through them. The nature of their ministry derives from the servant form of Jesus Christ the Incarnate and Crucified Son of God, and is thus always a humble and never a lordly form of ministry. This Holy Ministry which cannot be separated from the Word and Mystery of Christ which it ministers is thus of divine origin, character and institution. It does not originate with the Church, but with Christ himself who set it in the Church and makes it efficacious through his own Presence and Spirit, promising it perpetuity and continuity throughout the ages in the building up of the Church and the extension of the Gospel throughout the world until he comes again.

In the historical tradition of the Reformed Churches, attempts were made at the Reformation to re-form the ministry and practice of the Church, which in the culture of Western countries had often become deformed in such a way as to obscure the true Face of in his Church. But this reforming of the ministry and practice of the Church took place—such was the intention and claim made—in accordance with the Apostolic Foundation and Pattern of the Church as it was discerned in the New Testament Scriptures and in the practice of the Early Church. It became distinctive of the Reformed Church that *episcope* was held to be lodged not individually in persons but corporately in the body of Presbyters, i.e., in the Presbytery as a whole. The 'Bishop' was understood to be the presiding Presbyter (*Proestos*), while ordination through 'the laying on of hands by the Presbytery' was mediated from generation to generation by the *diadoche episkopon/presbuteron*—that is to say, the Reformed Church sought to take its pattern of reform from the pattern of the Early Church before the bishop became separated from the presbytery over which he presided and attained the character of a 'lordly' figure exercising a juridical and magisterial function independently of the Presbyters over whom he presided. While in the

Western tradition, theologically there was held to be no higher 'order' than that of the Presbyter, who was ordained 'in order to the Eucharist', so that the Bishop was not held to be superior in order but only in jurisdiction, actually the Bishop became invested by canon law with princely powers so that he came to exercise a lordly function in his own independent right. Since that practice had given rise to so much worldliness and abuse in the Western Church, the Reformers sought to recover the 'servant form' of the ministry after the pattern of 'the Servant Form of Christ himself', and the humble, evangelical form of the early Church Bishop who did not lord it over the Eucharist but served Christ in the Eucharist as a steward of the mysteries of God.

In this way the Reformed Church came to operate with a twofold pattern of ministry: that of the presbyter or bishop who dispenses the mysteries of God in Word and Sacrament, and that of elder or deacon who prompts the congregation or people to receive the mysteries of God in Word and Sacrament. Each local Church has a council of these elder-deacons, presided over by the Presbyter-Bishops, after the pattern of the Eucharistic celebration in the Early Church. The local Councils of Churches are subordinate to the Presbytery which comprises all the ordained Presbyters and one representative from the elder-deacons, but the Presbytery has its own elected President known as the 'Moderator'. This Presbytery is recognised as a 'sacral court' having magisterial function, but in its turn it is subordinate along with other Presbyteries to a General Assembly, similarly comprised, which is presided over by its 'Moderator'. The national Reformed Churches are autocephalous like Orthodox Churches. But all the Reformed Churches are united through common Apostolic Faith and Practice (as they understand it), in a world-wide union known as 'The Alliance of Reformed Churches', in which, however, there are no special prerogatives of seniority, as in the Orthodox Church, and which constitutes no more than a *Communion* or Family of Reformed Churches. It is not claimed by the Reformed Churches that their order is derived from some Biblical 'blueprint', but only that it is 'agreeable to the Word of God', as they interpret the New Testament in the light of the Apostolic and early Catholic tradition, and that it is always open to revision and re-form in obedience to Jesus Christ and the Apostolic Foundation of the Church in him. The Reformed Churches have, therefore, a rather open outlook (perhaps more open than the Anglican and the Lutheran in certain respects) and it is this character they seek to maintain in all ecumenical discussion and all proposals for intercommunion or Church union. It is the theological foundation for Church life and order that is important for them, which requires Church law to be subordinated to the Gospel so that it may be used only to serve the rule of Christ and his Spirit in the Church.

There are clearly differences in ethos, practice and order between the Reformed and the Orthodox Churches, but the agreement in basic theology would appear to be deeply grounded. Hence it would seem best for serious discussions between the Orthodox and the Reformed to concern themselves with these fundamental issues in doctrine and from an agreement or consensus there to carry the discussion into the areas of Church, Ministry and Sacraments where divergences are most apparent.

In this case, it would be most helpful if discussions began with the doctrine of the *Holy Trinity*: and then moved from there into the doctrines of *the Son* and *the Spirit*, and then to the doctrine of the Eucharist. That would provide the right context for discussion about the Church and the Ministry. The conversations could aim at a clarification of the understanding which East and West, in this case the Orthodox and the Reformed, have of their common foundation in the Alexandrian and Cappadocian theology, to which the Conciliar Statements are so heavily indebted. At first glance it is suggested that deepest agreement could be reached on the basis of the Athanasian-Cyrilline theology, which is impeccably Orthodox, and which is so basic to the Reformed Church. The Cappadocian theology also deeply influenced the Reformed Church, not least through John Calvin, whose teaching was so indebted to and so close to that of St. Gregory Nazianzen that he was given the title 'ho theologos' by Philip Melanchthon. The Athanasian-Cyrilline theology carries a deeper grasp of the Vicarious Humanity of Christ which is of special significance for the Reformed, as also for the modern liturgical renewal, in which we are all engaged in some measure. It may well be the case that by approaching the doctrine of the Trinity in this way, we could cut behind the difference between East and West over the 'Filioque' clause, and establish full and deep agreement on the doctrine of the Holy Spirit as well as the doctrine of the Son—not least if we followed the Cappadocians (cf. Nazianzen's *Fifth Oration on the Spirit*), Hilary of Poitiers, and Calvin, in the 'apophatic' reserve they maintained in handling the 'images' used in elucidation of the Trinitarian relations in God.

From this basis it may be possible to cut behind the damaging dualism that separated the traditional 'Antiochene' and 'Alexandrian' approaches to

Christology and Soteriology, affecting the understanding of the Priesthood of Christ, and consequently of 'priesthood' in the Church and the Liturgy; but from this basis also it may be possible to cut behind the divergences not only between East and West but between the 'Chalcedonian' and 'non-Chalcedonian' positions in the East, which, it is now evident, have to do with deep epistemological and cosmological dualisms which have left their mark on later Byzantine thought in the East and Augustinian thought in the West. Further, this line of approach opens up classical Greek theology to fresh appreciation in the context of the modern scientific world, as that theology which is the most relevant of all for our modern scientific world, in its rejection of the ancient, mediaeval and modern dualisms, and in recovering the unitary understanding of the created universe so deeply embedded especially in the great Alexandrian understanding of the Incarnation and Creation. One steady effect of such a clarification would be the sifting clear of the central and basic Christian convictions from pseudo-theological and obsolete scientific notions derived from time-conditioned notions of a past culture. Out of this would emerge, in a deeper way than East/West or Roman Catholic/Evangelical Churches have been able to achieve so far, a common basis for agreement on the questions of authority in the Church and in the formulation and development of Christian doctrine, and if we can reach a deeper Trinitarian understanding of the creation, a common basis also for the relation between Christian Faith and the modern scientific world. It would appear that modern scientific understanding of the created universe which cuts away the old damaging dualisms of the past can help us to bridge the gap between *icon* and *word*, for example, which is so symptomatic of the divergence between the Orthodox and the Reformed.

MEMORANDUM B

Obviously in the ecumenical context, discussions on the Church, Ministry and Sacraments will have to take place. Certainly Reformed theology is well based for this, because of the work of Calvin, and of its classical 'de fide' understanding of these doctrines. Calvin was the first in the West to break with the Augustinian/Thomist dualist notion of the Church as body/soul (which yielded the dualism between legal institution and 'mystical body'), and the first really to give an adequate *theological* account of the Church as the Body of Christ in history, and thus to link the doctrine of the Church profoundly with the doctrine of Christ, the incarnate Son of God. (Calvin was here partially followed by the Tridentine Catechism, but that more realist and Christological conception of the Church remained abortive until Vatican II). At the same time Calvin was the first theologian in the West after Hilary (with the partial exception of St. Anselm) to lay the basis for a more adequate doctrine of the Holy Spirit, which is closely linked to the doctrine of Christ. Again, Calvin was the only one of the Reformers who broke with the Boethian/Thomist 'individualist' notion of 'person'. Here he follows in the tradition of Hilary of Poitiers and Richard of St. Victor (as well as Athanasius and Cyril of Alexandria), whose doctrine of the Trinity is the nearest in the West to the classical position of the Greek Church. These doctrines stand behind Calvin's understanding of the Church and Sacraments. Here another point of primary importance must be noted: Calvin's radical break with the Roman and Lutheran notion of 'space' or 'place' (determined by Aristotle's conceptions in the fourth book of his *Physics*), in which he followed closely the teaching of the Greek Fathers, Athanasius, Nazianzen, Nyssa and Cyril of Alexandria. It is at this point that divergences in the understanding of the Incarnation and the Real Presence arise between Calvin and the Latin tradition, which again throws Calvin's theology into the Eastern type.

There are, of course, problems in Calvin's theology, to which we must not shut our eyes. The most obvious relates to his doctrine of predestination with its apparent split in the doctrine of God, which gives a 'Nestorian' appearance: that is, a duality between the eternal God as he is in himself, and God as he manifests himself in his incarnate and redemptive form in Jesus Christ. The strangest thing is that Calvin does not follow the Latins (apart from Irenaeus and Hilary, who were really 'Greek' in their outlook and theology) in his Christology and Soteriology, but Athanasius and Cyril of Alexandria; so that this element of 'Nestorianism' does not derive from his Christology as such (although we should bear in mind the Scotist reaction against Thomist 'Eutychianism', mediated to Calvin through John Major along with his doctrine of the Trinity). Calvin learned from Cyril of Alexandria (specifically from Oecolampadius' Latin edition of Cyril's works) the enormous emphasis, which he made his own (including Cyril's vocabulary) on the servant obedience of the incarnate Son, which is so characteristic of the Reformed doctrine of Christ and Salvation. How then did the 'Nestorian' dualism in his doctrine of God come into Calvin's thought? Evidently it came partly from Augustine, to whom he was indebted for much of his doctrine of predestination, but also from the influence of Antiochene exegetes upon him, notably St. Chrysostom, reinforced by Calvin's openness to Jewish OT scholarship. But perhaps the decisive thing here is that he was influenced by the distinction begun by the Cappadocians between the eternal 'Being' of God and his 'Energies' (Calvin's thought stood so close to Nazianzen that Melanchthon actually transferred to Calvin the title the ancients gave to Nazianzen, 'ho theologos'). It was, alas, that dualism, backed by a resurrected Origenism and by Neoplatonic influence, which led Byzantine thought into a dualist outlook basically similar to the Augustinian. It would seem to me that at some time the ultimate doctrine of God behind Christology would require to be looked at, if we are to enter into any basic and fruitful discussions with the Orthodox. This could, in my view, be done best by reference to the teaching of St. Athanasius.

The Orthodox Church has problems of its own, which are deeper than most Orthodox theologians realise, and which may be summarised briefly by saying that its theology has tended in recent centuries (but going back to the post-Chalcedonian period) to rest upon the Cappadocian rather than upon the Athanasian-Cyrilline axis. It was owing to the Cappadocian basis, e.g. its tendency toward the double notion of 'substance', a generic and a particular (which was deepened by the Dionysian and Neoplatonic developments together with the revival of Aristotelian thought in the schools from Byzantium to Gaza), that Greek theology became trapped in a position in which those post-Chalcedonians who were opposed to dualism and who resented the Latin/Leonine interpretation of Chalcedon were denigrated as 'monophysite' heretics—a disastrous misunderstanding which resulted in the schism of the Copts from the Byzantines. The Copts and other 'non-Chalcedonians', were not really monophysite, for they grounded their theology very rigorously on Cyril of Alexandria, as is evident, for example, in the physics of John Philoponos of Alexandria (not to be confused with 'John the Grammarian'). The rejection by the Greek Orthodox, now Byzantine, of these 'non-Chalcedonians', had the effect of deepening the dualism in their own thought, in which they were prone, with emphasis upon the apophatic side of that dualism, to oppose the Latins with their emphasis on the cataphatic side of the same dualism.

These are problems that require to be solved, if deep ecumenical relations are to be achieved. The modern Greek Orthodox have already taken considerable steps in this direction, largely through Methodios of Aksum (now of Thyateira and Great Britain), in respect of the difference between the 'Chalcedonians' and 'non-Chalcedonians' (especially the Coptic, Ethiopic and Syrian Christians), which augurs well for their discussions with us. The depth of the problem we face in the West can be seen from the decisively Latin and distorted Leonine and Augustinian slant given to the interpretation of the Greek Fathers one finds in such a work as that of the great Grillmeier, almost wholly uncritically accepted by Western scholars!

It would seem to me in view of all this that a deep-going dialogue on the most fundamental issues between the Reformed and the Orthodox would serve the whole Faith and Order work of the Ecumenical movement, and lay a sounder basis for agreement and unity in the area of Church, Ministry and Sacraments.

My proposal, therefore, which I have already outlined to the Greek Orthodox Patriarchs and Archbishops in the Middle East, is that our discussions should begin with the doctrine of the *Holy Trinity*; and move from there into the doctrines of the Son and the Spirit, and then into the doctrines of the Eucharist and the Church and the Ministry (probably in that order). The basic question I would set down for this discussion would be whether there is not a far-reaching difference between the teaching of Athanasius and Cyril on the one hand and that of the Cappadocians on the other hand. The problem is sharpest at the point where the Cappadocians speak of God the Father unreservedly in terms of *aitia, pege* and *arche,* but not of the Son or of the Spirit, whereas Athanasius' great principle ran that we say of the Son everything we say of the Father, except 'Father'. Bound up with this difference is the fact that the Cappadocians formalised the meaning of the terms *'ousia'* and *'hypostasis'* in the formula: *'One ousia, three hypostaseis'*, thereby moving in an Aristotelian direction, whereas for Athanasius the use of these terms does not depend on any formal defining of them but on that to which they refer and by which their meaning is wholly governed—which represents a more elastic and dynamic use of theological terms. The danger of the Cappadocian position was pointed out by Cyril of Alexandria in protesting against the use of *aitia* of intra-Trinitarian relations. The Cappadocians were in a difficulty, for their formula could easily lead into an apparently 'tritheist' position, since they tended to use *'ousia'* in a generic and not in a concrete sense; consequently they had to defend themselves against such a charge and did so (see especially Nyssa's work 'That There are not Three Gods') . But they did so at the expense of a distinction between the Deity of the Father as wholly underived, 'uncaused' Deity, and the Deity of the Son and of the Spirit as eternally 'caused ' or derived. At the same time, this led to the tendency to identify 'Father' = the Godhead with 'Father' = the Person of the Father. It was, in my view, this Cappadocian distinction that provided the ground for the problem of the understanding of the procession of the Spirit when East and West split over the notorious '*filioque*' clause added by the West to the Nicene-Constantinopolitan Creed, without the authority of an Ecumenical Council, and the Greeks responded by insisting on the procession of the Spirit from 'the Father *only*' which implied 'from the *Person* of the Father'. If the Son and the Spirit are eternally 'caused' by the Father, how can it be said that the Spirit proceeds from the Son so described? But if the Spirit does not proceed from the Son as well as the Father, then, for the West, that would import a damage to belief in the unqualified Deity of the Son. Moreover the problem arose on both sides of whether the One God that is the Godhead can be thought of as 'Person', or whether 'Person' is to be restricted to the three 'Persons' of the Father, the Son and the Spirit. For the Greeks that difficulty was not so acute as for the Latins, since the Greek formula 'from the Father only' identified the 'Father' with the 'Person of the Father'. Other questions enter into this '*filioque*' dispute, with some right and some wrong on both sides, but the basic difficulty which ought not to have arisen comes from the Cappadocian distinction in the Trinity—which is, incidentally, allied at a second-order level to their distinction between the 'Being' of God and his 'Energies'. I would maintain that had the Greek Church remained steadfast to the Athanasian-Cyrilline basis, the whole problem, and the division that followed it, would probably not have risen: nor would the Greeks have lapsed into their characteristic Byzantine dualism. In other words, by returning to the impeccably Orthodox and non-dualist basis of Athanasius and Cyril we ought to be able to cut behind the schism between East and West over the '*filioque*', and at the same time provide a deeper basis for the healing of the rift between Evangelical and Catholic wings of Church, not to mention the rift between the Orthodox and the so-called 'Monophysite' Churches.

I believe that if we can agree on a basic doctrine of the Trinity, which must be far nearer to the traditional doctrine of the East and West (cf. *'An Ecumenical Consensus on the Doctrine of the Trinity'* prepared by the Académié Internationale des Sciences Religieuses), and we can go on to clear up problems regarding Christology, cut behind the damaging dualism which severs theology into 'Antiochene' and 'Alexandrian' camps, with unfortunate effects in the liturgy as well. For example, the Byzantine liturgy through Chrysostom's influence has taken on dualist Antiochene elements, evident not least in the notion of the Priesthood of Christ and the priest hood of the Church—cf. here the Commentary on the Liturgy by Nicholas Cabasilas. But we must also deal especially with the insidious effect of the Aristotelian doctrine of space/ place, reintroduced into the Greek Church, against the Athanasians, Cappadocians, and Cyrillians, by John of Damascus, with serious problems in Christology and even in the doctrine of the Trinity, not to mention epistemology and cosmology. Thus I believe we could more or less settle certain basic issues in Christology—which cannot but help East and West, and which would cut behind those divergences in the doctrine of the Eucharist and the Ministry which are related to the doctrines of Grace, the Real Presence, Sacrifice, etc., but also to the concept of the continuity of the Church and its Ministry in the Eucharistic Life of the People of God. Far from weakening the notion of the real presence of the risen Christ in the Church and the Sacraments, and far from damaging the notions of continuity and dynamic stability of the ministry throughout history, this can only deepen and strengthen them.

Finally, I would argue that this line of approach opens up classical Greek theology to fresh appreciation in the context of the modern scientific world, which makes it clear that that theology is the most relevant of all for our modern scientific world, as well as for the union of the whole Church in Christ today. One steady effect it has is to help us to cleanse our thought of pseudo-theological concepts which are little more than passing, time-conditioned notions derived from an obsolete culture that have, unfortunately, been given the sanction of ecclesiastical authority in the past. Out of this there would naturally emerge, in a deeper way than the East/West or Roman Catholic/Evangelical Churches have been able to treat of it so far, the problem of *authority* in the formulation and development of Christian doctrine. I see no reason why we should not at this tricky point also come to a closer agreement than has hitherto been possible in the traditional patterns of ecumenical discussion, in which we begin from the wrong end. But it would involve a radical rethinking of the basis of canon law, which in West and East, has taken into itself (e.g., through Leo the Great and Justinian) the dualist orientation of Stoic legal thought. This could be undermined with considerable effectiveness by reference to the non-du a list notions of physical law which we see already in John Philoponos and now in the post-Einsteinian non-dualist understanding of the created order. This would have immense benefit for the Roman Catholic

Church in the impasse in which they find themselves with respect to the projected *Lex Fundamentalis Ecclesiae,* but also for the Orthodox, who not only behind the Iron Curtain but in the Middle East and Ethiopia have to face the problems posed by Marxist thought. The latter will clearly be of increasing significance for the Orthodox Church in Muslim countries. To reach any really significant fruit in this direction we would have to develop, as the Church has not yet done, a *Trinitarian understanding of the creation.*

CHAPTER 4

Agreed Statement on the Holy Trinity

WE CONFESS TOGETHER THE evangelical and ancient Faith of the Catholic Church in 'the uncreated, consubstantial and coeternal Trinity', promulgated by the Councils of Nicaea (AD 325) and Constantinople (AD 381). 'This is the Faith of our baptism that teaches us to believe in the Name of the Father, of the Son and of the Holy Spirit. According to this Faith there is one Godhead, Power and Being of the Father, of the Son, and of the Holy Spirit, equal in Honour, Majesty and eternal Sovereignty in three most perfect Subsistences (en trisi teleiotatais hypostasesin), that is, in three perfect Persons'(trisi teleiois prosopois) (Ep. Syn. Constantinopolitanae, AD 382).

THE SELF-REVELATION OF GOD AS FATHER, SON AND HOLY SPIRIT

According to the Holy Gospel God has revealed himself in the Father, the Son and the Holy Spirit, as *'through the Son we have access to the Father in one Spirit'* (Eph 2.18). Of decisive importance in the Church's formulation of belief in the Holy Trinity was the dominical institution of Baptism *'in the name of the Father and of the Son and of the Holy Spirit '* (Mt 28.19). As Basil expressed it: '*We are bound to be baptized in the terms we have received and to profess faith in the terms in which we have been baptized*' (Ep.125.3). Other triadic formulations in the New Testament reinforced this belief, such as the benediction: '*The grace of the Lord Jesus Christ and the love of God and the communion of the Holy Spirit be with you all*' (2 Cor

12.14). The ancient Catholic Church laid great stress on the words of our Lord: *'All things have been delivered to me by my Father; and no one knows the Son except the Father; and no one knows the Father except the Son, and any one to whom the Son chooses to reveal him'* (Mt 11.27; Lk 10.22). With this they conjoined the words of St Paul about *'what God has revealed to us through the Spirit; for the Spirit searches everything, even the depths of God'* (1 Cor 2.10) (Thus John of Damascus, *De fide orthodoxa* 1.1). This is the foundation of the Apostolic doctrine of the Trinity in Unity and the Unity in Trinity: one Being, three Persons.

To believe in the Unity of God apart from the Trinity is to limit the truth of divine Revelation. It is through the divine Trinity that we believe in the divine Unity, and through the divine Unity that we believe in the divine Trinity. *'There is one eternal Godhead in Trinity, and there is one glory of the Holy Trinity... If the doctrine of God* (he theologia) *is now perfect in Trinity, this is the true and only divine worship* (theosebeia), *and this is the beauty and the truth, it must have always been so'* (Athanasius, *Con. Ar.* 1.18).

THREE DIVINE PERSONS

In the New Testament witness to God's Revelation *'the Father'*, *'the Son'*, and *'the Holy Spirit'* are unique and proper names denoting three distinct Persons or real Hypostases which are neither exchangeable nor interchangeable while nevertheless of one and the same divine Being. There is one Person of the Father who is always the Father, distinct from the Son and the Spirit; and there is another Person of the Son who is always the Son, distinct from the Father and the Spirit; and another Person of the Holy Spirit who is always the Spirit distinct from the Father and the Son. In this Trinity *'One is not more or less God, nor is One before and after Another'*, *'for there is no greater or less in respect of the Being or the consubstantial Persons'* (Gregory the Theologian, *Or.* 31.14; 40.43). All three Persons are coeternal and coequal. They are all perfectly one in the identity of their Nature and perfectly consubstantial in their Being. Each Person is himself Lord and God, and yet there are not three Lords or Gods, but only one Lord God, and there is only one and the same eternal Being of the Father, the Son and the Holy Spirit. The Father, the Son and the Holy Spirit are perfectly and completely consubstantial in their mutual indwelling of one another and in their containing (*perichoresis*) of one another. *'The Trinity praised, worshipped and adored, is one and indivisible and without degrees* (aschematistos), *and he is united without confusion, just as the Monad also is distinguished in thought without division. For the threefold doxology, "Holy, Holy, Holy is the Lord" offered by those venerable living beings, denotes the three perfect Persons, just as in the word "Lord" they indicate his one Being'* (Athanasius, In ill. om. 6). The Holy Trinity is thus perfectly homogeneous and unitary, both in the threeness and oneness of God's activity, and in the threeness and oneness of his own eternal unchangeable Being. What God the Father is toward us in Christ and in the Spirit he is inherently and eternally in himself, and what he is inherently and eternally in himself he is toward us in the Incarnation of his Son and in the Mission of the Spirit. *'As it always was, so it is even now; and as it now is, so it always was and is the Trinity, and in him* (en aute) *Father, Son and Holy Spirit'* (Athanasius, Ad Ser. 3.7). *'In the Godhead alone the Father is properly Father, and since he is the only Father, he is and was, and always is. And the Son is properly the Son, and the only Son. And of them it holds good that the Father is always called Father, and the Son is and always called Son. And the Holy Spirit is always the Holy Spirit, whom we have believed to be of God, and to be given from the Father through the Son. Thus the Holy Trinity remains invariable, known in one Godhead'* (Athanasius, Ad Ser. 4.6).

While the three Divine Persons differ from one another precisely as Father, Son and Holy Spirit, they are nevertheless conjoined in all their distinctiveness, for the entire and undivided Godhead resides in each Person, and each Person dwells in or inheres in the Other; so that the whole of one Person is imaged in the whole of the Other. In the terms used by Athanasius, *'There is only one Form* (eidos) *of Godhead'* (Athanasius, De syn. 52; Con. Ar. 3.16). Thus the Son reveals the Father as his complete image, and the Spirit does the same to the Son. The Father is revealed through the Son in the Holy Spirit, and it is in the Spirit and through the Son that we come to the Father. Each and all reveal the whole Godhead, and thus none can be regarded as being partial in any way as compared with the other two: each Person is '*whole God*' and the '*whole God*' is in each Person. Since '*God is Spirit*' (John 4.24) the '*whole God*' and '*each Person*' and all relations within the Holy Trinity are to be understood in a completely spiritual way.

ETERNAL RELATIONS IN GOD

The three Divine Persons are also conjoined through their special relations. Thus the Son is eternally begotten of the Father and the Spirit eternally proceeds from the Father and abides in the Son, in ineffable ways that are beyond all time (*achronos*), beyond all origin (*anarchos*), and beyond all cause (*anaitios*). The generation of the Son and the procession of the Spirit are unknowable mysteries which cannot be explained by recourse to human or creaturely images, although some images (e.g. Light from Light) may provide a way for us to grasp some aspects of the reality to which they are used to refer (cf. Athanasius, *Con. Ar.* 2.36; Cyril of Jerusalem, *Cat.* 11.11). They indicate distinctions in relations not partitions or divisions. '*Differentiated as the Persons are, the entire and undivided Godhead is one in Each*'. '*Each of these Persons is entirely united to those with whom he is conjoined, as he is with himself, because of the identity of Being and Power that is between them*' (Gregory the Theologian, *Or.* 31.14, 16). The three Persons of the Holy Trinity are thus to be heard and known, worshipped and glorified 'as one Person (prosopon)' (Didymus, *De Trin.* 2.36; Cyril of Alexandria, *In Jn.* 15.1).

The three Divine Persons are also inseparably conjoined in all the manifestations of God's activity, in creation, providence, revelation, and salvation, as they are consummated in the Incarnate Economy of the Son. In fact all divine activity begins with the Father, extends through the Son and reaches its fulfilment in the Spirit. Thus, as St Basil taught, creation is initiated by the Father, effected by the Son and perfected by the Spirit (*De Spir. Sanct.* 16.38).

THE ORDER OF DIVINE PERSONS IN THE TRINITY

In the Trinitarian formulae of the New Testament, as Gregory the Theologian, among others, pointed out, there is a variation in the order in which 'the Father', 'the Son', and the 'Holy Spirit' are mentioned, which indicates that the order does not detract from full equality between the three Divine Persons (Gregory the Theologian, *Or.* 36.15). Nevertheless, as we learn from the institution of Holy baptism, there is a significant coordination which places the Father first, the Son second, and the Spirit third (cf. Athanasius, *Ad Ser.* 3.5 ; Basil, *Ep.* 125.3). The priority of the Father does not imply that there is something more in him compared to the Son, for all that the Father is the Son is apart from 'Fatherhood', and likewise all that the Son is the Spirit is apart from 'Sonship'. Thus the order inherent in the Trinitarian relations is grounded on the fact that the Son is begotten of the Father and the Spirit proceeds from the Father. This applies also to the unique revelation of the Father through the Incarnation of his only begotten Son and the sending of the Holy Spirit by the Father in the name of the Son.

This priority of the Father or Monarchy of the Father within the Trinity does not detract from the fact that the Father is not properly (*kurios*) Father apart from the Son and the Spirit, that the Son is not properly Son apart from the Father and the Spirit, and that the Spirit is not properly Spirit apart from the Father and the Son. Hence the *Monarchia* of the Father is perfectly what it is in the Father's relation to the Son and the Spirit within the one indivisible Being of God. '*The perfection of the Holy Trinity is an indivisible and single Godhead*' (Athanasius, *Ad Ser.* 1.33).

TRINITY IN UNITY AND UNITY IN TRINITY, THE ONE MONARCHY

Since there is only one Trinity in Unity, and one Unity in Trinity, there is only one indivisible Godhead, and only one *Arche* (arche) or *Monarchia* (monarchia). As such, however, Gregory the Theologian reminds us, '*It is a Monarchy that is not limited to one Person*' (Or. 29.2). '*The Godhead is one in Three, and the Three are One, in whom all the Godhead is, or, to be more precise, who are the Godhead*' (Or. 39.11). '*Each person is God when considered in himself; as the Father, so the Son, and as the Son, so the Holy Spirit; the Three One God when contemplated together; Each God because consubstantial; one God because of the Monarchy. I cannot think of the One without being enlightened by the splendour of the Three; not can I distinguish them without being carried back to the One*' (Gregory the Theologian, Or. 40.41). '*In proclaiming the divine Monarchia we do not err, but confess the Trinity, and Trinity in Unity, One Godhead of the Father, Son and Holy Spirit* (ten triada, monada en triadi, kai triada en monadi, mian theoteta patros kai huiou, kai hagiou pneumatos) (Epiphanius, *Haer.* 62.3). The *mia arche* or *Monarchia* is inseparable from the Trinity, the *Monas* from the *Trias*. As such the Monarchy of the Father within the Trinity is not exclusive of the Monarchy of the whole undivided Trinity in relation to the whole of creation. Hence all worship and glorification by the creature is offered '*to God the Father through the Son and in the Spirit* ' or '*to the Father with the Son and together with the Holy Spirit* ', that is, to the one indivisible God who is Three in One and One in Three, the Holy Trinity who is blessed for ever.

PERICHORESIS: THE MUTUAL INDWELLING OF FATHER, SON AND HOLY SPIRIT

The Holy Trinity remains invariable, known in one Godhead and one Monarchy, but in which Each of the three Divine Persons indwells and is indwelt by the Others. *'They reciprocally contain One Another, so that One permanently envelopes, and is permanently enveloped by, the Other whom he yet envelopes'* (Hilary, *De Trin.* 3.1). It is in the light of this eternal *perichoresis* of the three Divine Persons in God, or the co-indwelling and co-inhering of the Father, the Son and the Holy Spirit in One Another, that we are to understand the mission of the Holy Spirit from the Father and the gift of the Holy Spirit by the Son. The Holy Spirit proceeds from the Father, but because of the unity of the Godhead in which each Person is perfectly and wholly God, he proceeds from the Father through the Son for the Spirit belongs to and is inseparable from the Being of the Father and of the Son. He receives from the Son and through him is given to us. Thus *'We believe in the Holy Spirit, the Lord and Giver of Life, who proceeds from the Father, who with the Father and the Son is worshipped and glorified, who spoke by the prophets.'* (The Nicene-Constantinopolitan Creed). It is precisely with the doctrine of the consubstantiality and Deity of the Holy Spirit that the proper understanding of the Holy Trinity is brought to its completion in the theology and worship of the Church. And it is with the doctrine of the Trinity that the adoration and knowledge of God reach their perfection. This is the faith of the One, Holy, Catholic and Apostolic Church, that we worship One God in Trinity and Trinity in Unity.

ONE BEING, THREE PERSONS

The faith and confession of the *'One Being* (ousia), *Three Persons'* (Synod of Alex, 362/1) does not rest on any preconception or definition of the Divine Being, but on the very Being of God as he has named himself *'I am who I am/I shall be who I shall be'* (Ex 3.14), the ever-living and self-revealing God who truly and really is, besides whom there is no other God. This revelation of God as *'he who is who he is'* is mediated to us in the Gospel through the one act of God the Father, through the Son and in the Spirit. Thus in the doctrine of the Holy Trinity the 'One Being' of God does not refer to some abstract essence, but to the 'I am' (*ego eimi*) of God, the eternal living Being which God is of himself (Athanasius, *Con. Ar.* 3.6; 4.1; *De syn.* 34–36;

De decr. 22). Similarly the faith and confession of the Unity in Trinity and Trinity in Unity does not presuppose some prior definition of the relation of the three Divine Persons to the one Divine Being or vice versa; it rests on the one revelation of God the Father which is given us through Jesus Christ and his Spirit.

Thus in confessing the Divine Unity in Trinity we do not presuppose precise knowledge of 'what' God is in his One Being or 'how' he is Three in One and One in Three, but we believe in him as One God, the Father, the Son and the Holy Spirit, and profess knowledge of him in accordance with this one revelation handed on to the Church through the Apostles. That is the one Faith in which we are baptized and on which the whole Church rests.

THE APOSTOLIC AND CATHOLIC FAITH

In the words of St Athanasius: 'It is the very tradition, teaching and faith of the Catholic Church from the beginning, which the Lord gave, the Apostles preached and the Fathers kept upon which the Church is founded . . . that there is a Trinity, Holy and complete, confessed to be God in Father, Son and Holy Spirit, having nothing foreign or external, nor composed of one who creates and one who is originated, but all creative, consistent, indivisible in nature, one in activity. The Father does all things through the Word in the Holy Spirit. Thus, the Unity of the Holy Trinity is preserved and thus One God is preached in the Church, who is over all and through all and in all (Eph 4.16)—"over all" as Father, as beginning and fountain; "through all" through the Word; but "in all" in the Holy Spirit. It is a Trinity not only in name and form of speech, but in truth and actuality. For as the Father is he who he is, so also his Word is one who is God over all, and the Holy Spirit is not without existence but truly exists and subsists.' (*Ad Ser.* 1.28)

Chapter 5

Significance Features
A Common Reflection on the Agreed Statement

—Thomas F. Torrance

THE THEOLOGICAL ORIENTATION OF the Agreed Statement is governed by the fact that it is only through God that God may be known. The self-revelation of God as the Father, the Son, and the Holy Spirit provides the framework within which alone it is to be interpreted. It is fidelity to the supreme truth that through Christ and in one Spirit we have access to the Father which opens a way through divergent traditions in the East and West for ecumenical agreement.

(1) TRINITARIAN LANGUAGE

Throughout the Statement attention is given to the fact that human language when applied to God is inevitably and rightly stretched beyond its ordinary or conventional sense if it is to serve the purpose intended. Accordingly terms like οὐσία, ὑπόστασις and φύσις borrowed by the Church from Greek are consistently handled in the new shape given to them as they are harnessed in the service of God's trinitarian self-revelation. Thus no use is made of Aristotle's distinction between primary and secondary substance which has troubled western theology, while Latin translations like 'substance' or 'essence' of more concrete Greek notions of being are usually avoided. Similarly the terms οὐσία and φύσις are not used in an abstract generic sense. The doctrine of the Holy Trinity expounded here is: One God, Three Persons, not Three Persons, One Nature.

Care has been taken in this Statement to recall our Lord's teaching that 'God IS Spirit'. This means that terms like οὐσία, ὑπόστασις or φύσις when applied to God must be understood in a wholly spiritual, personal yet genderless way. It also means that any images taken from creaturely being have to be understood in a diaphanous or 'see-through' way, in which they are used like lenses through which vision take place, but which are not themselves projected into Deity. They are used like all biblical and theological terms spiritually beyond the images themselves to truth independent of them. Hence when the incarnate Son is said to be the Image of the Father, and the Holy Spirit is spoken of as the Image of Christ, stress is laid upon a wholly spiritual way of understanding the consubstantial relation of the incarnate Son to the Father and of all hypostatic relations in God, which cuts away arguments advanced by the Arians in reading back the Images of creaturely sonship and fatherhood into God.

Of particular significance is the deepening of the Nicene conception of οὐσία through its coordination with the divine 'I am who I am/I shall be who I shall be', on the one hand, and with the coinherence of the three Persons in the unity of the Godhead, on the other hand. The effect of this to give the term οὐσία a personal meaning under the impact of divine Revelation, and to develop the understanding of οὐσία as being in its internal relations along with ὑπόστασις as being in objective relations. Thus ὑπόστασις is used to denote the three divine Persons in the distinctive otherness of their relations with one another within the oneness of the οὐσία of the Godhead. The words for 'face' (πρόσοπον) and 'name' are also allied to ὑπόστασις which has the effect of giving it the meaning of self-identifying personal being. It was through this unique coordination of the concepts of οὐσία and ὑπόστασις together with the coinherent relations of the divine hypostases divine hypostases who are the consubstantial Trinity, that birth was given to the concept of 'person' and of 'personal' unknown before in the ancient tradition of either the Hebrews of the Greeks. The relations between persons are integral to what persons are—which holds uncreated way in the Trinity and in creaturely way way in human being. It is in this sense, not in a subjective or psychological sense, that the Statement on the Holy Trinity uses the terms 'person' and 'personal'.

(2) THE MONARCHY

Of far-reaching importance is the stress laid upon the Monarchy of the Godhead in which all three divine Persons share, for the whole indivisible Being of God belongs to each of them as it belongs to all of them together. This is reinforced by the unique conception of coinherent or perichoretic relations between the different Persons in which they completely contain and interpenetrate one another while remaining what they distinctively are in their otherness as Father, Son and Holy Spirit. God is intrinsically Triune, Trinity in Unity and Unity in Trinity. There are no degrees of Deity in the Holy Trinity, as is implied in a distinction between the underived Deity of the Father and the derived Deity of the Son and the Spirit. Any notion of subordination in God is completely ruled out. The perfect simplicity and the indivisibility of God in his Triune Being mean that the ἀρχή or μοναρχία cannot be limited to one Person, as Gregory the Theologian pointed out. While there are inviolable distinctions within the Holy Trinity, this does not detract from the truth that the whole Being of God belongs to each divine Person as it belongs to all of them and belongs to all of them as it belongs each of them, and thus does not detract from the truth that the Monarchy is One and indivisible, the Trinity in Unity and the Unity in Trinity.

The doctrine of the Monarchy that is not limited to one Person, and the doctrine of the περιχώρησις of the three Divine Persons, or their reciprocal containing of one another, when taken together, may help toward a fuller understanding of the mission of the Holy Spirit from the Father and gift of the Holy Spirit by the Son. As the Agreed Statement says: 'The Holy Spirit proceeds from the Father, but because of the unity of the Godhead in which each Person is perfectly and wholly God, he proceeds from the Father through the Son for the Spirit belongs to and is inseparable from the Being of the Father and of the Son'. A further study in depth of this procession might help us to find ways of cutting behind the division between the East and the West over the so-called '*filioque*', for it does not allow of any idea of the procession of the Spirit from two ultimate principles or ἀρχαι.

(3) ECUMENICAL SIGNIFICANCE

The Statement on the Holy Trinity is thus of considerable ecumenical significance in offering an approach to the doctrine of the Trinity which is neither from the Three Persons to the One Being of God, nor from the One Being of God to the Three Persons. The account of the Trinity given by the Statement stresses at one and the same time the Trinity and the Unity of God, through guidance taken mostly from Athanasius and Gregory the Theologian. As such it cuts across mistaken polarised views of the doctrine of the Holy Trinity according to which Latin theology moves from the Oneness of God to the three Persons of the Father, the Son and the Holy Spirit, while Greek theology moves from the three Persons of the Father, the Son and the Holy Spirit to the Oneness of God. What is provided by the Agreed Statement of the Orthodox theologians in the East and the Reformed theologians in the West is preeminently a Statement on the Triunity of God as Trinity in Unity and Unity in Trinity.

Chapter 6

Photos

From the back of the photo: "Photograph taken at the Greek Consulate General commemorating H. E. the Archbishop Methodios of Thyateira and Great Britain's visit to Edinburgh in May 1980." Archbishop Methodios is on Torrance's right.

Part 2: Primary Sources from the Orthodox-Reformed Theological Dialogue

This photo depicts a gathering hosted by Sir Reo Stakis in Edinburgh to celebrate the Honorary Doctor of Divinity degree granted to The Ecumenical Patriarch Bartholomew in 1996. Front row from left: two unknown Greek women; Rev Dr Margaret Forrester; Archbishop Mario Conti (Roman Catholic Archbishop of Glasgow); The Rt Rev Dr John McIndoe (Moderator of the General Assembly in 1996); The Ecumenical Patriarch; Sir Reo Stakis; Archbishop be Methodius Fouyas; unknown Greek woman; unknown Greek man

Middle row from left: Rev Charles Robertson; unknown man in a tie; 2 unknown bearded Greek priests; Metropolitan John Zizioulas; unknown clean shaven man; unknown Greek priest with shaded glasses; unknown man with a moustache; unknown bearded Greek priest

Back row from left: unknown Greek man with a bow tow; the Very Rev Dr James Harkness (who had been Moderator the previous year); Prof Iain Torrance; the Rt Rev Richard Holloway (Bishop of Edinburgh of the Scottish Episcopal Church); five unknown men; Greek priest with the white forked beard is the Rev John Maitland-Moir (a Scot who became an Orthodox priest); T. F. Torrance; Rev Maxwell Craig ; Fr George Dragas; three unknown men

Torrance wearing his protopresbyter cross

Torrance and Patriarch Bartholomew I embracing at the 1996 celebration of the anniversary of New College

Part 2: Primary Sources from the Orthodox-Reformed Theological Dialogue

Torrance conversing with unknown Orthodox priests

From the left: Archbishop Methodios, Dr. Hew Torrance (Iain and Morag Torrance's son, Patriarch Bartholomew I, and T. F. Torrance in the back

According to Iain Torrance (in personal correspondence), Torrance was given this protopresbyter cross by Archbishop Methodios. It was specially and very carefully designed by Archbishop Methodios in blue, which Archbishop Methodios thought was a Church of Scotland color, and in design it used the cross/crosslets of Jerusalem which also appear in Torrance's coat of arms. Archbishop Methodios also designed the cross to depict the *Salvator Mundi* rather than the *Theotokos*, in light of Torrance's great Christological emphasis in his theology.

Bibliography

Anatolios, Khaled. *Athanasius: The Coherence of His Thought*. New York: Routledge, 2004.
———. *Retrieving Nicaea: The Development and Meaning of Trinitarian Doctrine*. Grand Rapids: Baker Academic, 2011.
Athanasius the Great, St., and Didymus the Blind. *Works on the Spirit PPS43*, translated by Mark DelCogliano, Andrew Radde-Gallwitz, and Lewis Ayres and edited by John Behr. Crestwood, NY: St. Vladimir's Seminary Press, 2011.
Ayres, Lewis. *Augustine and the Trinity*. Cambridge: Cambridge University Press, 2010.
———. "The Fundamental Grammar of Augustine's Trinitarian Theology." In *Augustine and His Critics: Essays in Honour of Gerald Bronner*, edited by Robert Dodaro and George Lawless, 51–76. London: Routledge, 2000.
———. *Nicaea and Its Legacy*. Oxford: Oxford University Press, 2004.
———. "Remember that you are Catholic (serm 52.2): Augustine on the Unity of the Triune God." In *Journal of Early Christian Studies* 8, no. 1 (2000) 39–82.
Baker, Matthew. "The Eternal 'Spirit of the Son': Barth, Florovsky and Torrance on the Filioque." *International Journal of Systematic Theology* 12, no. 4 (2010) 382–403.
———. "Correspondence between Torrance and Florovsky." In *T. F. Torrance and Eastern Orthodoxy*, edited by Matthew Baker and Todd Speidell, 286–324. Eugene, OR: Pickwick, 2015.
———. "Introductory Essay." In *T. F. Torrance and Eastern Orthodoxy*, edited by Matthew Baker and Todd Speidell, vi–xi. Eugene, OR: Pickwick, 2015.
———. "The Place of St. Irenaeus of Lyons in Historical and Dogmatic Theology according to Thomas F. Torrance." *Participatio: The Journal of the Thomas F. Torrance Theological Fellowship* 2 (2010) 5–43.
Baker, Matthew, and George Dragas. "Interview Regarding T. F. Torrance." *Participatio: The Journal of the Thomas F. Torrance Theological Fellowship* 4 (2013) 30–46.
———. "Interview with Protopresbyter George Dion. Dragas regarding T. F. Torrance." In *T. F. Torrance and Eastern Orthodoxy*, edited by Matthew Baker and Todd Speidell, 1–18. Eugene, OR: Pickwick, 2015.
Baker, Matthew, and Todd Speidell. *T. F. Torrance and Eastern Orthodoxy*. Eugene, OR: Pickwick, 2015.
Barnes, Michel René. "Augustine in Contemporary Trinitarian Theology." *Theological Studies* 56 (1995) 237–50.
———. "De Régnon Reconsidered." *Augustinian Studies* 26, no. 2 (1995) 51–79.
———. "One Nature, One Power: Consensus Doctrine Pro-Nicene Polemic" *Studia Patristica* 29 (1997) 205–23.

Bibliography

———. *The Power of God: Dynamis Theology in Gregory of Nyssa's Trinitarian Theology.* Washington, DC: Catholic University of America, 2001.

———. "Rereading Augustine's Theology of the Trinity." In *The Trinity: An Interdisciplinary Symposium on the Trinity*, edited by Stephen T. Davis, Daniel Kendall, and Gerald O'Collins, 145–78. New York: Oxford University Press, 1999.

Barth, Karl. *Church Dogmatics.* 14 vols. Edited by T. F. Torrance. Translated by G. T. Thomson et al. 2nd ed. Edinburgh: T. & T. Clark, 1975–1977.

———. "Preface." Translated by G. W. Bromiley. In *Church Dogmatics*, edited by Geoffrey W. Bromiley and Thomas F. Torrance, I/1:xi–xvii. 2nd ed. Edinburgh T. & T. Clark, 1975.

British Council of Churches. *The Forgotten Trinity, Volume 1: The Report of the BCC Study Commission on Trinitarian Doctrine Today.* London: British Council of Churches, 1989.

———. *The Forgotten Trinity.* Vol. 2, *A Study Guide on Issues Contained in the Report of the BCC Study Commission on Trinitarian Doctrine Today.* London: British Council of Churches, 1989.

———. *The Forgotten Trinity.* Vol. 3, *A Selection of Papers Presented to the BCC Study Commission on Trinitarian Doctrine Today.* Edited by Alasdair I. C. Heron. London: British Council of Churches, 1991.

Behr, John. "Calling upon God as Father: Augustine and the Legacy of Nicaea." In *Orthodox Readings of Augustine*, edited by Aristotle Papanikolaou and George E. Demacopoulos, 153–65. Crestwood, NY: St. Vladimir's Seminary Press, 2008.

———. "Introduction." In *Saint Athanasius the Great: On the Incarnation: (Greek/English) PPS44a*, translated and edited by John Behr, 19–49. Greek/English. Crestwood, NY: St. Vladimir's Seminary Press, 2012.

———. *The Mystery of Christ: Life in Death.* Crestwood, NY: St. Vladimir's Seminary Press, 2006.

———. *The Nicene Faith: Part I.* Crestwood, NY: St. Vladimir's Seminary Press, 2004.

———. *The Nicene Faith: Part II.* Crestwood, NY: St. Vladimir's Seminary Press, 2004.

———. "Review of *Divine Meaning: Studies in Patristic Hermeneutics*, by T. F. Torrance." *St Vladimir's Theological Quarterly* 42, no. 1 (1998) 104–8.

———. *The Way to Nicaea.* Crestwood, NY: St. Vladimir's Seminary Press, 2001.

Brown, Andrew. "Sacked Greek Orthodox Leader Attacks Church." *The Independent*, April 21, 1988.

Coakley, Sarah. "Afterword: 'Relational Ontology,' Trinity, and Science." In *The Trinity in an Entangled Word: Relationality in Physical Science and Theology*, edited by John Polkinghorne, 184–99. Grand Rapids: Eerdmans, 2010.

Colyer, Elmer. *How to Read T. F. Torrance: Understanding His Trinitarian & Scientific Theology.* Downers Grove, IL: InterVarsity, 2001.

Davis, Stephen T., Daniel Kendall, and Gerald O'Collins, eds. *The Trinity: An Interdisciplinary Symposium on the Trinity.* Oxford: Oxford University Press, 1999.

Dean, Benjamin. "Person and Being: Conversation with T. F. Torrance about the Monarchy of God." *International Journal of Systematic Theology* 15, no. 1 (2013) 58–77.

Dimitrios I, His All-Holiness The Ecumenical Patriarch. "Address to the Delegation of the World Alliance of Reformed Churches." Istanbul, 1979. Contained in The Thomas F. Torrance Manuscript Collection. Special Collections, Princeton Theological Seminary Library.

Bibliography

Daley, Brian. "The Church Fathers." In *The Cambridge Companion to John Henry Newman*, edited by Ian Ker and Terrence Merrigan, 29–46. Cambridge: Cambridge University Press, 2009.
Dragas, George. "The Eternal Son." In *The Incarnation: Ecumenical Studies in the Nicene-Constantinopolitan Creed*, edited by Thomas F. Torrance, 16–57. Edinburgh: Handsel, 1981.
———. *Saint Athanasius of Alexandria: Original Research and New Perspectives*. Rollinsford, NH: Orthodox Research Institute, 2005.
———. "The Significance for the Church of Professor Torrance's Election As Moderator of the General Assembly of the Church of Scotland." ΕΚΚΛΗΣΙΑΣΤΙΚΟΣ ΦΑΡΟΣ 58, nos. 3–4 (1976) 214–31.
———. "St. Athanasius contra Apollinarem." PhD thesis, University of Durham, 1985.
———. "St Athanasius on the Holy Spirit and the Trinity." In *Theological Dialogue between Orthodox & Reformed Churches*, edited by Thomas F. Torrance, 2:39–60. Edinburgh: Scottish Academic, 1993.
Ellis, Brannon. "The Spirit From the Father, Of Himself God." In *Ecumenical Perspectives on the Filioque for the 21st Century*, edited by Myk Habets, 87–106. London: T. & T. Clark, 2014.
Ernest, James D. *The Bible in Athanasius of Alexandria*. Leiden: Brill, 2004.
Esser, Hans-Helmut. "The Authority of the Church and Authority in the Church according to the Reformed Tradition." In *Theological Dialogue between Orthodox & Reformed Churches*, edited by Thomas F. Torrance, 1:50–57. Edinburgh: Scottish Academic, 1985.
Fairbairn, Donald. "Review of *Thomas F. Torrance and the Church Fathers*, by Jason Radcliff." *Participatio: The: Journal of the Thomas F. Torrance Theological Fellowship* 5 (2015) 115–18.
Florovsky, Georges. "Gregory Palamas and the Tradition of the Fathers." In *Bible, Church, Tradition: An Eastern Orthodox View*, 105–20. Norway: Nordland, 1972.
Fouyas, Methodios. *Orthodoxy, Roman Catholicism, and Anglicanism*. London: Oxford University Press, 1972.
Gledhill, Ruth, and Clifford Longley. "Methodios Tells of 'Envious Rivals.'" *The Times*, April 21, 1988.
Goodliff, Andy. "Review of *The Holy Trinity Revisited: Essays in Response to Stephen R. Holmes*." Edited by Thomas A. Noble and Jason S. Sexton. *Regent's Reviews* 18, no. 1 (2016) 26–27.
Gunton, Colin. "T. F. Torrance's Doctrine of God." *The Promise of Trinitarian Theology*, edited by Colin Gunton. Edinburgh: T. & T. Clark, 1991.
Habets, Myk. *Ecumenical Perspectives on the Filioque for the 21st Century*. London: T. & T. Clark, 2014.
———. "The Essence of Evangelical Theology: Critical Introduction to Thomas F. Torrance, *The Trinitarian Faith: The Evangelical Theology of the Ancient Catholic Church*." In The *The Trinitarian Faith: The Evangelical Theology of the Ancient Catholic Church*, by Thomas F. Torrance, vi–xxxii. 2nd ed. London: T. & T. Clark, 2016.
———. "Getting beyond the *Filioque* with Third Article Theology." In *Ecumenical Perspectives on the Filioque for the 21st Century*, edited by Myk Habets, 211–30. London: T. & T. Clark, 2014.
Habets, Myk, and Phillip Tolliday, eds. *Trinitarian Theology after Barth*. Eugene, OR: Wipf & Stock, 2011.

Bibliography

Hennessy, Kristin. "An Answer to de Régnon's Accusers: Why We Should Not Speak of 'His' Paradigm," *Harvard Theological Review* 100 (2007) 179–97.

Heron, Alisdair. "Homoousios with the Father,." In *The Incarnation: Ecumenical Studies in the Nicene-Constantinopolitan Creed*, edited by Thomas F. Torrance, 58–87. Edinburgh: Handsel, 1981.

Holmes, Stephen R. *The Holy Trinity: Understanding God's Life*. Milton Keynes, UK: Paternoster, 2011.

———. "Response: In Praise of Being Criticized." In *The Holy Trinity Revisited: Essays in Response to Stephen R. Holmes*, edited by Thomas A. Noble and Jason S. Sexton, 137–55. Milton Keynes, UK: Paternoster, 2015.

Hunsinger, George. "Foreword." In *T. F. Torrance and Eastern Orthodoxy: Theology in Reconciliation*, edited by Matthew Baker and Todd Speidell, iii–iv. Eugene, OR: Wipf and Stock, 2015.

Him Ip, Pui. "'Back to the Fathers': The Nature of Historical Understanding in 20th century Patristic *Ressourcement*." *Reviews in Religion and Theology* 23, no. 1 (2016) 4–13.

Hussey, Edmund. "The Palamite Trinitarian Models." *St. Vladimir's Theological Quarterly* 16 (1972) 83–89.

Irving, Alex. "Fr. Georges Florovsky and T. F. Torrance on the Doctrine of Creation." *St. Vladimir's Theological Quarterly*, 61, no. 3 (2017) 301–22.

Kaiser, Christopher B. "The Biblical and Patristic Doctrine of the Trinity." In *Theological Dialogue between Orthodox & Reformed Churches Volume 2*, edited by Thomas F. Torrance, 161–92. Edinburgh: Scottish Academic, 1993.

Kilby, Karen. "Aquinas, the Trinity, and the Limits of Understanding," *International Journal of Systematic Theology* 7, no. 4 (2005) 414–27.

Koev, Totju. "The Teaching about the Holy Trinity on the Basis of the Nicene-Constantinopolitan Symbol of Faith." In *Theological Dialogue between Orthodox & Reformed Churches*, edited by Thomas F. Torrance, 2:61–85. Edinburgh: Scottish Academic, 1993.

Konstantinidis, Chrysostomos S. "Authority in the Orthodox Church." In *Theological Dialogue between Orthodox & Reformed Churches*, edited by Thomas F. Torrance, 1:58–75. Edinburgh: Scottish Academic, 1985.

Kreeft, Peter. *Protestants and Catholics in Dialogue: What Can We Learn From Each Other?* San Francisco: Ignatius, 2017.

Lampe, G. W. H., ed. *A Patristic Greek Lexicon*. London: Oxford University Press, 1969.

Lewis, C. S. "Priestesses in the Church?" In *God in the Dock: Essays in Theology and Ethics*. Grand Rapids: Eerdmans, 1970.

Letham, Robert. "Old and New, East and West, and a Missing Horse" In *The Holy Trinity Revisited: Essays in Response to Stephen R. Holmes*, edited by Thomas A. Noble and Jason S. Sexton, 11–26. Milton Keynes, UK: Paternoster, 2015.

Lossky, Vladimir. *The Mystical Theology of the Eastern Church*. Crestwood, NY: St. Vladimir's Seminary Press, 1976.

Mastrantonis, George. *Augburg and Constantinople: The Correspondence between the Tübingen Theologians and Patriarch Jeremiah II of Constantinople on the Augsburg Confession*. Brookline, MA: Holy Cross Greek Orthodox, 2005.

McDowell, John C. "On Not Being Spirited away: Pneumatology and Critical Presence." In *Ecumenical Perspectives on the Filioque for the 21st Century*, edited by Myk Habets, 167–84. London: T. & T. Clark, 2014.

McGrath, Alistair. *T. F. Torrance: An Intellectual Biography*. Edinburgh: T. & T. Clark, 1999.

———. "Trinitarian Theology." In *Where Shall My Wond'ring Soul Begin?*, edited by Mark A. Noll and Ronald F. Thieman, 51–60. Grand Rapids: Eerdmans, 2000.

McLelland, Joseph, ed. *New Man: An Orthodox and Reformed Dialogue*. New Brunswick: Agora, 1973.

Meyendorff, Jean. *Byzantine Theology: Historical Trends and Doctrinal Themes*. London: Mowbrays, 1974.

———. *Christ in Eastern Christian Thought*. Crestwood, NY: St. Vladimir's Seminary Press, 1975.

———. *Introduction A l'étude de Grégoire Palamas*. Paris: Patristica Sorbonensia, 1959.

———. "Introduction." In *Gregory Palamas: The Triads*, translated by Nicholas Grendle, 1–22. New York: Paulist, 1983.

Meyendorff, Jean, ed. *Grégoire Palamas: Défense des saints hésychastes: Introducion, texte critique, traduction et notes*. Louvain: Spicilegium Sacrum Lovaniense, 1959.

Meredith, Anthony. "The Idea of God in Gregory of Nyssa." In *Studien zur Gregor von Nyssa und der Christlichen Spätantike*, edited by Hubertus R. Drobner and Christoph Klock, 127–47. Leiden: Brill, 1990.

Migne, J. P. *Patrologia Cursus Completus Series Graeca*. 165 vols. Paris: 1857–1886.

———. *Patrologia Cursus Completus Series Latina*. 217 vols. Paris: 1844–1864.

Molnar, Paul. "Introduction to the Second Edition of Thomas F. Torrance *The Christian Doctrine of God: One Being, Three Persons*." In *The Christian Doctrine of God: One Being, Three Persons*, by Thomas F. Torrance, ix–xxxii. London: T. & T. Clark.

———. "Theological Issues Involved in the *Filioque*." In *Ecumenical Perspectives on the Filioque for the 21st Century*, edited by Myk Habets, 20–39. London: T. & T. Clark, 2014.

———. *Thomas F. Torrance: Theologian of the Trinity*. Farnham: Ashgate, 2009.

Nesteruk, Alexei V. "Universe, Incarnation, and Humanity: Thomas Torrance, Modern Cosmology, and Beyond." *Participatio Journal* 4 (2013) 213–39.

Newell, Roger J. "Apollinarianism in Worship Revisited: Torrance's Contribution to the Renewal of Reformed Worship." *Princeton Theological Review* 14, no. 2/39 (2008) 49–63.

Noble, T. A. *Holy Trinity: Holy People: The Theology of Christian Perfecting*. Eugene, OR: Wipf and Stock, 2013.

———. "T. F. Torrance on the Centenary of His Birth: A Biological and Theological Synopsis With Some Personal Reminiscences." *Participatio: The Journal of the Thomas F. Torrance Theological Fellowship* 4 (2013) 8–29.

Noble, Thomas A., and Jason S. Sexton *The Doctrine of the Holy Trinity Revisited: Essays in Response to Stephen R. Holmes*. Milton Keynes, UK: Paternoster, 2015.

Papanikolaou, Aristotle, and George E. Demacopoulos, "Augustine and the Orthodox: The 'West' in the East." In *Orthodox Readings of Augustine*, edited by Aristotle Papanikolaou and George E. Demacopoulos, 11–40. Crestwood, NY: St. Vladimir's Seminary Press, 2008.

Parvis, Sara. *Marcellus of Ancyra and the Lost Years of the Arian Controversy 325–345*. Oxford: Oxford University Press, 2006.

Prestige, G. L. *God in Patristic Thought*. London: SPCK, 1952.

Quasten, Johannes. *Patrology*. 5 vols. Notre Dame: Ave Maria, 2000.

Radcliff, Jason. "Does the Church in Scotland Still Need Theology?" *Theology in Scotland* 21, no. 2 (2014) 47–63

———. "A Reformed Asceticism." *Theology in Scotland* 20, no. 1 (2013) 43–56.

Bibliography

———. "T. F. Torrance and the Patristic Consensus on the Doctrine of the Trinity" in *The Doctrine of the Holy Trinity Revisited: Essays in Response to Stephen R. Holmes*, edited by T. A. Noble and J. S. Sexton, 68–81. Milton Keynes, UK: Paternoster, 2015.

———."T. F. Torrance in light of Stephen Holmes's Critique of Contemporary Trinitarian Thought," *Evangelical Quarterly* 86, no. 1 (2014) 21–38.

———. *Thomas F. Torrance and the Church Fathers*. Eugene, OR: Pickwick, 2014.

———."Thomas F. Torrance's Conception of the Consensus Patrum on the Doctrine of Pneumatology" in *Studia Patristica LXIX*, 417–34. Leuven: Peeters, 2013.

Rae, Murray, and Graham Redding. *More Than a Single Issue: Theological Considerations Concerning the Ordination of Practising Homosexuals*. Adelaide: ATF: 2000.

Rahner, Karl. *The Trinity*. Danvers, MA: Crossroad, 1997.

Régnon, Théodore de. *Études de théologie positive sur la Sainte Trinité*. Paris: Retaux, 1898.

Rigdon, Bruce. "Worship and the Trinity in the Reformed Tradition." In *Theological Dialogue between Orthodox & Reformed Churches*, edited by Thomas F. Torrance, 2:211–18. Edinburgh: Scottish Academic, 1993."

Rist, John M. *Augustine: Ancient Thought Baptized*. Cambridge: Cambridge University Press, 1994.

Roldanus, Johannes. *Le Christ et l'Homme dans la Théologie d'Athanase d'Alexandrie*. Leiden: Brill, 1968.

Romanides, John. *The Ancestral Sin*. Ridgewood, NJ: Zephyr, 2008.

———. *Franks, Romans, Feudalism, and Doctrine: An Interplay between Theology and Society. Patriarch Athenagoras Memorial Lectures*. Brookline, MA: Holy Cross Orthodox Press, 1981.

Rossum, Joost Van. "Creation-Theology in Gregory Palamas and Theophanes of Nicaea, Compatible or Incompatible?" *Studia Patristica* 69 (2013) 373–78.

Schaff, Philip. *History of the Church: Reformation A.D. 1517–1530*. Edinburgh: T. & T. Clark, 1888.

Shapland, C. R. B. "Introduction." In *The Letters of Saint Athanasius concerning the Holy Spirit,* translated by C. R. B. Shapland, 11–47. New York: Philosophical Library, 1951.

Shapland, C. R. B., trans. *The Letters of Saint Athanasius concerning the Holy Spirit*. New York: Philosophical Library, 1951.

Siecienski, Edward. *The Filioque: History of a Doctrinal Controversy*. Oxford: Oxford University Press, 2010.

Simon, Archbishop. "The Trinity and Prayer," In *Theological Dialogue between Orthodox & Reformed Churches,* edited by Thomas F. Torrance, 2:193–210. Edinburgh: Scottish Academic, 1993.

Sinkewicz, Robert E. *Saint Gregory Palamas: The One Hundred and Fifty Chapters*. Toronto: The Pontifical Institute of Mediaeval Studies, 1988.

Small, Joseph D. "Orthodox and Reformed in Dialogue: The Agreed Statement on the Holy Trinity." In *The Witness of Bartholomew I: Ecumenical Patriarch*, 102–27. Grand Rapids: Eerdmans, 2013.

Smith, Richmond. "Official Minutes from the Orthodox-Reformed Dialogue." In The Thomas F. Torrance Manuscript Collection. Special Collections, Princeton Theological Seminary Library, Box 170.

Speidell, Todd. *Fully Human in Christ: The Incarnation as the End of Christian Ethics*. Eugene, OR: Wipf and Stock, 2016.

Speidell, Todd, and Matthew Baker, eds.. *T. F. Torrance and Orthodoxy: Theology in Reconciliation*. Eugene, OR: Wipf and Stock, 2015.

Studer, Basil. Translated by Matthew J. O'Connell. *The Grace of Christ and the Grace of God in Augustine of Hippo.* Collegeville: Michael Glazier, 1997.

Timiadis, Emilianos. "God's Immutability and Communicability." In *Theological Dialogue between Orthodox & Reformed Churches,* edited by Thomas F. Torrance, 1:23–49. Edinburgh: Scottish Academic, 1985.

———. "The Trinitarian Structure of the Church and Its Authority." In *Theological Dialogue between Orthodox & Reformed Churches,* edited by Thomas F. Torrance, 1:121–56. Edinburgh: Scottish Academic, 1985.

Torrance, David W., and Jock Stein. *Embracing Truth: Homosexuality and the Word of God.* Edinburgh: Handsel, 2012.

Torrance, Thomas F. "Agreed Statement on the Holy Trinity." In *Theological Dialogue between Orthodox & Reformed Churches,* edited by Thomas F. Torrance, 2:219–26. Edinburgh: Scottish Academic, 1993.

———. "Another 'Wall' Comes Down: Historic Agreement by Reformed and Orthodox on the Doctrine of the Holy Trinity." *Ministers' Forum* 138 (1991) 2–3.

———. "Athanasius: A Study in the Foundations of Classical Theology." In *Theology in Reconciliation: Essays towards Evangelical and Catholic Unity in East and West,* 215–56. Grand Rapids: Eerdmans, 1996.

———. *Atonement: The Person and Work of Christ.* Edited by Robert T. Walker. Milton Keynes, UK: Paternoster, 2009.

———. *The Christian Doctrine of God: One Being Three Persons.* Edinburgh: T. & T. Clark, 1996.

———. "Commentary on the Agreed Statement on the Holy Trinity." In *Trinitarian Perspectives: Toward Doctrinal Agreement,* by Thomas F. Torrance, 127–44. London: T. & T. Clark, 1994.

———. "Concluding Affirmation: Agreed Understanding of the Theological Development and Eventual Direction of the Orthodox/Reformed Conversations Leading to Dialogue." In *Theological Dialogue between Orthodox & Reformed Churches,* edited by Thomas F. Torrance, 1:157–58. Edinburgh: Scottish Academic, 1985.

———. *Conflict and Agreement in the Church.* Vol. 1, *Order & Disorder.* London: Lutterworth, 1959.

———. *Conflict and Agreement in the Church.* Vol. 2, *The Ministry and the Sacraments of the Gospel.* London: Lutterworth, 1960.

———. *Gospel, Church, and Ministry.* Edited by Jock Stein. Eugene, OR: Wipf and Stock, 2012.

———. "His Eminence Archbishop Methodios of Thyateira and Great Britain." Rotary Club Speech, 1984. In The Thomas F. Torrance Manuscript Collection. Special Collections, Princeton Theological Seminary Library, Box 172.

———. *Incarnation: The Person and Life of Christ.* Edited by Robert T. Walker. Milton Keynes, UK: Paternoster, 2008.

———. "Introduction." In *The Mystery of the Lord's Supper: Sermons on the Sacrament Preached in the Kirk of Edinburgh by Robert Bruce in AD 1589,* edited by Thomas F. Torrance, 13–36. London: Clarke, 1958.

———. "Introduction." In *The School of Faith: The Catechisms of the Reformed Church,* edited by Thomas F. Torrance, xi–cxxvi. Reprint. Eugene, OR: Wipf and Stock, 1996.

———. "Introduction." In *Theological Dialogue between Orthodox & Reformed Churches,* edited by Thomas F. Torrance, 1:ix–xxvii. Edinburgh: Scottish Academic, 1985.

Bibliography

———. "Introduction." In *Theological Dialogue between Orthodox & Reformed Churches*, edited by Thomas F. Torrance, 2:ix–xxvi. Edinburgh: Scottish Academic, 1993.

———. *Itinerarium Mentis In Deum: T. F. Torrance—My Theological Development*. In The Thomas F. Torrance Manuscript Collection. Special Collections, Princeton Theological Seminary Library, Box 10.

———. "Karl Barth and the Latin Heresy." *Scottish Journal of Theology* 39, no. 4 (1986) 461–82.

———. "The Legacy of Karl Barth." In *Karl Barth: Biblical and Evangelical Theologian*, edited by Thomas F. Torrance, 160–81. Edinburgh: T. & T. Clark, 1990.

———. "Memoranda on Orthodox/Reformed Relations." In *Theological Dialogue between Orthodox & Reformed Churches*, edited by Thomas F. Torrance, 1:3–21. Edinburgh: Scottish Academic, 1985.

———. "The Ministry of Women." In *Gospel, Church, and Ministry*, by Thomas F. Torrance and edited by Jock Stein, 201–19. Eugene, OR: Wipf and Stock, 2012.

———. "My Interaction with Karl Barth." In *Karl Barth: Biblical and Evangelical Theologian*, edited by Thomas F. Torrance, 121–35. Edinburgh: T. & T. Clark, 1990.

———. "The One Baptism Common to Christ and His Church." In *Theology in Reconciliation: Essays towards Evangelical and Catholic Unity in East and West*, 82–105. Grand Rapids: Eerdmans, 1996.

———. "The Orthodox Church in Great Britain." In *T. F. Torrance and Eastern Orthodoxy: Theology in Reconciliation*, edited by Matthew Baker and Todd Speidell, 325–31. Eugene, OR: Wipf and Stock, 2015.

———. *Preaching Christ Today: The Gospel and Scientific Thinking*. Grand Rapids: Eerdmans, 1994.

———. "Preface to Theological Dialogue Between Orthodox and Reformed Churches Volume 2." In *Theological Dialogue between Orthodox & Reformed Churches*, edited by Thomas F. Torrance, 2:vii–viii. Edinburgh: Scottish Academic, 1993.

———. *Reality & Evangelical Theology: The Realism of Christian Revelation*. Reprint. Eugene, OR: Wipf and Stock, 1999.

———. "The Relevance of Orthodoxy." In *T. F. Torrance and Eastern Orthodoxy: Theology in Reconciliation*, edited by Matthew Baker and Todd Speidell, 332–40. Eugene, OR: Wipf and Stock, 2015.

———. *Royal Priesthood: A Theology of Ordained Ministry*. Edinburgh: T. & T. Clark, 1993.

———. *Scottish Theology: From John Knox to John McLeod Campbell*. London: T. & T. Clark, 1996.

———. "Significant Features, a Common Reflection on the Agreed Statement on the Holy Trinity." In *Theological Dialogue between Orthodox & Reformed Churches*, edited by Thomas F. Torrance, 2:229–232. Edinburgh: Scottish Academic, 1993.

———. *Theological Dialogue between Orthodox & Reformed Churches*. Vol. 1. Edinburgh: Scottish Academic, 1985.

———. *Theological Dialogue between Orthodox & Reformed Churches*. Vol. 2. Edinburgh: Scottish Academic, 1993.

———. *Theology in Reconciliation: Essays towards Evangelical and Catholic Unity in East and West*. Reprint. Eugene, OR: Wipf and Stock, 1996.

———. *Theology in Reconstruction*. Reprint. Eugene, OR: Wipf and Stock, 1996.

———. *The Trinitarian Faith: The Evangelical Theology of the Ancient Catholic Church*. Edinburgh: T. & T. Clark, 1988.

---. "The Trinitarian Foundation and Character of Faith and of Authority in the Church." In *Theological Dialogue between Orthodox & Reformed Churches*, edited by Thomas F. Torrance, 2:79–120. Edinburgh: Scottish Academic, 1993.

---. *Trinitarian Perspectives: Toward Doctrinal Agreement*. London: T. & T. Clark, 1994.

---. "The Triunity of God." In *Theological Dialogue between Orthodox & Reformed Churches*, edited by Thomas F. Torrance, 2:3–37. Edinburgh: Scottish Academic, 1993.

---. "Working Paper on the Holy Trinity." In *Theological Dialogue between Orthodox & Reformed Churches*, edited by Thomas F. Torrance, 2:109–121. Edinburgh: Scottish Academic, 1993.

Torrance, Thomas F., ed. *The Incarnation: Ecumenical Studies in the Nicene Constantinopolitan Creed A.D. 381*. Edinburgh: Handsel, 1981.

---. *The School of Faith: The Catechisms of the Reformed Church*. Edited by Thomas F. Torrance. Reprint. Eugene, OR: Wipf and Stock, 1996.

The Thomas F. Torrance Manuscript Collection. Special Collections, Princeton Theological Seminary Library.

Torrance, James. *Worship, Community, and the Triune God of Grace*. Downers Grove, IL: InterVarsity, 1997.

Walker, Robert T. Review of *Thomas F. Torrance and the Church Fathers: A Reformed, Evangelical, and Ecumenical Reconstruction of the Patristic Tradition*, by Jason Radcliff. *Theology in Scotland* 23, no. 2 (2016) 67–69.

Vischer, Lukas. "The Holy Spirit—Source of Sanctification, Reflections on Basil the Great's Treatise on the Holy Spirit." In *Theological Dialogue between Orthodox & Reformed Churches*, edited by Thomas F. Torrance, 2:86–108. Edinburgh: Scottish Academic, 1993.

Voulgaris, Christos. "The Biblical and Patristic Doctrine of the Trinity." In *Theological Dialogue between Orthodox & Reformed Churches*, edited by Thomas F. Torrance, 2:122–60. Edinburgh: Scottish Academic, 1993.

Walker, Robert T. "Recollections and Reflections." *Participatio: The Journal of the Thomas F. Torrance Theological Fellowship* 1 (2009) 39–48.

Webster, John. "Theologies of Retrieval." *The Oxford Handbook of Systematic Theology*, edited by John Webster, Kathryn Tanner, and Iain Torrance, 584–99. Oxford: Oxford University Press, 2007.

Weinandy, Thomas. *The Father's Spirit of Sonship: Reconceiving the Trinity*. Eugene, OR: Wipf and Stock, 2011.

Wendebourg, Dorothea. "From the Cappadocian Fathers to Gregory Palamas: The Defeat of Trinitarian Theology." *Studia Patristica* 17, no. 1 (1982) 194–99.

Ziegler, Geordie W. *Trinitarian Grace and Participation: An Entry into the Theology of T. F. Torrance*. Minneapolis: Fortress, 2017.

Yannaras, Christos. Yannaras, *Elements of Faith: An Introduction to Orthodox Theology*. Edinburgh, T. & T. Clark, 2000.

---. *Orthodoxy and the West: Hellenic Self-Identity in the Modern Age*. Brookline, MA: Holy Cross Orthodox Press, 2006.

Zizioulas, John. *Being as Communion: Studies in Personhood and the Church*. Crestwood, NY: St. Vladimir's Seminary Press, 1985.

---. *Communion and Otherness: Further Studies in Personhood and the Church*. London: T. & T. Clark, 2006.

Index of Names

Alexandria, Athanasius of, x. 1, 2, 4, 14, 15, 16, 25, 29, 30, 31, 32, 33, 38, 40, 41, 43, 45, 46, 49, 53, 54, 57, 59, 65, 66, 68, 70, 71, 72, 73, 74, 77, 82, 85, 86, 87, 88, 89, 90, 91, 92, 93, 95, 96, 97, 98, 104, 107, 108, 112, 138, 139, 140, 141, 145, 146, 147, 148, 149, 150, 154,

Alexandria, Cyril of, x, 1, 2, 25, 38, 40, 41, 43, 45, 51, 52, 53, 54, 57, 59, 70, 72, 73, 74, 82, 86, 90, 91, 101, 104, 108, 112, 114, 119, 136, 138, 139, 140, 141, 142, 147

Ayres, Lewis, 83, 84, 96, 97, 105, 106, 107

Baker, Matthew, 14, 15, 16, 22, 37, 44, 46, 48, 49, 60, 61, 72, 78, 91, 94, 95, 108, 113, 116,

Barnes, Michel René, 97, 106

Barth, Karl, 2, 6, 14, 22, 26, 30, 31, 32, 33, 43, 68, 71, 77, 81, 82, 89, 90, 91, 95, 107, 117

Bartholomew I, Patriarch, 156, 157, 158

Behr, John, 29, 97

Blind, Didymus the, 73, 86, 147

Breck, John, 59

Bucer, Martin, 17

Calvin, John, 2, 14, 17, 19, 24, 2527, 30, 31, 32, 42, 56, 63, 71, 77, 89, 125, 128, 130, 136, 137, 138, 139

Campbell, John McLeod, 26

Chrysostom, John, 70, 119, 139, 142

Coakley, Sarah, 22, 33, 34, 40, 83

Colyer, Elmer, 30

Damascus, John of, 72, 85, 90, 142, 145

Dimitrius 1, Patriarch, 47, 61

Dragas, George Dion., xi, 3, 6, 7, 9, 13, 14, 15, 16, 21, 26, 27, 28, 35, 37, 42, 44, 45, 46, 48, 49, 50, 59, 60, 61, 71, 72, 73, 74, 75, 77, 78, 79, 91, 94, 95, 105, 116, 118, 120, 156

Esser, Hans-Helmut, 58, 59, 65

Florovsky, Georges, 22, 32, 37, 44, 49, 54, 95, 125

Fouyas, Methodios, 3, 4, 6, 7, 8, 9, 10, 21, 35, 36, 37, 38, 40, 41, 45, 46, 47, 48, 49, 50, 51, 52, 55, 57, 72, 78, 98, 100, 120, 156

Goodliff, Andy, 80

Great, Basil the, 53, 70, 73, 77, 82, 86, 90, 104, 106, 114, 144, 147

Gregory Nazianzen, 24, 70, 71, 77, 85, 86, 87, 91, 92, 136138, 139,

Gunton, Colin, 13, 34, 40, 44, 95, 97, 114

Habets, Myk, 22, 33, 34, 73, 81, 89

Hippo, Augustine of, 31, 32, 44, 53, 54, 55, 83, 84, 89, 90, 92, 96, 97, 106, 107, 108, 109, 119, 138

Holmes, Stephen, 22, 34, 82, 83, 84, 89, 94, 96, 97, 104, 105, 106, 112

Hunsinger, George, 2, 14, 15

Index of Names

Istravridis, Vasil, 59

Juhasz, Istvan, 59

Kaiser, Christopher, 71, 76
Koev, Totju, 71, 73, 75
Konstantinidis, Chrysostomos, 58, 59, 61, 62, 65, 66

Limouris, Gennadios, 59
Lochman, Jan, 19, 20, 59

McCord, James, 9, 18, 45, 56, 59, 61, 62, 125
McLelland, Joseph, ix, 20, 24, 59
Meyendorff, John, 20, 95, 108
Molnar, Paul, 1, 3, 22, 31, 93, 95, 98, 102, 110

Newell, Roger, 115
Noble, Thomas, 3, 41, 81, 97, 98, 106

Palamas, Gregory, 53, 54, 55, 67, 70, 107, 108, 109, 113, 114
Papandreaou, Damaskinos, 59
Perret, Edmund, 59
Poitiers, Hilary of, 88, 90, 136, 138

Radcliff, Jason Robert, 2, 7, 18, 24, 26, 30, 34, 84, 104, 105, 106, 112, 113, 114, 116
Rahner, Karl, 32, 33, 43, 92, 112
Regnon, Théodore de, 22, 34, 81, 83, 89, 90, 97, 110
Riazon, Archbishop Simon of, 71
Rigdon, Bruce, 71, 76
Romanides, John, 90

Salamis, Epiphanius of, 73, 87, 91, 148
Schleiermacher, Friedrich, 90
Small, Joseph, 17, 63, 64, 66, 67, 68, 69, 73, 74, 75, 76, 84, 111,
Smith, Richmond, 59

Timiadis, Emilianos, 58, 59, 64, 66, 68, 70, 74, 104, 106
Torrance, Iain R., 119, 156

Vischer, Lukar, 24, 59, 71, 73, 75
Voulgaris, Christos, 71, 75, 76

Walker, Robert Torrance, 14, 27, 28, 41

Ziegler, Geordie, 81
Zizioulas, John, 6, 32, 34, 40, 47, 48, 96, 104, 105, 106, 109, 156
Zwingli, Huldrych, 17, 19, 56, 128

www.ingramcontent.com/pod-product-compliance
Lightning Source LLC
Chambersburg PA
CBHW071456150426
43191CB00008B/1362